LEARN JAPANESE
NEW COLLEGE TEXT

Mazamaza to
Amerika ni miru
Atarashiki
Mono e no hiyaku ni
Ikiru inochi o
　　—Nyozekan—

LEARN JAPANESE

NEW COLLEGE TEXT   VOLUME I

John Young and Kimiko Nakajima-Okano

Published for
University of Maryland University College

University of Hawaii Press
Honolulu

This volume is one in a series of Japanese language textbooks
prepared by the Asian Division of the University of Maryland
University College and published by the University of Hawai'i
Press.

00 01 02 03 04 05   14 13 12 11 10

Library of Congress Cataloging-in-Publication Data

Young, John, 1920–
   Learn Japanese.

   1. Japanese language—Text-books for foreign
speakers—English. I. Nakajima-Okano, Kimiko.
II. Title.
PL539.3.Y64   1984   495.68'3421   83-18060
ISBN 0-8248-0859-2

University of Hawai'i Press books are printed on acid-free
paper and meet the guidelines for permanence and durability
of the Council on Library Resources.

CONTENTS

ACKNOWLEDGMENTS

The authors are deeply indebted to the Japanese language faculty and administrative staff members of the University of Maryland and of more than one hundred universities and schools who have used the original *Learn Japanese: College Text* and offered many invaluable comments in the preparation of this revised text. We are also very grateful to the staff members of the Institute of Far Eastern Studies and of the Asian Bilingual Curriculum Development Center at Seton Hall University for their assistance.

We also wish to mention the following people whose assistance was very valuable in the preparation of the original *Learn Japanese: College Text:* Ms. Yoshiko Andō, Dr. Edgar A. Austin, Dr. Ivan Benson, Dr. Keiichirō Okutsu, Mr. Setsuo Sugimura, and Mr. Shōzō Kurokawa.

Yuku kumo ya
Hotaka no mine no
Nokori yuki
     —Seien—

Clouds drifting
Over the mountains of Hotaka
Snow lingers

INTRODUCTION

1. PURPOSE AND APPROACH

Since the Second World War, the teaching of languages has undergone a significant change in the United States, with primary stress now placed upon oral communication as the basis for learning a foreign language. This new emphasis resulted partly from new and improved methods of teaching a spoken language based on descriptive linguistic analysis of the target language and from a realization that there is among Americans a general and immediate need for an oral language capability. It was in line with these considerations that *Learn Japanese: College Text* was prepared, using an audio-lingual approach with some structural-cognitive adjustments. In addition to the stimulus-response training of language practices, the authors have also tried to stimulate conscious learning of new items by deliberate attention to patterns. *Learn Japanese: College Text* has been successful in helping many learners to acquire a structural as well as a communicative competence.

Twenty years have passed since we first started the compilation work in 1962. There is a need to revise the original text to: (1) keep the dialog more up-to-date; (2) incorporate users' constructive and valid comments; and (3) adopt some of the newest notional/functional ideas in language teaching. This new revised text, *Learn Japanese: New College Text,* has been prepared on the basis of the above-stated consideration. The notional/functional study was conducted by the Council of Europe in 1973. It stresses the importance of identifying individual purpose in using a language (what we talk *for* = functional), and the necessity for considering different types of language use and their connections with realization systems (what we talk *about* = notional). Thus, considerations are given to semantic options related to a set of behavioral options concerning what the language users can do within the social context of any situation, and linguistic options selected on the basis of language competence. This new text will, therefore, place more emphasis on "the generation of discourse" than on the mere "generation of sentences," and skills are viewed as competence in performing functional tasks necessary to language users. It will emphasize the interactive aspect of communication and Japanese culture. Therefore, special attention has been paid to the content selection and sequencing as well as to the learners' functions and roles in a Japanese-speaking environment.

2. SOME USEFUL CONSIDERATIONS

The Japanese presented herein represents the language most acceptable and widely adopted within Japan; that is, the dialect that may be more or less defined as being spoken by native speakers of a middle-class background, with a college education, residents of the Yamanote area of Tōkyō, and roughly falling into the 25–45 age group. Although certain vocabulary items or minor patterns may vary from locality to locality, no difficulty in communication should result from adhering to the materials presented here.

The "pattern approach" used in this text should not be confused with that used in other texts in this field. In essence, this text goes beyond the "formula-application" approach and develops a whole new presentation based upon association and repetition. There is no need to reiterate here the importance of repetition in language study, but repetition should not be enforced in isolation. We emphasize both association and repetition. Association reflects the connecting links between modes of utterances or patterns. Repetition formulates habits in uttering sentence patterns. A "pattern" is not a single item, occurring independently or to be learned in isolation. Rather, it is a structure related to other structures, and consequently must be associated with them in order to achieve complete mastery of the language. Associating these structures, or moving from one structure to another, is accomplished through principles of "transformation," utilized extensively in this text.

Additionally, a strong association is maintained between the patterns presented and the language as it used in living situations. The pattern is associated, then, with its functional role as a means of transferring ideas in real conversational situations as well as with its part in the structure of the language.

Furthermore, the material presented is based upon an error analysis and a contrastive study of English and Japanese structure, but effort has been made to relegate the differences to their proper places in the language. The grading of the material presented herein is based upon the degree of difficulty of learning it from the standpoint of English speakers. But the most difficult items are not necessarily the most important items, and they should not be unduly stressed out of proportion.

A dialog serves as the core of each lesson, and, in turn, the patterns introduced in each lesson serve as the backbone of the dialog. New patterns are introduced in each lesson in a natural and functional manner and are analyzed graphically. They are developed in the drills or exercises to the extent that the student should achieve a level of mastery reflected by almost automatic response.

The drills constitute an essential part of each lesson. It is through the drills that the student is given the opportunity to produce his/her own Japanese; the systematic transformation and expansion of the Japanese sentence structure are the vehicles through which the student absorbs the language for his own use. Too much emphasis cannot be given them nor can the necessity for always maintaining normal speed in the responses be ignored. Constant review also should be kept in mind as a means of insuring that the student has actually mastered the respective points of the drills. Going ahead too rapidly, before the student has completely mastered the point, must be avoided. Each successive pattern is dependent on the preceding material and presupposes an understanding of all that comes before it.

It should be borne in mind that the use of English in the classroom should be limited to the essentials. Valuable class time should be devoted to producing Japanese, not to explaining the logic of the language in English. Logic doesn't necessarily determine what is accepted in the language.

3. LESSON ARRANGEMENT

Volume I of *Learn Japanese: New College Text* consists of fifteen lessons, each of which requires a minimum of three hours of classroom work. The first two lessons provide an introduction to Japanese pronunciation and *kana,* and seek to emphasize creating a foundation in correct pronunciation, accent, and intonation habits, as well as an introduction to Japanese writing. Some useful classroom and daily expressions are introduced in these two lessons mainly for the purpose of practicing pronunciation. In addition to the lessons that constitute the main body of the text, there are special systematic review and application lessons, Lessons 6, 10, and 15, which cover the materials in the preceding lessons. The review lessons group the contents of previous lessons, such as vocabulary, expressions, and phrases, into pattern and conjugation categories, and provide Relational Checking Drills, and other types of drills as well as Review Exercises. The Relational Checking Drill is meant to check the use of Relationals. The learner should complete a sentence by inserting a proper Relational. The Review Drill deals with the pattern sentences covered in previous lessons. In addition, the review lessons also contain application exercises which apply the contents lessons to a variety of new situations, enabling the learners to develop communicative skills.

Lesson 14 provides an introduction to *kana* orthography and some mini dialog containing a few new structural items for recognition. This lesson has been introduced for "passive learning," and the student is not required to study the content for examination. If necessary, this lesson may be omitted. Other than in the phonology, *kana,* and review and application lessons, the following format is followed:

Part 1. Useful Expressions

These are contemporary expressions which are used idiomatically in conversation. They are not usually included in any pattern classification presented but are necessary for conversational purposes. They should be memorized.

Part 2. Dialog

Each dialog consists of a realistic conversation incorporating useful expressions and sentences based upon patterns either introduced in the respective lesson or in previous lessons. The student's first contact with the dialog should be aural. The ''mim-mem'' method—mimicking the instructor or tape and thus memorizing—is recommended for the purpose of mastering the dialog. After the drill work, the student should again repeat the dialog, memorize it, and develop his own controlled but situation-centered conversation.

Part 3. Pattern Sentences

New ''pattern sentences'' are broken down graphically into their respective components and the structural elements involved in a pattern are illustrated visually without subjecting the student to the intricacies of traditional grammar. These pattern sentences are fundamental to a rapid mastery of the oral language and should be memorized by the student. In this section, an arrow indicates modification: a box followed by an arrow always shows that it modifies the box following an arrow. In other words, the box before an arrow is the Predicate Modifier and the box after an arrow is the Predicate. When two or more Predicate Modifiers are positioned vertically, it means that the sequence of these Predicate Modifiers can be relatively changed, while horizontally arranged Predicate Modifiers show that their sequence is absolute. Grammatical points have been printed in capital letters and numbers in parenthesis in boxes indicate those of the following Notes.

Part 4. Notes

Brief structural explanations as well as other explanations such as cultural features are contained in this section. The student should familiarize himself with this section so that the instructor may concentrate upon drills during the class sessions. The analysis of the structure is to be considered as an aid to the student and should not be treated as an item to be memorized. Japanese words or phrases occuring within an English context will be indicated in italics, as will the English words that occasionally occur in Japanese contexts in the notes. Also, English translations or equivalents for Japanese expressions occurring in an English context are noted by quotation marks. Subscript and superscript numbers appearing in useful expressions, dialog, and pattern sentences refer to note numbers.

Part 5. Vocabulary

New words and phrases appearing in the dialog, notes, and drills are given their English equivalents in this section. It should be noted, however, that vocabulary items are normally not used independently. They are used as part of a sentence and their independent meanings should not be overemphasized.

Part 6. Hiragana Practice

Hiragana is introduced generally in certain of the vocabulary words already acquired by the student. This is merely intended to familiarize the student somewhat with the Japanese *hiragana* writing system. The student is responsible, however, for mastering the *hiragana* presented in each lesson.

Part 7. Drills

Various types of drills are included in this section, depending upon the language aspect being stressed. The left-hand column is for the instructor, and the right-hand column suggests varied responses which may be given by the student. The textbook should not be used by the student during the drills; the student should listen to the instructor carefully and respond according to instruction. The use of English should be limited to the English cues given in the E-J drill. New vocabulary items may also be added in this section so that sufficient or more realistic drill might be effected.

A.   Pronunciation Drill

This section is based upon the words and phrases in the lesson and stresses correct pronunciation, accent, and intonation. The purpose is to let the student understand the stream of sounds, hear the distinctive sound features, and approximate their production. The importance of understanding the language at a normal speed and of facilitating good pronunciation habits should not be underemphasized.

B.   Pattern Drill

This drill consists of important pattern sentences from the dialog as well as other sources. They should be repeated by the student until he/she has mastered them and can reproduce them automatically. Automatic habit formulation in the use of Japanese is the target of this drill.

C.   Substitution Drill

A code sentence is given first by the instructor. After mastering the pattern, the student substitutes that part of the sentence shown in italics by other words or phrases. This is a highly controlled drill and rapid response should be stressed at all times.

D.   Expansion Drill

This drill starts with short sentences which the student expands by adding words, Relationals, or phrases.

E.   Transformation Drill

This is a drill wherein the student makes changes of a structural transformation nature in the sentences given.

F.   Response Drill

This is a question and answer drill designed to encourage the student to respond utilizing his own Japanese as opposed to the previous drills, which were highly controlled in that the student was limited to producing one particular item or phrase.

G.   Mixed Drill

This includes any drill that combines elements of substitution or transformation with any of the other types of drills. It is a complicated type of drill, forcing the student to cope with several changes or structural differences simultaneously.

H.   Combination Drill

Two or more sentences are given by the instructor for the student to combine into one sentence. This is designed to affect the student's ability to formulate complicated sentences.

I. E-J Drill (English-Japanese Drill)

In this drill, the instructor, after giving the code sentence, gives the cues in English. The student should quickly respond with the Japanese sentence modeled on the code sentence. Should there be such a need, the instructor may convert other types of drill into this type by giving the cues in English. This drill is effective when used as a review drill. In this drill, substitution or transformation is signaled in English.

Part 8. Exercises

This part may be covered in the classroom or outside the classroom, depending upon the difficulty of the pattern sentences to be learned. Normally the student is expected to do the review exercises outside the classroom. The purpose is to help learners to internalize items and points learned so far.

4. OTHER CONSIDERATIONS

The above description of the various component parts of each lesson is designed to facilitate their most efficient and effective use by both the student and the instructor. There are several basic principles of application which should be constantly borne in mind by the instructor as well as the student.

First, in view of the fact that the students using these texts for the first time represent a wide range of proficiency in Japanese—from ''zero'' to a relatively fair degree—the contents of the lessons have been separated into two categories, one for ''active'' learning and the other for ''passive'' learning.

For our purposes, active learning reflects those portions of the lessons that should be thoroughly learned by the student, to the point where they can be both *recognized* and *produced* easily and naturally. This includes, for example, Useful Expressions, Dialogs, Pattern Sentences, and the contents of the drill portions of each lesson. Passive learning represents those parts that are included as supplementary information and should be learned by the student to the point where they can be *recognized* and *understood*. *Reproduction* will not be required. The parts for passive learning, for example, are the contents of Lesson 14, the analysis section included in the appendices, et cetera. The student is responsible for a thorough knowledge of all the materials contained in the active learning category but the material contained in the passive category will not be required.

As a second general principle, the instructor should adhere to the sequence of presentation followed in each lesson, moving on to the next part only when satisfied that the students have a thorough grasp of and facility with that particular material. The instructor may supplement the examples given in the drills but should exercise great caution not to burden the student with extra vocabulary items nor unconsciously introduce unfamiliar structural forms. In the review lessons, however, the instructor is free to exercise his or her discretion in emphasizing or de-emphasizing certain points, depending on an appraisal of the students' facility with that particular item.

Further, it is desirable that the textbook should be closed at all times in the classroom. The instructor is urged to avoid giving redundant explanations or directions for the various drills. For example, the simple term ''substitute'' followed by hand signals should be enough to effect a fast-moving substitution drill, as opposed to lengthy explanations about how the drill should be conducted. The importance of maintaining a brisk pace and not letting the class lag is fundamental. In the event that a student cannot answer in a reasonably short interval, the instructor should not hesitate to give further cues or hints, or even to ask someone else to answer the question and then come back to the original student for repeating the correct answer. Never permit the classroom atmosphere to become interrupted.

5. ROMANIZATION

The romanization system herein is the Hepburn system, together with two modifications. It was felt that the system used in *Beginning Japanese* by Dr. Jorden was superior from the standpoint of effecting an easier transition to the written language as well as facilitating morpho-phonemic and structural descriptions, but it was realized that a large number of students are already familiar with the Hepburn system and a sudden change to the *Beginning Japanese* system might create some initial confusion. As a result, the Hepburn system with the following two modifications was adopted for this text:

1. Long vowels are written as *aa, ii, uu, ei, oo* in this text. However, long vowel *ē* in a foreign word and three words—Sentence Interjective *ee*, Sentence Particle *nee*, and Noun *oneesan*—-are written as *ee*.

example:

Hepburn	Learn Japanese
ōkii	*oo*kii
kyū	ky*uu*
okāsan	ok*aa*san
bīru	b*ii*ru
tait*ei*	tait*ei*
onēsan	on*ee*san

2. Within a word, the nonfinal syllabic *n* will be written as *n'*:

example:

gen'in   kon'ban   shin'bun

At the same time, however, the following convention, distinguished by / / symbols, is adopted in explaining phonological and structural rules:

1) /t/ represents *t, ts,* and *ch;*

2) /s/ represents *s* and *sh;*

3) /h/ represents *f* and *h;* and

4) /z/ represents *j* and *z* (*j* covers /zy/ before *a, u,* or *o*).

LESSON 1
INTRODUCTION TO PRONUNCIATION

1.1 USEFUL EXPRESSIONS

Ohayoo gozaimasu.₁

"Good morning." This expression is a formal or polite greeting used in the morning. Informally, *Ohayoo* is used. The literal meaning is "It is early." Consequently, this expression may not be used later than 10 or 11 A.M.

Kon'nichi wa₁

"Hello." "Good day." This expression may be used roughly from 10 or 11 A.M. to 5 or 6 P.M. when it gets dark. Do not use this expression when you leave.

Kon'ban wa₁

"Good evening." This expression literally means "Tonight," and may be used after it gets dark. This greeting is not to be used when one leaves.

Sayoonara.₂

"Good-bye." This expression is sometimes contracted to *Sayonara.*

Oyasumi nasai.₂

"Good night." The literal meaning is "Rest," or "Go to sleep." Therefore, you use this expression when you leave if it is dark enough to go to sleep at night, or if you are going to sleep, or if you see someone going to sleep in the daytime. The contracted form is *Oyasumi.*

Doomo arigatoo gozaimasu.₃

"Thank you very much." This is a formal expression of thanks. Depending upon the degree of politeness, some parts of this expression may be omitted. Here are expressions of thanks listed from the formal to less formal:
Doomo arigatoo gozaimasu.
Arigatoo gozaimasu.
Doomo arigatoo.
Arigatoo.
Doomo.

Doomo₄ sumimasen.₃

"I am very sorry for what I am now doing, or I am going to do, or for what I have done." "Thanks a lot." Informally, the contracted form *Doomo* may be used. Originally, this expression was merely that of apology, but it is now common practice to use it as an expression of gratitude.

Gomen nasai.₃

"Forgive me." This expression is used as a colloquial expression of apology. Compared with *Sumimasen,* which is broad in use, *Gomen nasai* is used as a somewhat more hearty apology, usually on less formal occasions, and is somewhat more colloquial.

Doo itashimashite.₅

"Don't mention it." "Not at all." This expression is used as a formal reply not only to expressions of gratitude but also to those of apology. Sometimes, *Iie* "No" will precede this expression. In the most informal cases, only *Iie* is used.

1.2 PRONUNCIATION NOTES

1.2.1 Syllables

The Tōkyō dialect has, for the purpose of this text, 5 vowels, 13 consonants, and 2 semi-vowels. They formulate 105 syllables. Each syllable should be pronounced with equal length and more or less even stress, although some syllables may be pronounced with more prominence.

Syllables are formulated in one of the following ways:

Vowel	5
Consonant	5
Consonant+Vowel	58
Consonant+/y/*+Vowel	33
/y/ or /w/+Vowel	4
Total:	105

*The symbol / / is used to indicate a phoneme.

Chart 1   Syllables of Japanese

initial \ final	/a/	/i/	/u/	/e/	/o/	/ya/	/yu/	/yo/	/wa/	ZERO
ZERO	a	i	u	e	o	ya	yu	yo	wa	/
/p/	pa	pi	pu	pe	po	pya	pyu	pyo	/	p
/b/	ba	bi	bu	be	bo	bya	byu	byo	/	/
/t/	ta	chi	tsu	te	to	cha	chu	cho	/	t
/d/	da	/	/	de	do	/	/	/	/	/
/k/	ka	ki	ku	ke	ko	kya	kyu	kyo	/	k
/g/	ga	gi	gu	ge	go	gya	gyu	gyo	/	/
/s/	sa	shi	su	se	so	sha	shu	sho	/	s
/z/	za	ji	zu	ze	zo	ja	ju	jo	/	/
/h/	ha	hi	fu	he	ho	hya	hyu	hyo	/	/
/m/	ma	mi	mu	me	mo	mya	myu	myo	/	/
/n/	na	ni	nu	ne	no	nya	nyu	nyo	/	/
/r/	ra	ri	ru	re	ro	rya	ryu	ryo	/	/
/n'/	/	/	/	/	/	/	/	/	/	n'

1.2.2 Vowels and Semi-Vowels

There are five vowels /a/, /i/, /u/, /e/, and /o/, and two semi-vowels /y/ and /w/ in Japanese. Vowels are pronounced in the mouth as shown in the following:

Chart 2   Vowels

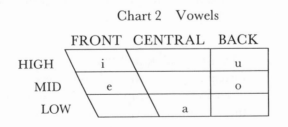

	FRONT	CENTRAL	BACK
HIGH	i		u
MID	e		o
LOW		a	

1.2.3 Single Vowels

/a/ is pronounced like ''a'' in ''father,'' but shorter.

/i/ is pronounced like ''i'' in ''machine,'' but shorter and clearer. Its sound is entirely different from ''i'' in ''knit,'' which occurs as a short ''i'' in English.

/u/ is pronounced like ''oo'' in ''hook.'' Japanese /u/ is produced without the lip-rounding.

/e/ is pronounced like ''e'' in ''pet,'' but shorter.

/o/ is pronounced like ''o'' in ''horse,'' but shorter and clearer.

1.2.4 Vowels in Sequence

Since a single vowel can be a syllable by itself in Japanese, a vowel can be followed by another vowel, and in pronunciation each vowel is short, clear, and even in length. Consecutive vowels can be different, such as /ai/, /ue/, /ie/, and /oi/, or the same, such as /aa/, /ii/, /uu/, /ee/, and /oo/. In the latter case, the vowels are called long vowels.

English-speaking people tend to pronounce the second of a two-different-vowels sequence, especially ''i'' and ''u,'' in an off-glide manner.

Compare:

ka-u . . . . cow	*o-u* . . . . owe	*ba-i* . . . . buy	*ma-i* . . . . my
ha-i . . . . high	*a-i* I	*so-u* . . . . sew	*to-i* . . . . toy

1.2.5 Long Vowels

English-speaking people often neglect to distinguish between long and short vowels but the distinction is extremely important in Japanese, as the length of the vowel may change the meaning of the word.

ooi   aa   iie   seeru   kuuki   Tookyoo

Compare:

ojisan	''uncle''	. . . . ojiisan	''grandfather'' or ''old man''
obasan	''aunt''	. . . . obaasan	''grandmother'' or ''old woman''
beru	''bell''	. . . . beeru	''veil''
biru	''building''	. . . . biiru	''beer''
Soko ni arimasu.	''It's there.''	. . . . Sooko ni arimasu.	''It's in the warehouse.''

1.2.6 Semi-Vowels

/y/ may be placed either in the initial position or between a consonant and a vowel in a syllable. /y/ appears only before /a/, /u/, and /o/.

/y/ is pronounced approximately like ''y'' in ''year,'' but it is more fully voiced.

yama   yuki   yoi   kyaku   kyuukoo   ryokan

/w/ is placed only at the initial position of a syllable. /w/ appears only before /a/.

/w/ is pronounced like ''w'' in ''want,'' but it is fully voiced.

warui   watakushi   kawa

1.2.7 Voiceless Vowels

Whenever an /i/ or /u/ vowel is placed between two of the voiceless consonants /k/, /s/, /t/, /p/, or /h/, the /i/ or /u/ becomes voiceless or is lost unless it is accented. In some cases, this phenomenon may occur when either *i* or *u* is placed between a voiceless consonant and a period.

s(u)-su-mu   ts(u)-ka-u   ma-ts(u)

Ko-re wa ho-n de-s(u).   Sh(i)-te imas(u).

Wa-ta-k(u)-shi mo i-ki-ma-s(u).

Chart 3   Consonants

manner of articulation	point of articulation	labial	apical	palatal	velar	glottal	others
plosive	voiceless	p	t -a -e -o		k		
plosive	voiced	b	d -a -e -o		g		
affricate			t (ts)* -u	t (ch) -i			
fricative	voiceless	h (f) -u	s -a -u -e -o	s (sh) -i	h -i	h -a -e -o	
fricative	voiced	w	z -a -u -e -o	y z (j) -i			
nasal	non-syllabic	m	n		g		
nasal	syllabic						n'
flap			r				

*Spellings in parentheses are those used in this text.

1.2.8 Consonants

There are 13 consonants in Japanese. All of these, except /n'/, may form syllables in combination with a vowel or a semi-vowel plus a vowel. However, of these 13 consonants, 5 do not necessarily require a combination of a vowel or semi-vowel to form a syllable. There are 58 cases of consonant+vowel syllables and 33 cases of consonant+semi-vowel+vowel combinations.

1.2.9 Single Consonant Syllables

The five consonants that can formulate a syllable alone are /k/, /s/, /t/, /p/, and /n'/. /k/, /s/, /t/, or /p/ as a syllabic consonant comes only before another identical consonant; that is, /kk/, /ss/, /tt/, or /pp/. These are conventionally called "double consonants," and are often difficult for English-speaking people to pronounce correctly. The tongue position for the pronunciation of the first consonant is held for one syllable beat before the tongue starts to move to produce the second consonant. The consonant syllable /n'/ will be explained later.

hakkiri   chotto   assari   yappari   massugu

Compare:

saka   "slope"   .... sakka   "writer"

ito   "thread"   .... itto   "one *to*"

keshi   "poppy"   .... kesshi   " 'do-or-die' spirit"

ita   "was (in a place)"   .... itta   "went"

ichi   "one"   .... itchi   "agreement"

1.2.10 Consonant + (Semi-Vowel) + Vowel Syllables

/p/ formulates nine syllables, *p, pa, pi, pu, pe, po, pya, pyu,* and *pyo.*

/p/ before *a, u, e* or *o* is pronounced like "p" in "poor" with less aspiration.

/p/ before *i, ya, yu,* or *yo* is pronounced like "p" in "pure."

apaato   piano   ippuu   peeji   ippo   ippyoo   pyuu

/b/ formulates eight syllables, *ba, bi, bu, be, bo, bya, byu,* and *byo.* It is pronounced like English "b," except that it is more fully voiced.

/b/ before *a, u, e,* or *o* is pronounced like "b" in "rebel," and *b* before *i, ya, yu,* or *yo* is pronounced like "b" in "abuse."

bai   tabi   byooki   byakuya

/t/ formulates nine syllables, *t, ta, chi, tsu, te, to, cha, chu,* and *cho.*

/t/ before *a, e,* or *o* is pronounced like "t" in "top," but the tongue touches the teeth. It has less aspiration than English "t."

taitei   ittoo   ittai

/t/ with /u/ is spelled *tsu* and /t/ is pronounced like "ts" in "cats." *Tsu* is one of the most difficult Japanese sounds for English-speaking people. Put your tongue in the position of producing English *t,* and before you pronounce *u* give a slight hiss. If you forget to start with *t,* it will sound like *su.*

Compare:

tsu   .... su   tsumi .... sumi

utsu   .... usu   tsuki .... suki

/t/ with /i/, /ya/, /yu/, or /yo/ is spelled *chi, cha, chu,* or *cho,* and /t/ is pronounced like "ch" in "cheap."

chichi   bachi   chittomo   itchi   itchaku   chotto

/d/ formulates three syllables, *da, de,* and *do.* /d/ is made by touching the alveolar ridge (behind the teeth) with the wider part of the tongue right behind the tip, but not as close to the tip as when one is sounding the English "d." To Americans, Japanese /d/ and /r/ may sound alike.

eda   ude   doko   kodomo

/k/ formulates nine syllables, *k, ka, ki, ku, ke, ko, kya, kyu,* and *kyo.*

/k/ is less aspirated than English "k." /k/ before *a, u, e,* or *o* is pronounced like "c" in "coot."

/k/ before *i, ya, yu,* or *yo* is pronounced like "c" in "cute."

      kokkai   kikyoo   iku   dake   kyaku   kekkyoku

/g/ formulates eight syllables, *ga, gi, gu, ge, go, gya, gyu,* and *gyo.*

/g/ is pronounced similarly to the hard English "g," when it is in initial position, but it is more fully voiced than in English.

/g/ before *a, u, e,* or *o* is pronounced approximately like "g" in "begone."

/g/ before *i, ya, yu,* or *yo* is pronounced like "g" in "regular," but it is more fully voiced.

      gyaku   gyuunyuu   gyookai   geki

      gakkoo   gikei   guchi   gochisoo

When /g/ appears in any other position than the initial, plosive /g/ changes into nasal /g/, the sound similar to "ng" in "singer." This is also true of the Relational *ga.* Although nasal /g/ is prominent in the Tōkyō speech of Japanese, there are quite a few Tōkyō people who don't use nasal /g/. Therefore, it isn't absolutely necessary to be able to pronounce it, but you should be able to recognize it.

      nagai   sugi   sugu   eigo   sagyoo   kaigyaku   toogyuu

      Kore ga hon desu.

/h/ formulates eight syllables, *ha, hi, fu, he, ho, hya, hyu,* and *hyo.*

/h/ before *i, ya, yu,* or *yo* is pronounced like "h" in "human," but it is more fricative.

      hito   koohii   hyaku   hyuuzu   hyooshi

/h/ before *a, e,* or *o* is pronounced like "h" in "hot."

      haha   heta   hoshi   chihoo

/h/ with *u* is spelled *fu* and produced with the lips close together and then by letting air come out in a puff. Since the upper teeth are not used at all, this pronunciation is unlike that of the English "f."

      fuufu   fuyu   fuchi   Koofu   Fujisan

/s/ formulates nine syllables, *s, sa, shi, su, se, so, sha, shu,* and *sho.*

/s/ before *a, u, e,* or *o* is pronounced like "s" in "see," but it is produced farther forward in the mouth.

      asa   sasa   susuki   gassaku   issei   soko

/s/ with /i/, /ya/, /yu/, or /yo/ is spelled *shi, sha, shu,* or *sho,* and /s/ is pronounced like "sh" in "she." But this is more aspirated than the above /s/.

      shichi   shishi   kushi   kesshite   shashoo   isshuu

/z/ formulates eight syllables, *za, ji, zu, ze, zo, ja, ju,* and *jo.*

/z/ with /i/, /ya/, /yu/, or /yo/ is spelled *ji, ja, ju,* and *jo* respectively, and /z/ is pronounced like "j" in "reject." But usually it is pronounced as if it were spelled "dz."

/z/ before *a, u, e,* or *o* is pronounced like "z" in "bazaar," but it is more fully voiced.

      jiko   jaa   kuji   juuji   koojoo

      zaseki   hazu   zehi   kazoku

/m/ formulates eight syllables, *ma, mi, mu, me, mo, mya, myu,* and *myo.*

/m/ is close to English "m," except for being more fully voiced.

/m/ before *a, u, e,* or *o* is pronounced like "m" in "mine," and /m/ before *i, ya, yu,* or *yo* is pronounced like "m" in "amuse."

mado   mimi   yomu   kome   motsu

myaku   Myuuzu   kimyoo

/n/ formulates eight syllables, *na, ni, nu, ne, no, nya, nyu,* and *nyo.*

/n/ before *a, u, e,* or *o* is pronounced like "n" in "deny" with the tongue touching the teeth and is fully voiced.

funa   inu   mune   kono

/n/ before *i, ya, yu,* or *yo* is pronounced like "n" in "menu."

nyooboo   niku   han'nya   gyuunyuu

/n'/ syllabic nasal, immediately before *p, b,* or *m,* is pronounced as a long "m."

en'pitsu   Shin'bashi   kin'mu

/n'/ immediately before /t/, /d/, /z/, /n/, or /r/ is pronounced as a long "n."

hon'too   san'ji   don'na   en'ryo   hon'dai

/n'/ before *k* or *g* is pronounced like the prolonged "ng" sound in "singer."

nan'gai   ben'kyoo   Ogen'ki desu ka /

Elsewhere, that is, before vowels, before *y, w,* glottal *h, s,* or at the end of a word, *n'* is pronounced with long nasalization. /n'/ at the end of a word is spelled *n* in this text.

hon   ten'in   kan'shin

/r/ formulates eight syllables, *ra, ri, ru, re, ro, rya, ryu,* and *ryo.* The Japanese /r/ is a flap /r/, made by flicking the tip of the tongue against the alveolar ridge.

Therefore, it is entirely different from American English "r," but is more like "l." This is rather similar to the British English pronunciation of "r" in "very."

raku   urusai   iroiro   rin'go   kirei   ryokan   Ryuukyuu

To American-English-speaking people, the Japanese /r/ may sound like /d/, but Japanese /r/ is shorter than /d/, and in producing /r/, the tip of the tongue touches the alveolar ridge, whereas in the production of /d/, the area of the tongue immediately behind the tip touches the upper teeth.

Compare:

Hara....hada   sore....sode   raku....daku   roku....doku

1.2.11 Syllabic Length

One of the most outstanding features in pronouncing Japanese is its syllabic length. A phrase or a sentence should be pronounced with an even and regular rhythm consisting of many beats, uttered with the same length. These beats are called syllables. About the same amount of time must be spent for each syllable. There is neither a speeding up nor a slowing down.

to-ko-ro	to-ki-do-ki	Yo-ko-ha-ma	ko-n'-ni-chi-wa
ki-t-to	yu-k-ku-ri	Na-ga-sa-ki	ko-n'-ba-n-wa

1.2.12 Accent

In English, if a syllable is accented, it shows that the accented syllable is produced with a strong stress. Therefore, English accent is called STRESS ACCENT. Furthermore, English vowels in a phrase or a sentence are not pronounced with the same duration. This contrasts with the Japanese language distinctly.

In English the stressed syllable is much more clearly uttered than others, and it is longer in time duration.

an Énglishman   an América

On the other hand, Japanese syllables are pronounced with more or less equal length and stress. Although some syllables are given more prominence, this has more to do with pitch than stress. Therefore, Japanese accent is called PITCH ACCENT.

1.2.13 Pitch Levels

For the purpose of this book two levels of pitch will be discussed, namely HIGHER PITCH and LOWER PITCH. They are not absolute pitch levels. They are higher or lower, relative to each other. Within one accent unit, syllables with higher pitch level will be marked by a horizontal bar over them.

yoofuku   den'wa

When there is a fall in pitch within one accent unit, a small superscript hook symbol will be attached to the end of the horizontal bar over the higher pitched level syllables. Any word with such a hook is called an accented word. Conversely, any word without such a hook is called an unaccented word.

tatemono   chookyori den'wa

However, when there is no fall in pitch within one accent unit, the superscript hook will not be attached to the superscript bar.

yoofuku   den'wa

1.2.14 Tokyo Pitch

In Tōkyō, pitch levels in one accent unit are governed by the following two conventions:

1) the pitch level of the first syllable must be different from that of the second syllable. Therefore, if the first syllable is higher in pitch, the second must be lower, and vice versa;

2) within one accent unit, whether it is a word, a phrase, or a clause, higher-pitched syllables can never be interrupted by any lower-pitched syllable.

Thus:

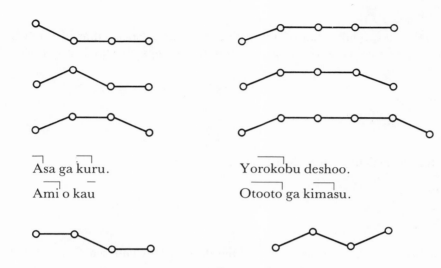

Asa ga kuru.

Yorokobu deshoo.

Ami o kau

Otooto ga kimasu.

But never:

1.2.15 Accent Variation

Many accented words lose their accent when used with other words forming one accent unit. Conversely, many accented words gain the accent when used with other words forming one accent unit.

arigatoo   +   gozaimasu   =   arigatoo gozaimasu

kaki   +   kata   =   kakikata

1.2.16 Intonation

The following marks are applicable only to useful expressions and dialogs.

1) Period (.)

This mark indicates that the final syllable of an utterance is pronounced with falling intonation. This is used at the end of a statement, a proposition, or an indirect question.

Soo desu.

Kabukiza de aimashoo ka.

Soo shimashoo.

2) Rising Intonation (_____/)

When a sentence or a phrase is uttered as a question or ends with a Sentence Particle *yo* or *ne,* et cetera, the final syllable is more or less pronounced in rising intonation.

10

English speakers tend to raise the pitch of the last several syllables or words in a gradually heightening pitch manner.

       Are you going?

Thus, Japanese intonation, especially that of a question, is different from that of English. The syllable next to the last is usually low-pitched and the rising intonation creeps into the last syllable while it is produced.

       Ikimasu ka /

3) Exclamation (!)

This mark indicates that the articulation of the final syllable ends abruptly.

       Yamada san!

4) Comma (,)

A comma indicates a break within the utterance. Therefore, when you see a comma after a word, a phrase, or a clause, you can pause between the expression and the word following. The comma is not equivalent in terms of function to its use in English.

       Hai, wakarimasu.

5) Question (?)

A question mark indicates that a sentence is uttered as a question.

       Ikimasu ka? /

1.3   DRILLS

1.3.1   General Pronunciation Drill

1. a ai au aoi i ii iie ie u ue uo o oi ooi

2. kau kao ou sou hai bai aiai taikai

3. tooi soo kookoo ookii tootoo

4. taitei seito sen'sei keisei meiji

5. yaya iya yuuki yuki yoi iwa waei

6. s(u)sumu mats(u) watak(u)shi ikimas(u) sh(i)tte imas(u)

7. sakka hassha happun tokkyo Hattori

8. gopeeji ippon pianisuto depaato

9. tabi byooki shibai

10. tatami totemo moto

11. Doozo dete kudasai.

12. kaki hokkyoku kyaku kyuukoo kokki kyoo

13. gaku Gin'za guchi geta goi gyaku gyuu gyookai

14. uchi ichi chakusoo chuui chotto

15. tsuyoi kutsu tsuru itsutsu tsutsu motsu yottsu

16. fuku fuufu fuuboo Fujisan yoofuku furui saifu

17. sesoo sasu issai issei

18. shichi yasashii shishakai shussho issho

19. hitotsu hima koohii hyaku hihyoo hyoohi hyuuzu

20. hachi heta fuhei

21. zasshi mazui zehi soozoo

22. jiko kujaku oji josei juuji

23. mada kumi muzukashii gimei

24. nani nuno nemasu gyuunyuu nyooboo

25. akan'boo kan'byoo shin'pai en'pitsu san'mai kin'mu Kon'nichi wa.

26. hon'too san'ji en'ryo kon'do ben'jo han'nyuu

27. nagai migi sugu agemasu gogo kaigyaku toogyuu sagyoo

28. nan'gai ben'kyoo hon'ki

29. hon ten'in kan'shin han'ei kan'sha hon'ya

30. raku kirai rin'go kuri rusu uru ren'shuu kore Roshia mochiron ryaku ryuukoo ichiryuu ryokoo kyooryoku ryooriya

1.3.2 Contrast Drill (Single Vowels *vs.* Long Vowels)

obasan	obaasan	seru	seeru
ojisan	ojiisan	beru	beeru
nisan	niisan	soko	sookoo
chizu	chiizu	toshin	tooshin
yuki	yuuki	yoko	yokoo
shuki	shuuki		

1.3.3 Contrast Drill (Consonant + Vowel Syllable *vs.* Syllabic Consonant)

ika	ikka	gaka	gakka
iku	ikku	isho	issho
saka	sakka	futa	futta
asari	assari	haka	hakka
kasai	kassai	bushi	busshi

nishi. . . . . nisshi	kita . . . . kitta
heta . . . . hetta	Okanai desu. . . . . Okkanai desu.
kata . . . . katta	Ito desu ka /. . . . . Itto desu ka /
soto . . . . sotto	Ite kudasai. . . . . Itte kudasai.

1.3.4   Sounds to be distinguished

a.   (shi)   (chi)

ishi. . . . . ichi	tashimasu . . . . tachimasu
kashi . . . . kachi	Hashi desu. . . . . Hachi desu.
kushi . . . . kuchi	Shikai desu ka/. . . . . . . Chikai desu ka/
toshi. . . . . tochi	Ushi o kaimasu. . . . . . Uchi o kaimasu.
jishin . . . . jichin	

b.   (su)   (tsu)

kasu . . . . katsu	sukimashita. . . . . tsukimashita
suru . . . . tsuru	Are wa suki desu. . . . . . Are wa tsuki desu.
suika . . . . tsuika	Den'sha ga sukimasu. . Den'sha ga tsukimasu.
sumi. . . . . tsumi	Suna ga arimasu ka/. . . Tsuna ga arimasu ka /
basu. . . . . batsu	

c.   (d)   (r)

doku . . . . roku	muda. . . . . mura
eda. . . . . era	sode . . . . sore
kodomo . . . . koromo	yudemasu . . . . yuremasu
kokuden . . . . kokuren	Hidoi desu nee. . . . . . Hiroi desu nee.
hadan . . . . haran	Tada desu. . . . . Tara desu.

d.   (i)   (e)

mai . . . . mae	kaimasu. . . . . kaemasu
aimasu. . . . . aemasu	kaerimasu . . . . kaeremasu
ikimasu . . . . ikemasu	

*   *   *   *   *   *   *   *   *   *   *   *

Tongue Twister: Tonari no kyaku wa yoku kaki kuu kyaku da

Boozu ga byoobu ni joozu ni boozu no e o kaita.

Nama mugi, nama gome, nama tamago.

e. (i)   (hi)

iru . . . . hiru   jii . . . . jihi

iso . . . . hiso   ikimasu . . . . hikimasu

mai . . . . mahi

f. (/y/ in the syllabic   (/y/ in the syllabic
    initial position)   noninitial position)

kiyoo . . . . kyoo   kiyaku . . . . kyaku

hiyoo . . . . hyoo   hiyaku . . . . hyaku

riyoo . . . . ryoo   shiyoo . . . . shoo

biyooin . . . . byooin

g. (syllabic /n'/)   (/n/)

bun'an . . . . bunan   ken'en . . . . kenen

gen'an . . . . genan   kin'en . . . . kinen

shin'an . . . . shinan

1.3.5   Pronunciation Drill (Practice the following numerals to familiarize yourself with them.)

page number

a.   1 . . . . ichi   ippeeji; ichipeeji

        2 . . . . ni   nipeeji

        3 . . . . san   san'peeji

        4 . . . . shi; yon   yon'peeji

        5 . . . . go   gopeeji

        6 . . . . roku   rokupeeji

        7 . . . . shichi; nana   shichipeeji; nanapeeji

        8 . . . . hachi   happeeji; hachipeeji

        9 . . . . ku; kyuu   kyuupeeji

        10 . . . . juu   jippeeji; juppeeji

        11 . . . . juuichi   juuichipeeji; juuippeeji

        12 . . . . juuni   juunipeeji

        13 . . . . juusan   juusan'peeji

        14 . . . . juushi; juuyon   juuyon'peeji

        15 . . . . juugo   juugopeeji

        16 . . . . juuroku   juurokupeeji

17. . . . . juushichi; juunana   juushichipeeji; juunanapeeji
18. . . . . juuhachi   juuhappeeji; juuhachipeeji
19. . . . . juuku; juukyuu   juukyuupeeji
20. . . . . nijuu   nijippeeji; nijuppeeji
21. . . . . nijuuichi   nijuu ichipeeji

30. . . . . san'juu   san'jippeeji; san'juppeeji
40. . . . . yon'juu   yon'jippeeji; yon'juppeeji
50. . . . . gojuu   gojippeeji; gojuppeeji
60. . . . . rokujuu   rokujippeeji; rokujuppeeji
70. . . . . shichijuu; nanajuu   shichijippeeji; nanajuppeeji
80. . . . . hachijuu   hachijippeeji; hachijuppeeji
90. . . . . kyuujuu   kyuujippeeji; kyuujuppeeji
100. . . . . hyaku   hyakupeeji
200. . . . . nihyaku   nihyakupeeji
300. . . . . san'byaku   san'byakupeeji
400. . . . . yon'hyaku   yon'hyakupeeji
500. . . . . gohyaku   gohyakupeeji
600. . . . . roppyaku   roppyakupeeji
700. . . . . nanahyaku   nanahyakupeeji
800. . . . . happyaku   happyakupeeji
900. . . . . kyuuhyaku   kyuuhyakupeeji
1,000. . . . . sen   sen'peeji

b. 1. . . . . hitotsu   6. . . . . muttsu
    2. . . . . futatsu   7. . . . . nanatsu
    3. . . . . mittsu   8. . . . . yattsu
    4. . . . . yottsu   9. . . . . kokonotsu
    5. . . . . itsutsu   10. . . . . too

1.3.6 General Accent Drill

a. e. . . . . E ga arimasu.   tomodachi. . . . . Tomodachi ni au.

    uchi. . . . . Uchi ga arimasu.   murasakiiro . . . . Murasakiiro no hana

    unagi. . . . . Unagi o taberu.

b.   e . . . . E ga arimasu.   yoi . . . . Yoi deshoo.

asa . . . . Asa ga suki desu.   Fujisan . . . . Fujisan ga mieru.

c.   ike . . . . Ike ga aru.   okaasan . . . . Okaasan ni iimasu.

aoi . . . . Aoi iro desu.   uma . . . . Uma ni norimasu.

d.   otoko . . . . Otoko ga imasu.   yorokobu . . . . Yorokobu deshoo

ureshii . . . . Ureshii desu.   kodomotachi. . . . . . . Kodomotachi ga kimasu.

e.   otooto . . . . Otooto deshita.   hazukashii . . . . Hazukashii desu.

dokukeshi . . . . Dokukeshi o nomu.   atatakai . . . . Atatakai tokoro.

1.3.7 General Intonation Drill

a.   Ohayoo gozaimasu.   Gomen nasai.   Itadakimasu.

Sayoonara.   Gomen kudasai.   Onegai shimasu.

Oyasumi nasai.   Okaeri nasai.   Omedetoo gozaimasu.

b.   Soo desu ka /   Ikimasen ka /   Moo naraimashita ne /   Gakkoo desu ne /

Ogen'ki desu ka /   Doko e ikimasu ka /   Soo desu ne /   Moshi moshi /

c.   A!   Moshi moshi!   Kon'nichi wa!

Sayoonara!   Soo desu yo!   Irasshai

d.   Gochisoo sama   Kon'ban wa

Tadaima   Iie   Kon'nichi wa

1.3.8 Contrastive Word Accent Drill

(The instructor may indicate the difference in meaning.)

ika . . . . ika   ichi . . . . ichi

uki . . . . uki   tsuma. . . . . tsuma

kaki . . . . kaki   kami . . . . kami

yooki . . . . yooki   kame . . . . kame

sake . . . . sake   kiri . . . . kiri

asa . . . . asa   iji . . . . iji

ishi . . . . ishi   igai. . . . . igai

hashi . . . . hashi   suzu . . . . suzu

kachi . . . . kachi   tabi . . . . tabi

16

1.3.9　Contrastive Sentence Accent Drill

(The instructor may indicate the difference in meaning.)

a.　E o mochimasu. . . . . E o mochimasu.

b.　Kaki o tabemasu. Kaki o tabemasu.

c.　Sake desu ne/. . . . . Sake desu ne/

d.　Kame desu ka/. . . . . Kame desu ka/

e.　Atsui mono desu. . . . . Atsui mono desu.

f.　Hana ga akai . . . . Hana ga akai

g.　Kono hashi desu. . . . . Kono hashi desu.

h.　Kore o kaite kudasai. . . . . Kore o kaite kudasai.

i.　Otte kudasai. . . . . Otte kudasai.

j.　Fuite kudasai. . . . . Fuite kudasai.

k.　Yon'de kudasai. Yon'de kudasai.

l.　Harete kimashita ne/. . . . . Harete kimashita ne/

m.　Kite kudasai. . . . . Kite kudasai.

n.　Ima desu ka/. . . . . Ima desu ka/

o.　Koori o kaimasu. . . . . Koori o kaimasu.

1.3.10　Contrastive Intonation Drill

a.　Soo desu ka. . . . . Soo desu ka/

b.　Soo desu ne/. . . . . Soo desu ne. . . . . .Soo desu nee.

c.　Soo desu yo. . . . . Soo desu yo/

d.　Moshi moshi. . . . . Moshi moshi/ . . . . .Moshi moshi!

e.　Kabukiza deshoo. . . . . Kabukiza deshoo/

f.　Goji han goro aimashoo ka. . . . . .Goji han goro aimashoo ka/

g.　Ikeda san . . . . .Ikeda san!

1.4　EXERCISES

1.4.1　One of the following words or expressions in each group will be pronounced by your instructor. Listen and underline the one pronounced.

a.　obasan　　obaasan　　　d.　soko　　sooko

b.　nisan　　niisan　　　e.　saka　　sakka

c.　yuki　　yuuki　　　f.　kasai　　kassai

g.	heta	hetta	q.	kaimasu	kaemasu
h.	bushi	busshi	r.	iru	hiru
i.	hiyoo	hyoo	s.	ikimasu	hikimasu
j.	kushi	kuchi	t.	kiyoo	kyoo
k.	kin'en	kinen	u.	biyooin	byooin
l.	suika	tsuika	v.	Ite kudasai.	Itte kudasai.
m.	kaerimasu	kaeremasu	w.	Ushi o kaimasu.	Uchi o kaimasu.
n.	kodomo	koromo	x.	Shikai desu.	Chikai desu.
o.	hadan	haran	y.	Hidoi desu nee.	Hiroi desu nee.
p.	mai	mae	z.	Den'sha ga sukimasu.	Den'sha ga tsukimasu.

1.4.2 In each group three words or expressions will be pronounced by your instructor. One of the three words or expressions is different from the other two. Work on this exercise with your book closed. Write the number representing the different word or expression.

Note: The following list is only for the use of the instructor. It is recommended that the instructor change the word order in each group to make this exercise effective. The instructor is also encouraged to make new lists based on the idea shown in the list.

a.	(1) chizu	(2) chizu	(3) chiizu
b.	(1) ojisan	(2) ojiisan	(3) ojisan
c.	(1) asari	(2) assari	(3) assari
d.	(1) gakka	(2) gaka	(3) gakka
e.	(1) tochi	(2) tochi	(3) toshi
f.	(1) Hashi desu.	(2) Hachi desu.	(3) Hashi desu.
g.	(1) basu	(2) basu	(3) batsu
h.	(1) kokuden	(2) kokuren	(3) kokuden
i.	(1) muda	(2) mura	(3) muda
j.	(1) sode	(2) sode	(3) sore
k.	(1) aimasu	(2) aimasu	(3) aemasu
l.	(1) iru	(2) hiru	(3) hiru
m.	(1) biyooin	(2) biyooin	(3) byooin
n.	(1) hiyaku	(2) hyaku	(3) hiyaku
o.	(1) bun'an	(2) bun'an	(3) bunan

18

1.4.3 Accent

In each group, three words or expressions will be pronounced by your instructor. Two types are included in this exercise: (A) In some groups two words or expressions are identical, while (B) In other groups three words are identical.

Write on your paper the numbers representing the identical items.

Example A: (1) ika   (2) ika   (3) ika

Write on your paper: (1)   (2)

Example B: (1) sake   (2) sake   (3) sake

Write on your paper: (1)   (2)   (3)

Note: The following list is for the use of the instructor. It is suggested that the word order be changed or new lists created to make this exercise effective.

a. (1) ishi   (2) ishi   (3) ishi

b. (1) maku   (2) maku   (3) maku

c. (1) asa   (2) asa   (3) asa

d. (1) hashi   (2) hashi   (3) hashi

e. (1) ichi   (2) ichi   (3) ichi

f. (1) kame   (2) kame   (3) kame

g. (1) toshi   (2) toshi   (3) toshi

h. (1) suru   (2) suru   (3) suru

i. (1) Kaki ga arimasu yo.   (2) Kaki ga arimasu yo.   (3) Kaki ga arimasu yo.

j. (1) Atsui mono desu.   (2) Atsui mono desu.   (3) Atsui mono desu.

k. (1) Kame desu.   (2) Kame desu.   (3) Kame desu.

l. (1) Yon'de kudasai.   (2) Yon'de kudasai.   (3) Yon'de kudasai.

m. (1) Kite kudasai.   (2) Kite kudasai.   (3) Kite kudasai.

n. (1) Ki ga tsukimashita.   (2) Ki ga tsukimashita.   (3) Ki ga tsukimashita.

o. (1) Ima desu ka/   (2) Ima desu ka/   (3) Ima desu ka/

1.4.4 Accent

One of the two words or expressions listed in each group will be pronounced by your instructor. Listen and check the right one with "X."

a. (1) uki   (2) uki

b. (1) kaki   (2) kaki

c. (1) kami   (2) kami

d. (1) suzu   (2) suzu

e. (1) tabi   (2) tabi

f. (1) Nihon desu ka /   (2) Nihon desu ka /

g. (1) Otte kudasai.   (2) Otte kudasai.

h. (1) Kono hashi desu.   (2) Kono hashi desu.

i. (1) Dare ga matte imasu ka /   (2) Dare ga matte imasu ka /

j. (1) Nani o katte imasu ka /   (2) Nani o katte imasu ka /

1.4.5 Intonation

One of the two words or expressions listed in each group will be pronounced by your instructor. Listen and check the right one with "X."

a. (1) Soo desu ka.   (2) Soo desu ka /

b. (1) Kirei desu yo /   (2) Kirei desu yo.

c. (1) A.   (2) A!

d. (1) Dooshite /   (2) Dooshite.

e. (1) Yoku wakarimashita ne /   (2) Yoku wakarimashita nee.

1.5 CULTURAL NOTES

1.5.1 Greeting

The use of the three greetings presented in Lesson 1 is governed by one or more of several considerations: the time of day, the normal or expected frequency of meeting, the relative status of the persons, and their degree of familiarity.

Unlike "Good morning," the use of *Ohayoo gozaimasu* is limited to the very early morning, from before dawn until about ten or eleven o'clock. In addition, it is used only upon the first encounter with any one person on a given day. It implies relative frequency of meeting; one would greet a person he had not seen for a few weeks differently. The full expression is formal and deferential, and its usage is mandatory in addressing one's superiors. *Ohayoo* by itself is acceptable among peers, and is also addressed to those of inferior status including inferior family members.

Kon'nichi wa covers the daylight hours, overlapping "Good morning" and "Good afternoon," and is neutral in respect to formality. Thus there is no real English equivalent, as "Hello" and "Hi" are both slightly weighted in respect to formality and are not limited to a time of day or night. In addition, *Kon'nichi wa* is occasionally used to get someone's attention when calling at their home. This use is similar to the expression "Is anyone home?" or "Hello?"

After dark, *Kon'ban wa* is used in greeting and, like *Kon'nichi wa,* is neither formal nor informal. It is similar to "Good evening" except that the latter carries a somewhat formal connotation in American culture.

In Japan, greetings are used as tools of social integration by establishing and reinforcing, through language, the hierarchical relationship between the speakers. As in its American usage, the greeting mediates initial contact between individuals in a specific time and place situation, smoothing their transition into actual conversation. The Japanese greeting, however, goes further by placing the speakers in their concrete social relation, through verbal acknowledgment (by the form it takes) of that social relation.

The form which a greeting takes is further determined by group consciousness within a group such as the family, where the intensity of in-groupness is very great. The greeting may be eliminated completely due to the great intimacy generated by the feeling of in-groupness. Within a group of less intense intimacy, an appropriate greeting is required. The absence of an appropriate greeting within a group of less intimacy, however, would be a breach of social etiquette and would be considered rude behavior.

The language used in greeting others, then, is a gauge of the intensity of in-groupness present in the relations of individuals.

1.5.2 Parting Expressions

The use of the two expressions of parting involves the same considerations as those of greeting. *Sayoonara* or "Good-bye" may be used at any time of the day, but it is not usually used with family members of the speaker. Occasionally it might be addressed to a relative, on parting for a period of time; if, for instance, the speaker's sister was going away on a trip. Among children and students, an intimate expression, *bai-bai* or "Bye-bye," which is very close to "See you later," is more common nowadays. *Jaa mata* is another of this kind of parting expression meaning "See you again," and will be presented in Lesson 3. See Note 3.4.17.

Oyasumi nasai is very similar in meaning and use to "Sleep well" or "Sleep tight." Used mostly among intimates, it carries warmth and suggests the hope or expectation of seeing the listener in the morning. *Oyasumi* alone is acceptable among peers as well as to inferiors.

1.5.3 Gratitude and Apology

The most common English expression of gratitude is "Thank you" or "Thanks," and the response is likely to be "You're welcome." Expressions of apology such as "I'm sorry" or "Pardon me" are answered with "That's all right" or some variant. The Japanese language, however, includes not only direct equivalents for the expressions "I'm sorry" and "Thank you," but also contains two expressions which may be applied to both situations.

Arigatoo and its polite form *Arigatoo gozaimasu* mean "Thank you" and *Gomen nasai* means "I'm sorry." *Sumimasen,* however, may mean either *Arigatoo* or *Gomen nasai,* or the combination of both. As an expression of gratitude, *Sumimasen* retains a distinctly apologetic character, as if to say, "Thank you for going to so much trouble." As an apology, it is equivalent to "Excuse me." Like "Excuse me," *Sumimasen* may also be used to catch someone's attention. *Doomo* may also be used alone to express either apology or gratitude.

A further distinction between *Gomen nasai* and *Sumimasen,* is that of relative formality. *Gomen nasai* is informal, casual, and colloquial, while *Sumimasen* is more formal. Furthermore, *Gomen nasai* exhibits a higher frequency of usage among children and, sometimes, women. If *Sumimasen* is translated as "Excuse me," *Gomen nasai* may be translated as "Forgive me." *Sumimasen,* then, can be used in three distinct contexts: to express gratitude, to express an apology, and to gain attention.

Expressions designed to attract someone's attention (*Sumimasen, Anoo,* and *Moshi moshi*) are always placed at the beginning of a sentence. To differentiate, *Gomen nasai* is never used at the beginning of a sentence, although it can be used by itself as a single expression.

As a whole, the Japanese readily demonstrate gratitude, using such expressions as *Arigatoo, Sumimasen,* and *Doomo.* In Japanese, apology occurs with a much greater frequency than in English—indicative of the display of modesty or the heteronomous tendency characteristic of the Japanese in their speech—in such expressions as *Doomo, Sumimasen,* and *Gomen nasai.*

1.5.4 Doomo or Vagueness

As stated above, *Doomo* may also be used alone to express either apology or gratitude. It is an abbreviated form of both *Doomo arigatoo* and *Doomo sumimasen,* thus embodying the traditional Japanese tendency to employ nonexplicit words or expressions, depending on the occasion.

1.5.5   Modesty or Heteronomy

Doo itashimashite may be used to respond to any of these expressions of gratitude and apology, in a manner similar to "Don't mention it" or "That's okay." Sometimes *Iie* "no" may be used either alone or preceding this expression. The use of *Iie* by itself as a response to an expression of gratitude or apology is less formal.

This heteronomous trait of the Japanese, whereby they attempt to show their consideration toward others in their speech, is especially true in the case of Japanese women, who tend to make their language more polite, more refined, and more modest than Japanese men. For women of a certain group, however, the distance between expressions used by males and those used by females may not be that great. For example, the mode of expression of female students among themselves is far less polite. We may regard this as a phenomenon of subcultures.

LESSON 2
INTRODUCTION TO KANA

2.1 USEFUL EXPRESSIONS

Wakarimasu ka₁ /	"Do you understand?" "Is that clear?"
(Hai,) wakarimasu.	"(Yes,) I understand."
(Iie,) wakarimasen.	"(No,) I do not understand."
Yoku dekimashita.	"Very good." "You did a good job." This is a compliment for good accomplishment.
Moo ichido itte kudasai.	"Please say it once more."
Ato ni tsuite itte kudasai.	"Please repeat after me."
Yoku kiite kudasai.	"Please listen carefully."
Yon'de kudasai.	"Please read it."
Kaite kudasai.	"Please write it."
Hanashite kudasai.	"Please speak." "Please talk."
Gopeeji o akete kudasai.	"Please open [the book on] page five."
Hon o tojite kudasai.	"Please close your book."
Chotto matte kudasai.	"Please wait for a moment."
Gomen kudasai.₂	"Pardon me." "Excuse me." This expression is commonly used by a visitor to someone's home to attract the resident's attention to the fact that the visitor is at the door. Or it may be used by a customer in a store to attract the sales clerk's attention. To answer this, *Hai* "Yes" is used.
Irasshai (mase).₂	"I am glad that you came." "Welcome." This expression is used for greeting a customer entering a store. *Irasshaimase* is more polite than *Irasshai* and is used by women, as well as by employees of stores, restaurants, hotels, et cetera.
Tadaima₃	"I've come home now." This expression literally means "Just now," and it implies that the speaker has safely come home.
Okaeri nasai.₃	"Welcome home." "I am glad to see you back." This expression is used by a person who is at home, as a reply to *Tadaima*. Informally, *Okaeri* is used.
Itadakimasu.₄	"I am going to eat or drink." This expression is used when a person is going to eat or drink. Literally it means "I will receive."
Gochisoo sama deshita.₄	"It was a feast." This expression is used after a person has eaten or drunk something and expresses his gratitude for it. *Deshita* may be omitted.

Onegai shimasu.₄

The literal translation is "I make a request." This expression is polite. Depending upon the context, this expression can be translated into various expressions in English, such as "Please do it for me," "Please take care of things," et cetera.

Omedetoo gozaimasu.₄

"Congratulations." This expression is used when someone has a birthday, has been promoted, or has had some other happy experience. It is also used as a New Year greeting. Informally, *Omedetoo* is used.

2.2 INTRODUCTION TO JAPANESE WRITING SYSTEM

Japan had no writing system before *kan'ji* (Chinese characters) were introduced from China. After the Japanese started to use *kan'ji* to write their language, two types of pronunciation were gradually developed in Japan.

One method was to attach Japanese meanings to certain *kan'ji* and use Japanese pronunciation for these *kan'ji*. Such pronunciation is called *kun* pronunciation. The other method was to pronounce the *kan'ji* according to their original Chinese sounds, with Japanese modification. Such pronunciation is called *on* pronunciation.

However, individual *kan'ji* were introduced to Japan at various times, and the original Chinese pronunciations of them differed, depending upon the time and place of origin. Thus, not only the southern Chinese sounds were introduced but also the northern sounds. Not only the Chinese pronunciations of one period were introduced but also those of other periods. This explains why there are generally at least two Japanese pronunciations for each *kan'ji*. *Kan'ji* are normally used for meanings, but some *kan'ji* are used as phonetic symbols without any meaning attached. The number of *kan'ji* used merely as phonetic symbols was gradually narrowed down to a few that represented certain Japanese sounds. Eventually the Japanese syllabary called *kana* replaced *kan'ji* as phonetic symbols.

Two types of *kana* were developed: *hiragana* and *katakana*. *Katakana* were developed on the basis of adopting just one portion of *kan'ji*, and *hiragana* were developed on the basis of modifying the shape of *kan'ji*.

Example:

kan'ji	伊	[i]	以	[i]
katakana	イ	[i]	↓	
hiragana			い	[i]

Today, *kana* and about two thousand *kan'ji* are used in the writing of Japanese. *Kan'ji* and *kana* are combined in writing. Usually Noun, Verb Base, and Adjective Base are written in *kan'ji*, and Sentence Interjectives, Pre-Nouns, Relationals, Adverbs, Copula, and Sentence Particles are written in *kana*. It is the readings of *kan'ji*, the orthographic arrangement of *kana*, and the suggested *kan'ji-kana* combinations that the student is to learn. They look rather cumbersome but they are not as chaotic as the English orthographic system.

2.3 HIRAGANA

In the postwar writing system of Japan, there are forty-six simple *hiragana* symbols and twenty-five variations. Since these *hiragana* have been practiced lesson by lesson, students are required to be able to recognize and produce all the *hiragana* at this stage. The following explanations are given only to systematize *hiragana* writing arrangements.

2.3.1 Simple Hiragana

Chart 1

dan¹ / gyoo²	/a/	/i/	/u/	/e/	/o/	zero³
a	あ	い	う	え	お	
ka /k/	か	き	く	け	こ	
sa /s/	さ	し	す	せ	そ	
ta /t/	た	ち	つ	て	と	
na /n/	な	に	ぬ	ね	の	
ha /h/	は	ひ	ふ	へ	ほ	
ma /m/	ま	み	む	め	も	
ya /y/	や	(い)⁴	ゆ	(え)	よ	
ra /r/	ら	り	る	れ	ろ	
wa /w/	わ	(ゐ)	(う)	(ゑ)	を	
n' /n'/						ん

1. *Kana* are classified into five *dan* according to the vowel final. Thus, あ、か、さ、た、な、は、ま、や、ら、and わ belong to /a/ *dan*.

2. *Kana* are also divided according to the consonant initial. The /t/ group of symbols is called, for instance, *ta gyoo* and た、ち、つ、て、and と are grouped as the *ta gyoo* sounds.

3. Zero means that there is no vowel final.

4. *Hiragana* in parentheses indicates that either it is not in current use or it is identical with *a gyoo* symbols both in shape and in pronunciation.

2.3.2 Two-dots Hiragana

There are twenty *hiragana* that represent voiced sounds. *Ga gyoo, za gyoo,* and *da gyoo* correspond to *ka gyoo, sa gyoo,* and *ta gyoo* respectively. *Ba gyoo* corresponds to *ha gyoo* in shape but it is not the voiced counterpart of *ha gyoo*.

Voiced *hiragana* have two dots at the upper right-hand corner of the corresponding *hiragana*.

Chart 2

	dan	/a/	/i/	/u/	/e/	/o/
ga	/g/	が	ぎ	ぐ	げ	ご
za	/z/	ざ	じ	ず	ぜ	ぞ
da	/d/	だ	ぢ*	づ*	で	ど
ba	/b/	ば	び	ぶ	べ	ぼ

* See Note 14.3.6.

2.3.3 One-circle Hiragana

Chart 3

	dan	/a/	/i/	/u/	/e/	/o/
pa	/p/	ぱ	ぴ	ぷ	ぺ	ぽ

They are the voiceless counterparts of *ba gyoo*.

2.3.4 A syllable composed of a consonant plus や、ゆ、or よ

Contracted sounds, such as /kya/, /syu/, /ryo/, et cetera, are represented by the combination of a *hiragana* of *i dan* and や、ゆ、or よ.

Usually the second symbol /ya/, /yu/, or /yo/ is written in a small character.

Chart 4

	/ya/	/yu/	/yo/
/k/	きゃ	きゅ	きょ
/s/	しゃ	しゅ	しょ
/t/	ちゃ	ちゅ	ちょ
/n/	にゃ	にゅ	にょ
/h/	ひゃ	ひゅ	ひょ
/m/	みゃ	みゅ	みょ

	/ya/	/yu/	/yo/
/r/	りゃ	りゅ	りょ
/g/	ぎゃ	ぎゅ	ぎょ
/z/	じゃ	じゅ	じょ
/b/	びゃ	びゅ	びょ
/p/	ぴゃ	ぴゅ	ぴょ

Note that the above combinations are written differently when a Japanese sentence is written vertically.

Compare: きゃく …… きゃく   しょり …… しょり   りゅう …… りゅう

2.3.5 How to write Hiragana

There is a slight difference between printed (as in the first column) and hand-written (as in the second column) *hiragana*.

Compare:

Chart 5   Stroke Order

a	あ	あ	ｰ	あ	te	て	て	て	
i	い	い	い	い	to	と	と	と	
u	う	う	｀	う	na	な	な	な	
e	え	え	｀	え	ni	に	に	に	
o	お	お	ｰ	おお	nu	ぬ	ぬ	ぬ	
ka	か	か	か	か	ne	ね	ね	ね	
ki	き	き	き	き	no	の	の	の	
ku	く	く	く		ha	は	は	は	
ke	け	け	け		hi	ひ	ひ	ひ	
ko	こ	こ	こ		fu	ふ	ふ	ふ	
sa	さ	さ	さ		he	へ	へ	へ	
shi	し	し	し		ho	ほ	ほ	ほ	
su	す	す	す		ma	ま	ま	ま	
se	せ	せ	せ		mi	み	み	み	
so	そ	そ	そ		mu	む	む	む	
ta	た	た	た		me	め	め	め	
chi	ち	ち	ち		mo	も	も	も	
tsu	つ	つ	つ		ya	や	や	や	

yu	ゆ	ゆ	ﬤ ゆ		ro	ろ	ろ	ろ
yo	よ	よ	￢よ		wa	わ	わ	しわ
ra	ら	ら	ゝら		o	を	を	￢ちを
ri	り	り	しり		n'	ん	ん	ん
ru	る	る	る		ga	が	が	つカかが
re	れ	れ	しれ		pa	ぱ	ぱ	いにはぱ

2.4 KATAKANA

With certain exceptions the use of *katakana* in the postwar standard Japanese writing system is limited to those names or words that are foreign in origin. Despite the increasing trend of using foreign words in everyday Japanese, *katakana* are considered secondary writing symbols. Therefore, this text is so arranged that the student learns *katakana* as they appear in lessons. The chart of *katakana* below is only for reference. It is suggested that the student consult Charts 6 through 10 whenever he encounters new *katakana* in this text.

2.4.1 Simple Katakana

Chart 6

dan / *gyoo*	/a/	/i/	/u/	/e/	/o/	zero
a	ア	イ	ウ	エ	オ	
ka /k/	カ	キ	ク	ケ	コ	
sa /s/	サ	シ	ス	セ	ソ	
ta /t/	タ	チ	ツ	テ	ト	
na /n/	ナ	ニ	ヌ	ネ	ノ	
ha /h/	ハ	ヒ	フ	ヘ	ホ	
ma /m/	マ	ミ	ム	メ	モ	
ya /y/	ヤ	（イ）	ユ	（エ）	ヨ	
ra /r/	ラ	リ	ル	レ	ロ	
wa /w/	ワ	（ヰ）	（ウ）	（エ）	ヲ	
n' /n'/						ン

2.4.2　Two-dots Katakana

Chart 7

dan / gyoo	/a/	/i/	/u/	/e/	/o/
ga　/g/	ガ	ギ	グ	ゲ	ゴ
za　/z/	ザ	ジ	ズ	ゼ	ゾ
da　/d/	ダ	(ヂ)	(ヅ)	デ	ド
ba　/b/	バ	ビ	ブ	ベ	ボ

2.4.3　One-circle Katakana

Chart 8

dan / gyoo	/a/	/i/	/u/	/e/	/o/
pa　/p/	パ	ピ	プ	ペ	ポ

2.4.4　A syllable composed of a consonant plus ヤ、ユ、or ヨ

Chart 9

	/ya/	/yu/	/yo/
/k/	キャ	キュ	キョ
/s/	シャ	シュ	ショ
/t/	チャ	チュ	チョ
/n/	ニャ	ニュ	ニョ
/h/	ヒャ	ヒュ	ヒョ
/m/	ミャ	ミュ	ミョ
/r/	リャ	リュ	リョ

	/ya/	/yu/	/yo/
/g/	ギャ	ギュ	ギョ
/z/	ジャ	ジュ	ジョ
/b/	ビャ	ビュ	ビョ
/p/	ピャ	ピュ	ピョ

2.4.5　How to write Katakana

There is a slight difference between printed (as in the first column) and hand-written (as in the second column) *kana*.

Chart 10　Stroke Order

a	ア	ア	⁻ ア	te	テ	テ	ー 二 テ
i	イ	イ	ノ イ	to	ト	ト	｜ ト
u	ウ	ウ	゛ ゛ ウ	na	ナ	ナ	ー ナ
e	エ	エ	ー エ エ	ni	二	二	ー 二
o	オ	オ	ー ナ オ	nu	ヌ	ヌ	フ ヌ
ka	カ	カ	フ カ	ne	ネ	ネ	゛ ナ オ ネ
ki	キ	キ	ー 二 キ	no	ノ	ノ	ノ
ku	ク	ク	ノ ク	ha	ハ	ハ	ノ ハ
ke	ケ	ケ	ノ ト ケ	hi	ヒ	ヒ	ー ヒ
ko	コ	コ	フ コ	fu	フ	フ	フ
sa	サ	サ	ー ナ サ	he	ヘ	ヘ	ヘ
shi	シ	シ	、 ‥ シ	ho	ホ	ホ	ー ナ オ ホ
su	ス	ス	フ ス	ma	マ	マ	フ マ
se	セ	セ	⁻ セ	mi	ミ	ミ	、 ミ ミ
so	ソ	ソ	、 ソ	mu	ム	ム	∠ ム
ta	タ	タ	ノ ク タ	me	メ	メ	ノ メ
chi	チ	チ	ノ ⁻ チ	mo	モ	モ	ー 二 モ
tsu	ツ	ツ	、 ゛ ツ	ya	ヤ	ヤ	フ ヤ

yu	ユ	ユ	㇅	ユ	ro	ロ	ロ	⼁	ㇹ ロ
yo	ヨ	ヨ	㇇	ヲ ヨ	wa	ワ	ワ	㇏	ワ
ra	ラ	ラ	￣	ラ	o	ヲ	ヲ	㇐	㇗ ヲ
ri	リ	リ	⼁	リ	n'	ン	ン	丶	ン
ru	ル	ル	ノ	ル	ga	ガ	ガ	㇇ カ ガ
re	レ	レ	レ		pa	パ	パ	ノ	ハ パ

2.5 CULTURAL NOTES

2.5.1 Classroom Usage

We assume that our learners are non-Japanese adults. Those useful classroom usages listed in 2.1 may, therefore, not be the normal expressions exchanged between a Japanese teacher and Japanese children. Please use these Japanese expressions in the classroom and avoid using English.

2.5.2 Irasshaimase

Irasshaimase may be translated as "Welcome" or "Come in," but it occurs with a much greater frequency in Japan than its equivalent forms in America. Used to receive a guest into one's home, both the English and the Japanese expressions occur with about the same frequency. In Japan, however, it is essential that *Irasshaimase* be addressed to every customer on entering a restaurant, bar, or shop. As explained in the Useful Expressions section, *Gomen kudasai* is used by a visitor or a customer. To answer this, *Hai* or *Irasshaimase* is used.

2.5.3 Tadaima

Tadaima and *Okaeri nasai* are exchanged in much the same fashion as Americans might say "Hi, I'm home" and "Oh, hi." The Japanese expressions are much more formalized, however, and function primarily as signals: that is, exactly the same words will probably be used each time, and the words themselves convey no information beyond a mutual acknowledgment of the fact that one has returned. *Tadaima* is used mainly upon returning home, and the length of absence, whether one has returned from an errand or from a long trip, makes no difference. *Okaeri nasai*, on the other hand, may be used to greet someone returning to his home, his office, or any other "base."

2.5.4 Itadakimasu and Gochisoo sama

Itadakimasu, in addition to other usages, is an expression of thanks for receiving and starting to eat or drink a meal or beverage. This expression is frequently used: one would almost always say *Itadakimasu* when receiving and starting to eat or drink a meal or beverage. Although it resembles grace that is said prior to eating, *Itadakimasu* carries no religious implications and simply expresses one's humbleness and gratitude for receiving food. The word derives from an expression meaning "to place on one's head" referring to the now outdated symbolic Japanese gesture of raising one's food or drink above one's head before starting to eat. It should be noted that the host or cook does not say it in his own home.

After the meal *Gochisoo sama deshita* is usually said, much as an American might say "Thank you, that was an excellent meal." It may also be used to thank someone for paying for a meal or beverage.

In summary, the Japanese seem to be inclined to use verbal cues for change in action, encounter and parting, such as *Irasshai, Tadaima, Okaeri nasai, Itadakimasu, Gochisoo sama deshita,* and *Omedetoo gozaimasu.* These also show the Japanese heteronomous tendency. They constantly try not to embarrass or inconvenience the other party and try to consider others' feelings.

LESSON 3
AFTER CLASS

3.1 USEFUL EXPRESSIONS

Jaa₁₇, mata ashita

"Well, I'll see you again tomorrow." *Jaa* is the contracted and informal equivalent of *dewa* "well, then." *Dewa, mata* "See you again" may be used in polite speech.

3.2 DIALOG

Mr. Yamada: Ishii san₁, issho ni kaerimasen₂ ka₃ /

Miss Ishii: Kore kara, chotto₄ Kan'da e₅ ikimasu₂.

Mr. Yamada: Kan'da e₆ /

Miss Ishii: Ee₇, hon o₈ kaimasu. Yamada san wa₉ nani₁₀ o shimasu ka/ Sugu₄ uchi e kaerimasu ka/

Mr. Yamada: Iie₇, kissaten de₁₁ koohii o nomimasu.

Miss Ishii: Yamada san wa yoku₄ kissaten e ikimasu ne₁₂.

Mr. Yamada: Ee, mainichi₁₃ ikimasu₁₄. Ishii san, ashita₁₃ gakkoo e kimasu₁₄ ka/

Miss Ishii: Ee, kimasu₁₅.

Mr. Yamada: Jaa, mata ashita.

Miss Ishii: Ee, sayoonara.

3.3 PATTERN SENTENCES⁽¹⁶⁾

Superior numbers refer to note numbers.

3.3.1

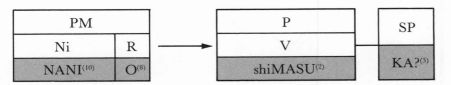

PM		→	P		SP
Ni	R		V		
NANI⁽¹⁰⁾	O⁽⁸⁾		shiMASU⁽²⁾		KA?⁽³⁾

3.3.2

PM		→	P
N	R		V
Uchi	E⁽⁵⁾		kaeriMASEN.⁽²⁾

3.3.3

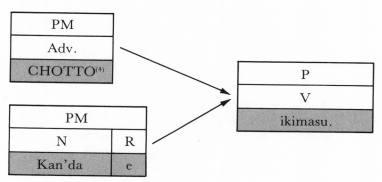

3.3.4

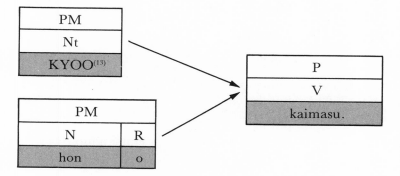

3.3.5

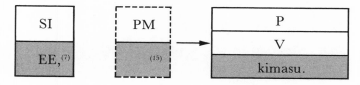

3.4 NOTES

3.4.1 The *-san*** in *Ishii san* is a dependent Noun attached to a family name or to the first name of someone else. With a family name it may mean either Mr., Mrs., or Miss. Note also that in Japanese one's family name is always said first.

Ishii san   ''Miss Ishii''

Yamada san   ''Mr. Yamada''

Do not use the *-san* with your own name.

*A hyphen before or after a word indicates that the word is used dependently.

Forms of Address

Mr. Yamada's form of addressing Miss Ishii immediately indicates his relationship to her. The use of her last name followed by *-san* indicates politeness, and therefore distance, thus revealing that they are classmates only, not necessarily close friends. In general, a man addressing a woman will use either her first name plus -san, or her last name plus -san, with the former showing less formality and less distance between them and used far less than the latter. For a man addressing another man, there are three possible forms of address: either the last name alone, the last name plus -kun, or the last name plus -san. These three forms are progressively more polite, with the last being the most polite form.

3.4.2   The -masu as in ikimasu occurs in a normal-style statement as the affirmative imperfect* tense form ending of a verbal Predicate. The -masu is a verbal Derivative and represents either a future action or a habitual action, depending on the circumstance. With such time expressions as ashita "tomorrow," ikimasu means "[I] am going" or "[I] will go," and kaerimasu with mainichi "every day" will mean "[I] go back" as a habitual action.

Ashita kaerimasu.	"[I] am going back tomorrow."
Mainichi kaerimasu.	"[I] go back every day."
Ashita ikimasu.	"[I] am going [there] tomorrow."
Mainichi ikimasu.	"[I] go [there] every day."

*The imperfect tense form (some books call it the present tense) shows that an action has not been completed. The perfect tense form (some books call it the past tense) means that the action has been completed. More details will be explained later.

The -masen in kaerimasen is the negative of -masu. The -masen also represents either a future action or a habitual action.

Verb(-masu) ⟶ Verb(-masen)

Sugu kaerimasu.	⟶	Sugu kaerimasen.
"[I] am going back soon."		"[I] am not going back soon."
Kyoo kimasu.	⟶	Kyoo kimasen.
"[He] will come today."		"[He] will not come today."

3.4.3   In changing a statement into a question, it is not necessary in Japanese to change the word order as one does in English. The addition of the Sentence Particle ka to the end of a statement turns it into an interrogative sentence.

Predicate ⟶ Predicate + ka?

Uchi e kaerimasu.	⟶	Uchi e kaerimasu ka?
"[I] am going home."		"Are [you] going home?"
Gin'za e ikimasu.	⟶	Gin'za e ikimasu ka?
"[I] am going to the Ginza."		"Are [you] going to the Ginza?"

The negative imperfect tense form of a Verb plus the interrogative Sentence Particle ka can mean "Won't you (do)?" It is a softer expression compared to any affirmative imperfect tense form of a Verb as it is more suggestive and less imperative.

Verb(-masu) + ka? ⟶ **Verb(-masen) + ka?**

Issho ni ikimasen ka?	"Won't [you] go with me?"
Koohii o nomimasen ka?	"Won't [you] have coffee?"
Issho ni kaerimasen ka?	"Won't [you] go home [with me]?"

3.4.4 Like *sugu* "soon" and *yoku* "often," *chotto* is an Adverb. The Adverb *chotto* "for a while" is often used in sentences of request, proposition, action, or invitation, to make them sound casual.

Chotto Kan'da e ikimasu.	"[I] am going to Kanda."
Chotto ocha o nomimasen ka?	"Won't [you] stop for a while and have some tea?"
Chotto uchi e kimasen ka?	"Won't [you] drop in at my house?"

Chotto serves as a buffer, softening conversation. This function will be explained in connection with the combination *Chotto shitsurei* in Lesson 5. (See Note 5.4.11.) As an Adverb, *chotto* has several meanings:

1) short or brief, referring to time and space

2) small or little, referring to quantity, quality

3) easily, readily

4) hardly

5) rather, to some extent, kind of

6) to catch another's attention, similar to *Sumimasen* in Lesson 1. See Note 1.5.3.

Americans use a number of words for the same purpose: "It's a bit far, but . . ." or, for example, "Would you wait a second, please." In neither English nor Japanese does the speaker mean that he will return in one second. In English, however, this modifier is optional: it would be entirely acceptable to say simply, "Would you please wait." In Japanese, on the other hand, it would be considered desirable to use a softener. For another example of the softening function of *chotto,* see the discussion of *sorosoro* in Note 7.4.17.

3.4.5 Kanda is called a student town because of the large number of bookstores and universities one finds there. Until the 1950s, Japanese students used bookstores more often, as the libraries generally weren't as well stocked as those found in the United States. A Japanese scholar would be more apt to purchase his books than to check them out from a library.

The *e* is a Relational that denotes direction, and is equivalent to the English preposition "to" as in "to (a place)." It follows a place Noun or a Noun that may indicate a place. The place Noun followed by *e* formulates a Predicate Modifier that modifies a Predicate following. The Predicate following this Predicate Modifier is always a verbal Predicate, and particularly that of motion Verbs, such as *ikimasu* "go," *kimasu* "come," *kaerimasu* "go (come) back," et cetera.

36

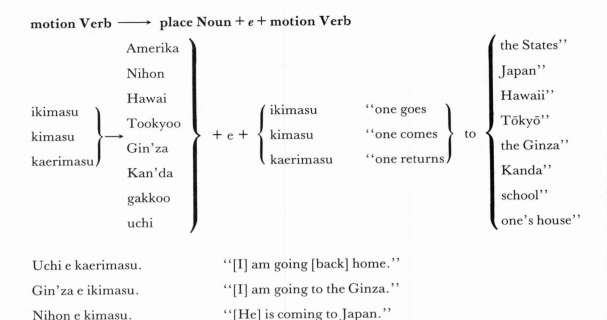

motion Verb ⟶ place Noun + *e* + motion Verb

Uchi e kaerimasu.	"[I] am going [back] home."
Gin'za e ikimasu.	"[I] am going to the Ginza."
Nihon e kimasu.	"[He] is coming to Japan."

3.4.6 In speaking Japanese, as with English, you may sometimes repeat part of the other speaker's speech with rising intonation when you get unexpected information, or you can use part of a sentence when the rest of the sentence is understood.

Kan'da e ikimasu.	"[I] am going to Kanda."
Kan'da e?	"To Kanda?"
Ashita Amerika e ikimasu.	"[I] am going to the States tomorrow."
Ashita?	"Tomorrow?"
Amerika e?	"To the States?"

Omission of Subject and other Predicate Modifiers

In this dialog there are a number of instances where subjects are omitted. This reveals a characteristic feature of the Japanese language, whereby all Predicate Modifiers can be omitted if they are implied by the context and therefore understood in the sentence. It is, then, necessary to develop this mutual understanding within the framework of Japanese culture.

3.4.7 In most cases the Sentence Interjective *iie* corresponds to "no" and *ee* to "yes." *Ee* has a more formal equivalent, *hai*. *Ee* is more commonly used than *hai* in conversation, but *hai* should be used to answer a knock at the door or the calling of one's name.

Uchi e kaerimasu ka?	"Are [you] going [back] home?"
Ee, (uchi e) kaerimasu.	"Yes, [I] am going [back] (home)."
Iie, (uchi e) kaerimasen.	"No, [I] am not going [back] (home)."
Teacher: Yamada san!	"Mr. Yamada!"
Yamada: Hai!	"Yes!" "Here."

3.4.8 Verbs such as *ikimasu* "go," *kaerimasu* "go back," *kimasu* "come" normally occur with the direction Relational *e* "to" according to the nature of the Verbs. Likewise, there are Verbs that normally occur with the Relational *o,* and they will be called transitive Verbs. The Relational *o* presented in this lesson indicates that the preceding Noun is the direct object of a transitive Verb, such as *kaimasu* "buy," *shimasu* "do," *nomimasu* "drink," *tabemasu* "eat," et cetera.

transitive Verb ⟶ **Noun (object) +** *o* **+ transitive Verb**

$$
\left.\begin{array}{l}\text{tabemasu}\\\text{nomimasu}\\\text{kaimasu}\\\text{shimasu}\end{array}\right\} \longrightarrow \text{OBJECT} + o + \left\{\begin{array}{l}\text{tabemasu}\\\text{nomimasu}\\\text{kaimasu}\\\text{shimasu}\end{array}\right.
$$

Taipuraitaa o kaimasu.	"[I] am going to buy a typewriter."
Mizu o nomimasu.	"[I] will drink water."
Ten'pura o tabemasu ka?	"Are [you] going to eat tempura?"

Note that some Japanese transitive Verbs do not correspond to English transitive Verbs, and vice versa. Those Verbs will be noted when they appear.

3.4.9 *Yamada san wa nani o shimasu ka?* means "Mr. Yamada, what are you going to do?" The Relational *wa* following a Noun functions to turn the Noun into the topic (often the one already under discussion) of what is about to be mentioned or described in the following part of the sentence. *Wa* will be explained more fully in Notes 4.4.8, 7.4.2, 7.4.3, and 9.4.2.

3.4.10 *Nani* "what?" is an interrogative Noun. An interrogative sentence with an interrogative Noun is formed by replacing a Noun with a corresponding interrogative Noun.

Noun + Relational + Predicate + *ka?* → **interrogative Noun + Relational + Predicate +** *ka?*

Ten'pura o tabemasu ka?	⟶	*Nani* o tabemasu ka?
"Are [you] going to eat tempura?"		"What are [you] going to eat?"
Gakkoo e ikimasu ka?	⟶	*Doko* e ikimasu ka?
"Are [you] going to school?"		"Where are [you] going?"

3.4.11 A place Noun followed by the Relational *de* indicates where an action takes place. This Relational will be more fully explained in Note 4.4.6 and drilled in Lesson 4.

Uchi de gohan o tabemasu.	"[I] am going to have a meal at home."
Gin'za de kamera o kaimasu.	"[I] am going to buy a camera at the Ginza."

3.4.12 *Ne* said with a rising intonation is a Sentence Particle, and means the strong expectation of the hearer's agreement to what the speaker has mentioned. It often corresponds to "isn't it?" "aren't you?" "don't you think?" et cetera.

Yoku kissaten e ikimasu ne?	"[You] go to the coffee shop often, don't you?"
Gyuunyuu o nomimasu ne?	"[You] drink milk, don't you?"

When the *ne* is said lightly, it merely functions to add softness or friendliness to speech. This is common practice in informal speech, particularly of women.

3.4.13 *Ashita* "tomorrow," *mainichi* "every day," and *kyoo* "today" are called time Nouns. They may be used adverbially without any Relational following.

Ashita gakkoo e kimasu ka?	"Are [you] coming to school tomorrow?"
Mainichi ikimasu.	"[I] go [there] every day."
Kyoo jisho o kaimasu.	"[I] am going to buy a dictionary today."

3.4.14 The use of *ikimasu* and *kimasu* is a little different from that of English "go" and "come." It is always speaker centered in the Japanese language. *Ikimasu* means motion away from the speaker's position, and *kimasu* always means motion toward the speaker. Therefore, "I will come to (your) house" will be *(Anata no) uchi e ikimasu,* when the speaker is not at the house, but if he is there, he should say *(Anata no) uchi e kimasu.*

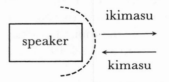

Kaerimasu, however, may mean either "go back" or "come back."

3.4.15 In Japanese the subject of a sentence such as "I," "you," "he," "she," et cetera, is optional: it may be expressed or it may be omitted when it is understood. *Kimasu* may be either "I come," "You come," "He comes," et cetera, and the situation usually makes it clear which person the speaker is referring to.

3.4.16 As you see in the PATTERN SENTENCES, a Predicate in Japanese occurs at the end of a sentence, and Predicate Modifiers such as *koohii o* precede the Predicate. Words with capital letters in boxes indicate that they are new grammatical points to be studied as "pattern structure." When they are indicated in other than capital letters, they are either not new grammatical points, or should be studied later.

3.4.17 *Jaa* is used by men with more frequency than any of its equivalent forms. It is less formal than *Sore dewa.* Although Japanese women use *Jaa* too, they, especially older women, use this word with less frequency than other equivalent forms. This indicates the traditional tendency of the Japanese to emphasize the dominant role of the man in relation to the woman. Whereas a woman must use more polite and more refined expressions in most situations, a man is allowed to use less polite forms with greater frequency dependent upon the situation.

3.5 VOCABULARY

Dialog

Ishii	.......N	family name
-san	......Nd	Mr.; Mrs.; Miss (see 3.4.1)
issho ni	....Adv.	together; with [me, us, etc.]
kaerimasen	V	do not go (come) back (negative of *kaerimasu* ← *kaeru*) (see 3.4.2)
ka	......SP	(see 3.4.3)
kore kara	....Adv.	from now
chotto	....Adv.	for a while (see 3.4.4)
Kan'da	.......N	Kanda Street or book center of Tōkyō
e	.......R	to (a place) (see 3.4.5)
ikimasu	V	go (normal form of *iku*) (see 3.4.14)
ee	.......SI	yes (see 3.4.7)
hon	.......N	book
o	.......R	(see 3.4.8)
kaimasu	V	buy (normal form of *kau*)
Yamada	.......N	family name
wa	.......R	(see 3.4.9)
nani	......Ni	what? (see 3.4.10)
shimasu	V	do (normal form of *suru*)
sugu	....Adv.	soon
uchi	.......N	home; house
kaerimasu	V	go back; come back (normal form of *kaeru*) (see 3.4.14)
iie	.......SI	no (see 3.4.7)
kissaten	.......N	coffee shop
de	.......R	at; in (see 3.4.11)
koohii	.......N	coffee
nomimasu	V	drink (normal form of *nomu*)
yoku	....Adv.	often; a good deal
ne	......SP	(see 3.4.12)
mainichi	.......N	every day
ashita	.......N	tomorrow (see 3.4.13)
gakkoo	.......N	school
kimasu	V	come (normal form of *kuru*) (see 3.4.14)

Notes

-masen	......Dv	(see 3.4.2 and 3.4.3)	
-masu	......Dv	(see 3.4.2)	
kyoo	......N	today	
Gin'za	......N	Ginza Street or a shopping center of Tōkyō	
ocha	......N	tea; green tea	
Amerika	......N	the United States of America; America	
Nihon	......N	Japan	
Hawai	......N	Hawaii	
Tookyoo	......N	capital of Japan	
hai	......SI	yes (formal equivalent of *ee*) (see 3.4.7)	
tabemasu	V	eat (normal form of *taberu*)	
taipuraitaa	......N	typewriter	
mizu	......N	water	
ten'pura	......N	tempura; Japanese fry; fritter	
doko	......Ni	what place?; where? (see 3.4.10)	
gohan	......N	meal; boiled rice	
kamera	......N	camera	
gyuunyuu	......N	cow's milk	
jisho	......N	dictionary	

Drills

bifuteki	......N	beefsteak
pan	......N	bread
biiru	......N	beer

3.6 HIRAGANA PRACTICE

3.6.1 Recognize the difference or similarity between two *hiragana* in each of the following pairs:

へ......へ	く......ん	く......し	い......い
へ......く	つ......つ	て......ん	り......い
つ......へ	つ......て	ん......ん	り......り
く......く	て......て	し......ん	り......こ
て......く	し......し	こ......こ	
つ......く	し......つ	い......こ	

3.6.2 Practice writing the following *hiragana*:

1. へ [he] へ へ
2. く [ku] く く
3. つ [tsu] つ つ
4. て [te] て て
5. ん [n'] ん ん
6. し [shi] し し
7. こ [ko] こ こ
8. い [i] い い
9. り [ri] り り

3.7 DRILLS

3.7.1 Pronunciation Drill

kaerimasú   kaerimasú ka/   ikimasú   ikimasú ka/
kimasú   kimasú ne/   nomimasú   nomimasú ne/
shimasú   shimasú ne/   tabemasú   tabemasú ne/
kaimasú   kaimasú ne/

3.7.2 Pattern Drill

1. Doko e ikimasu ka?
2. Kan'da e ikimasu.
3. Nani o shimasu ka?
4. Hon o kaimasu.
5. Hon o kaimasu ka?
6. Ee, kaimasu.
7. Sugu uchi e kaerimasu ka?
8. Iie, kaerimasen.
9. Yoku kissaten e ikimasu ne.
10. Issho ni kaerimasen ka?

3.7.3 Transformation Drill (statement ⟶ question *ka?*)

1. Uchi e kaerimasu. ⟶ Uchi e kaerimasu *ka?*
2. Gohan o tabemasu. ⟶ Gohan o tabemasu ka?
3. Nihon e ikimasu. ⟶ Nihon e ikimasu ka?
4. Hon o kaimasu. ⟶ Hon o kaimasu ka?
5. Gakkoo e kimasu. ⟶ Gakkoo e kimasu ka?
6. Koohii o nomimasu. ⟶ Koohii o nomimasu ka?

3.7.4 Transformation Drill (statement ⟶ question *ne?*)

1. Bifuteki o tabemasu.   ⟶ Bifuteki o tabemasu *ne?*
2. Tookyoo e kimasu.   ⟶ Tookyoo e kimasu ne?
3. Mizu o nomimasu.   ⟶ Mizu o nomimasu ne?
4. Jisho o kaimasu.   ⟶ Jisho o kaimasu ne?
5. Gin'za e ikimasu.   ⟶ Gin'za e ikimasu ne?
6. Amerika e kaerimasu.   ⟶ Amerika e kaerimasu ne?

3.7.5 Response Drill (negative response)

1. Gin'za e *ikimasu* ka?   . . . . *Iie, ikimasen.*
2. Koohii o nomimasu ne?   . . . . Iie, nomimasen.
3. Gakkoo e kimasu ka?   . . . . Iie, kimasen.
4. Amerika e kaerimasu ne?   . . . . Iie, kaerimasen.
5. Jisho o kaimasu ka?   . . . . Iie, kaimasen.
6. Nihon e kimasu ka?   . . . . Iie, kimasen.
7. Mizu o nomimasu ka?   . . . . Iie, nomimasen.
8. Uchi e kaerimasu ne?   . . . . Iie, kaerimasen.
9. Bifuteki o tabemasu ka?   . . . . Iie, tabemasen.
10. Kissaten e ikimasu ne?   . . . . Iie, ikimasen.
11. Hon o kaimasu ka?   . . . . Iie, kaimasen.
12. Gohan o tabemasu ne?   . . . . Iie, tabemasen.

3.7.6 Transformation Drill (N ⟶ Ni)

1. *Gakkoo* e ikimasu.   ⟶ *Doko* e ikimasu ka?
2. *Pan* o tabemasu.   ⟶ *Nani* o tabemasu ka?
3. Gyuunyuu o nomimasu.   ⟶ Nani o nomimasu ka?
4. Uchi e kaerimasu.   ⟶ Doko e kaerimasu ka?
5. Jisho o kaimasu.   ⟶ Nani o kaimasu ka?
6. Uchi e kimasu.   ⟶ Doko e kimasu ka?
7. Ocha o nomimasu.   ⟶ Nani o nomimasu ka?
8. Ten'pura o tabemasu.   ⟶ Nani o tabemasu ka?
9. Amerika e kaerimasu.   ⟶ Doko e kaerimasu ka?
10. Nihon e ikimasu.   ⟶ Doko e ikimasu ka?
11. Hon o kaimasu.   ⟶ Nani o kaimasu ka?
12. Gakkoo e kimasu.   ⟶ Doko e kimasu ka?

3.7.7 Substitution Drill

Gakkoo e *ikimasu.*

1. *Tookyoo*   . . . . *Tookyoo* e ikimasu.
2. *kimasu*   . . . . Tookyoo e *kimasu.*
3. uchi   . . . . Uchi e kimasu.
4. kaerimasu   . . . . Uchi e kaerimasu.

5. kimasen	. . . . Uchi e kimasen.	10. kaerimasu ka?	. . . . Uchi e kaerimasu ka?
6. Amerika	. . . . Amerika e kimasen.	11. Nihon	. . . . Nihon e kaerimasu ka?
7. kaerimasen	. . . . Amerika e kaerimasen.	12. doko	. . . Doko e kaerimasu ka?
8. ikimasu ka?	. . . . Amerika e ikimasu ka?	13. ikimasu ka?	. . . Doko e ikimasu ka?
9. uchi	. . . . Uchi e ikimasu ka?	14. kimasu ka?	. . . . Doko e kimasu ka?

3.7.8   Substitution Drill

Jisho o *kaimasu.*

1. *pan*	. . . . *Pan* o kaimasu.	8. tabemasen	. . . . Ten'pura o tabemasen.
2. koohii	. . . . Koohii o kaimasu.	9. gohan	. . . . Gohan o tabemasen.
3. nomimasu	. . . . Koohii o nomimasu.	10. tabemasu ka?	. . . . Gohan o tabemasu ka?
4. nomimasen	. . . . Koohii o nomimasen.	11. nani	. . . Nani o tabemasu ka?
5. ocha	. . . . Ocha o nomimasen.	12. nomimasu ka?	. . . . Nani o nomimasu ka?
6. kaimasen	. . . . Ocha o kaimasen.	13. kaimasu ka?	. . . . Nani o kaimasu ka?
7. ten'pura	. . . . Ten'pura o kaimasen.	14. shimasu ka?	. . . . Nani o shimasu ka?

3.7.9   Response Drill

1. Kyoo doko e ikimasu ka? / Tookyoo	. . . . (Kyoo) Tookyoo e ikimasu.
2. Koohii o nomimasu ka? / ee	. . . . Ee, (koohii o) nomimasu.
3. Nani o tabemasu ka? / ten'pura	. . . . Ten'pura o tabemasu.
4. Mainichi gakkoo e kimasu ka? / hai	. . . . Hai, (mainichi gakkoo e) kimasu.
5. Ashita uchi e kaerimasu ka? / iie	. . . . Iie, (ashita uchi e) kaerimasen.
6. Nani o kaimasu ka? / hon	. . . . Hon o kaimasu.
7. Ashita kimasu ka? / iie	. . . . Iie, (ashita) kimasen.
8. Amerika e kaerimasu ka? / iie	. . . . Iie, (Amerika e) kaerimasen.
9. Kyoo nani o shimasu ka? / gakkoo e ikimasu	. . . . (Kyoo) gakkoo e ikimasu.
10. Doko e ikimasu ka? / uchi	. . . . Uchi e ikimasu.

3.7.10   Expansion Drill

1. Ikimasu.	. . . . Ikimasu.
Kan'da e	. . . . Kan'da e ikimasu.
kore kara	. . . . Kore kara Kan'da e ikimasu.

2. Tabemasen. . . . . Tabemasen.

 gohan o . . . . Gohan o tabemasen.

 sugu . . . . Sugu gohan o tabemasen.

3. Ikimasu ka? . . . . Ikimasu ka?

 doko e . . . . Doko e ikimasu ka?

 mainichi . . . . Mainichi doko e ikimasu ka?

4. Kaimasu ka? . . . . Kaimasu ka?

 nani o . . . . Nani o kaimasu ka?

 kyoo . . . . Kyoo nani o kaimasu ka?

5. Kaerimasen. . . . . Kaerimasen.

 uchi e . . . . Uchi e kaerimasen.

 kyoo . . . . Kyoo uchi e kaerimasen.

6. Kimasu ka? . . . . Kimasu ka?

 gakkoo e . . . . Gakkoo e kimasu ka?

 mainichi . . . . Mainichi gakkoo e kimasu ka?

7. Shimasu ka? . . . . Shimasu ka?

 nani o . . . . Nani o shimasu ka?

 ashita . . . . Ashita nani o shimasu ka?

8. Nomimasu. . . . . Nomimasu.

 biiru o . . . . Biiru o nomimasu.

 yoku . . . . Yoku biiru o nomimasu.

3.7.11 Relational Checking Drill

1. Tookyoo, ikimasu . . . . Tookyoo *e* ikimasu.

2. mizu, nomimasu . . . . Mizu *o* nomimasu.

3. uchi, kaerimasen . . . . Uchi e kaerimasen.

4. nani, shimasu ka? . . . . Nani o shimasu ka?

5. gohan, tabemasu . . . . Gohan o tabemasu.

6. doko, ikimasu ka? . . . . Doko e ikimasu ka?

7. jisho, kaimasu . . . . Jisho o kaimasu.

8. ocha, nomimasu ka? . . . . Ocha o nomimasu ka?

9. uchi, kimasen . . . . Uchi e kimasen.

10. nani, tabemasu ka? . . . . Nani o tabemasu ka?

11. kamera, kaimasen . . . . Kamera o kaimasen.

12. doko, kaerimasu ka? . . . . Doko e kaerimasu ka?

3.7.12 E-J Substitution Drill

Gakkoo e *ikimasu* ka?

1. to the States . . . . *Amerika* e ikimasu ka?

2. return . . . . Amerika e kaerimasu ka?

3. home . . . . Uchi e kaerimasu ka?

4. come . . . . Uchi e kimasu ka?

5. go	. . . . Uchi e ikimasu ka?	10. come	. . . . Tookyoo e kimasu ka?
6. to Hawaii	. . . . Hawai e ikimasu ka?	11. to the Ginza	. . . . Gin'za e kimasu ka?
7. to Japan	. . . . Nihon e ikimasu ka?	12. where	. . . . Doko e kimasu ka?
8. return	. . . . Nihon e kaerimasu ka?	13. go	. . . . Doko e ikimasu ka?
9. to Tōkyō	. . . . Tookyoo e kaerimasu ka?	14. return	. . . . Doko e kaerimasu ka?

3.7.13 E-J Substitution Drill

Gohan o *tabemasu* ka?

1. beefsteak	. . . . *Bifuteki* o tabemasu ka?	8. drink	. . . . Ocha o nomimasu ka?
2. what	. . . . Nani o tabemasu ka?	9. coffee	. . . . Koohii o nomimasu ka?
3. buy	. . . . Nani o kaimasu ka?	10. cow's milk	. . . . Gyuunyuu o nomimasu ka?
4. book	. . . . Hon o kaimasu ka?	11. what	. . . . Nani o nomimasu ka?
5. dictionary	. . . . Jisho o kaimasu ka?	12. do	. . . . Nani o shimasu ka?
6. camera	. . . . Kamera o kaimasu ka?	13. eat	. . . . Nani o tabemasu ka?
7. tea	. . . . Ocha o kaimasu ka?	14. buy	. . . . Nani o kaimasu ka?

3.8 EXERCISES

3.8.1   Rearrange each group of the following words into a good Japanese sentence:

1. e   issho ni   Kan'da   ka   ikimasen

2. tabemasu   mainichi   o   nani   ka

3. kaerimasu   ne   uchi   e   sugu

3.8.2   Make appropriate questions which will lead to the following answers:

1. Bifuteki o tabemasu.   5. Hai, ocha o nomimasu.

2. Iie, uchi e kaerimasen.   6. Iie, mainichi koohii o nomimasu.

3. Jisho o kaimasu.   7. Ee, Nihon e ikimasu.

4. Gakkoo e ikimasu.   8. Iie, kaimasen.

3.8.3   Insert an appropriate item in each of the following blanks:

1. Doko (   ) ikimasu (   )?

2. Ocha (   ) nomimasu.

3. Amerika (   ) kaerimasen.

4. Uchi (   ) kimasen (   )?

5. Nani (   ) shimasu (   )?

3.8.4 Carry on the following conversations in Japanese:

1. Ishii: Good morning.

   Yamada: Good morning.

   Ishii: Where are you going today?

   Yamada: I am going to Tōkyō, Miss Ishii. What are you going to do?

   Ishii: I am going home.

2. Ishii: Are you going to have a meal?

   Yamada: Yes, I am.

   Ishii: What are you going to eat?

   Yamada: I am going to eat tempura. Won't you eat it with me?

   Ishii: Yes, I will.

3.8.5 Answer the following questions in Japanese:

1. Ashita gakkoo e kimasu ne?

2. Sugu uchi e kaerimasu ka?

3. Mainichi ocha o nomimasu ka?

4. Kyoo hon o kaimasu ka?

5. Ashita doko e ikimasu ka?

6. Kore kara nani o shimasu ka?

3.8.6 Answer the following questions on the basis of the Dialog:

1. Ishii san wa kyoo nani o shimasu ka?

2. Yamada san wa sugu uchi e kaerimasu ka?

3. Yamada san wa mainichi doko e ikimasu ka?

4. Yamada san wa ashita gakkoo e kimasu ka?

LESSON 4
MONDAY AT SCHOOL

4.1   USEFUL EXPRESSIONS

Erai desu nee.

"Good!" This is an expression of praise used when the speaker is impressed by someone's hard work or effort.

Soo desu ka /

"Is that so?" "Really?" This is one of the expressions used most frequently among Japanese. According to the intonation or situation, this expression is interpreted in various ways.

Ii desu ne.

"Sounds nice." This is said when the speaker agrees to someone's idea or proposal.

4.2   DIALOG

Mr. Itō:	Koyama san, kinoo dekakemashita₁ ka /
Miss Koyama:	Iie, dekakemasen deshita₂. Ashita shiken ga₃ arimasu₄.
	Sore de₅, uchi de₆ ichinichijuu ben'kyoo o₇ shimashita.
Mr. Itō:	Erai desu nee. Watashi₈ wa zen'zen ben'kyoo shimasen deshita.
Miss Koyama:	Soo desu ka / Nani o shimashita ka /
Mr. Itō:	Shin'juku de eiga o mimashita. Sore kara₅, depaato de kaimono mo₉ shimashita.
Miss Koyama:	Soo desu ka.
Mr. Itō:	Koyama san, asatte kurasu ga arimasu ka /
Miss Koyama:	Iie, arimasen kedo₁₀.
Mr. Itō:	Jaa, issho ni Kamakura e ikimasen ka / Soshite₅, yoru resutoran de shokuji o
	shimashoo₁₁.
Miss Koyama:	Ii desu ne. Ikimashoo.

4.3   PATTERN SENTENCES

4.3.1

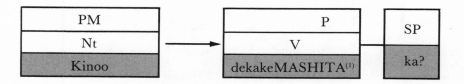

4.3.2

SI		PM	→	P	
				V	C
Iie,				dekakeMASEN	DESHITA.[2]

4.3.3

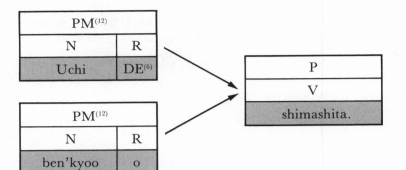

4.3.4

PM		→	P
N	R		V
Kaimono	MO[9]		shimashita.

4.3.5

PM		→	P
N	R		V
Shokuji	o		shiMASHOO.[11]

4.4 NOTES

4.4.1 The -*mashita* in *dekakemashita* indicates the perfect tense form or normal TA form of -*masu*.

Predicate Modifier + Verb*(-masu)* ⟶ Predicate Modifier + Verb*(-mashita)*

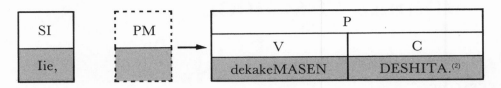

mimasu	"see"	mimashita	"saw"
kimasu	"come"	kimashita	"came"
kakimasu	"write"	kakimashita	"wrote"
kikimasu	"listen to"	kikimashita	"listened to"

Terebi o mimashita.	"[I] watched television."
Kinoo Tookyoo e ikimashita.	"[I] went to Tōkyō yesterday."
Ototoi tegami o kakimashita.	"[I] wrote a letter the day before yesterday."

4.4.2 *Dekakemasen deshita* is the perfect tense form of *dekakemasen* "(someone) does not go out," or the negative perfect form of *dekakemasu* "(someone) goes out." The negative perfect tense form of a Verb is formulated by adding *deshita,* the perfect tense form of the Copula *desu,* to the negative imperfect tense form of the Verb.

Verb(-masen) ⟶ **Verb(-masen) + *deshita***

dekakemasu	"[He/She] goes out."
dekakemasen	"[He/She] does not go out."
dekakemashita	"[He/She] went out."
dekakemasen deshita	"[He/She] did not go out."
Kyoo teepu o kikimashita ka?	"Did [you] listen to the tape today?"
Iie, kikimasen deshita.	"No, [I] didn't."
Kinoo kurasu e ikimashita ka?	"Did [you] go to the class yesterday?"
Iie, ikimasen deshita.	"No, [I] didn't."

4.4.3 The Relational *ga* that stands after a Noun is the subject Relational, and singles out the Noun as the subject of the following Predicate. Note that the subject followed by *ga* is equally emphasized as the following Predicate. As for the topic subject, see Note 3.4.9. *Ga* will be formally introduced in Note 5.4.3.

4.4.4 The Verb *arimasu* may be used in a pattern that does not have any place expression. In this case, *arimasu* corresponds to "(someone) has (something)." See Notes 5.4.2 and 5.4.6 for *arimasu* with a place expression.

Terebi ga arimasu ka?	"Do [you] have a TV set?"
Ashita kurasu ga arimasen.	"[I] do not have any class tomorrow."
Kinoo shiken ga arimashita.	"[I] had an examination yesterday."

4.4.5 *Sore de* "consequently," *sore kara* "and then," "afterwards," and *soshite* "and then" are Sentence Interjectives. Like *hai, ee,* and *iie,* they are usually placed at the beginning of an utterance. Normally they serve the purpose of connecting two utterrances.

Ashita shiken ga arimasu.	"[I] am going to have an exam tomorrow.
Sore de, ben'kyoo shimasu.	So, [I] am going to study."

Eiga o mimashita. Sore kara,   "[I] saw a movie. Afterwards, [I] had lunch."

 hirugohan o tabemashita.

Heya e ikimashita. Soshite,   "[I] went to [my] room. And, [I] studied

 ben'kyoo shimashita.   [there]."

4.4.6 A place Noun followed by the Relational *de* indicates where an action takes place. This Relational precedes an action Verb or a Verb of happening. See Note 5.4.2 for *ni*.

place Noun + *de* + (~ o) + action Verb

	(kaimono o)	shimasu	"do shopping	in Tōkyō"
Tookyoo	(terebi o)	kaimasu	"buy a TV set	at the department store"
depaato	(asa gohan o)	tabemasu	"have breakfast	
koko	(biiru o)	nomimasu	"drink beer	here"
gakkoo	(eiga o)	mimasu	"see a movie	at school"
heya	(tegami o)	kakimasu	"write a letter	in the room"
	(rekoodo o)	kikimasu	"listen to the record	

(de connects the left column to the middle)

Gakko de anata o mimashita. "[I] saw you at the school."

Doko de kaimono o shimasu ka? "Where are [you] going shopping?"

Uchi de tegami o kakimashita. "[I] wrote a letter at home."

Gakkoo de teepu o kikimasu. "[I] will listen to tapes at school."

Depaato de kaimashita. "[I] bought [it] at the department store."

Gakkoo de nihon'go o ben'kyoo shimasu. "[I] study Japanese at school."

4.4.7 The Relational *o* in *ben'kyoo o shimasu* is optional. Some Nouns, such as *shokuji* "eating (a meal)," *kaimono* "shopping," *ben'kyoo* "study," can form their verbal expressions by adding the Verb *shimasu* ⟵ *suru* "do" to the Nouns without the Relational *o*. These combinations may be treated as single Verbs.

kaimono (o) shimasu   "go shopping"

ben'kyoo (o) shimasu   "study"

shokuji (o) shimasu   "eat (a meal)"

No difference in meaning occurs when the Relational *o* is inserted. When there is *o*, however, *shokuji* or *kaimono* is the object of the Verb *shimasu*, while *ben'kyoo*, *shokuji*, or *kaimono* is part of the Verb when *o* is not used.

51

4.4.8 *Watashi* is a contracted form of *watakushi* and is less polite than the latter. The Relational *wa* after *watashi* indicates that *watashi* is the topic that the speaker is referring to and, in this case, the Predicate is in a negative form. See Notes 3.4.9, 7.4.2, and 7.4.3.

Watashi wa mainichi gakkoo e ikimasu.   "I go to school every day."

Watakushi wa soko de Itoo san o mimashita.   "I saw Mr. Itō there."

4.4.9 The Relational *mo* may occur after a Noun and, in an affirmative sentence, it adds the meaning of "also" or "too" to the Noun. *Mo* can take the place of the Relational *o*. See Note 7.4.10 for *mo* replacing *wa* or *ga*. Also see Notes 8.4.8, 11.4.5, and 12.4.5 for other functions of *mo*.

Noun + *o* + Verb ⟶ Noun + *mo* + Verb

Watashi wa nihon'go *o* ben'kyoo shimashita.   "I studied Japanese."

Watashi wa nihon'go *mo* ben'kyoo shimashita.   "I studied Japanese also (as well as some other language)."

Mainichi teepu o kikimasu. Rekoodo mo kikimasu.   "[I] listen to tapes every day. I also listen to records."

4.4.10 *Kedo* is a clause Relational meaning "although." The clause followed by *kedo* is a subordinate clause meaning "although . . ." See Note 12.4.7. However, when the main clause is not stated and the utterance ends with *kedo,* then the meaning "although" becomes vague and the listener will have to judge the speaker's intent.

Ashita kurasu ga arimasu ka?   "Do [you] have classes tomorrow?"

Iie, arimasen kedo . . .   "No, [I] don't. (Why did you ask that?)"

Ototoi Shin'juku e ikimashita ka?   "Did [you] go to Shinjuku the day before yesterday?"

Ee, ikimashita kedo . . .   "Yes, [I] did. (How do you know?)"

4.4.11 The *-mashoo* in *shimashoo* is the OO form of *-masu*. In this lesson, this form is used propositionally as equivalent for "let's (do)." Therefore, the *-mashoo* followed by the Sentence Particle *ka* corresponds to "Let's (do), shall we?" or "Shall we (do)?" See *Yobimashoo ka?* in Lesson 5 and *Nomimashoo ka?* in Lesson 7. The use of OO form other than the above will be explained in Note 13.4.9.

Predicate Modifier + Verb*(-masu)* ⟶ Predicate Modifier + Verb*(-mashoo)* (+ *ka?*)

Ban'gohan o tabemashoo.   "Let's eat supper."

Depaato de kaimono o shimashoo.   "Let's do [some] shopping at the department store."

Ikimashoo ka?   "Shall we go?"

Uchi e kaerimashoo ka?   "Shall we go [back] home?"

Ee, kaerimashoo.   "Yes, let's go [back]."

Uchi de terebi o mimashoo ka?　　　"Shall we watch TV at home?"

Ashita eiga o mimashoo.　　　"Let's see a movie tomorrow."

As this usage of -mashoo is limited to the speaker's proposition of doing something with the hearer, arimashoo never occurs in this meaning.

4.4.12 Most Japanese sentences have more than one Predicate Modifier.

1)　Kinoo　　depaato e　　ikimashita.
　　(PM)　　　(PM)　　　　(P)

2)　Issho ni　　uchi de　　ban'gohan o　　tabemashoo.
　　(PM)　　　(PM)　　　(PM)　　　　(P)

Even if the order of the Predicate Modifiers is changed in the above sentences, the sentences will still be grammatically correct, and the meanings will not differ. There will be only a slight change in the place of emphasis. Generally speaking, the Predicate Modifier that is closer to the Predicate will be the more emphatic.

1)　Depaato e kinoo ikimashita.

2)　Uchi de issho ni ban'gohan o tabemashoo.
　　Ban'gohan o uchi de issho ni tabemashoo.
　　Issho ni ban'gohan o uchi de tabemashoo.

This flexible transposition is called "relative sequence." The cases in which the above procedure cannot be applied will be explained in Note 8.4.10.

4.5 VOCABULARY

Dialog

Koyama	. . . . . . .N	family name	
kinoo	. . . . . . .N	yesterday	
dekakemashita	V	went out; set out (TA form of *dekakemasu*←*dekakeru*) (see 4.4.1)	
dekakemasen 　deshita	V	did not go out (negative perfect tense form of 　*dekakemasu*←*dekakeru*) (see 4.4.2)	
shiken	. . . . . . .N	examination; test	
ga	. . . . . . .R	(see 4.4.3)	
arimasu	V	have (see 4.4.4)	
sore de	. . . . . . .SI	so; accordingly (see 4.4.5)	
de	. . . . . . .R	at; in (see 4.4.6)	
ichinichijuu	. . . . . . .N	all day long; throughout the day	
ben'kyoo	. . . . . . .N	study	
ben'kyoo (o) 　shimashita	V	studied (TA form of *ben'kyoo (o) shimasu*←*ben'kyoo (o) suru*) 　(see 4.4.7)	

watashi	.......N	I (the contracted form of *watakushi*) (see 4.4.8)
zen'zen	....Adv.	not at all (see 7.4.15)
ben'kyoo (o) shimasen deshita	V	did not study (negative perfect tense form of *ben'kyoo (o) shimasu←ben'kyoo (o) suru*)
shimashita	V	did (TA form of *shimasu←suru*)
Shin'juku	.......N	a shopping center in Tōkyō
eiga	.......N	movie
mimashita	V	saw (TA form of *mimasu←miru*) (or "watch" as in "watch TV")
sore kara	.......SI	afterwards; and (then)
depaato	.......N	department store
kaimono	.......N	shopping
mo	.......R	also; too (see 4.4.9)
kaimono (o) shimashita	V	did shopping (TA form of *kaimono (o) shimasu←kaimono (o) suru*)
asatte	.......N	the day after tomorrow
kurasu	.......N	class
arimasen	V	do not have (negative of *arimasu←aru*) (see 4.4.4)
kedo	......Rc	(see 4.4.10 and 12.4.7)
jaa	.......SI	well
Kamakura	.......N	a historical city near Tōkyō
soshite	.......SI	and
yoru	.......N	night
resutoran	.......N	restaurant (Western style)
shokuji	.......N	meal; eating a meal
shokuji (o) shimashoo	V	let's dine (OO form of *shokuji (o) shimasu←shokuji (o) suru*) (see 4.4.11)
ikimashoo	V	let's go (OO form of *ikimasu←iku*)

Notes

-mashita	.....Dv	TA form of *-masu* (see 4.4.1)
kakimasu	V	write (normal form of *kaku*)
kikimasu	V	listen to; hear (normal form of *kiku*) (*Kikimasu* is a transitive Verb: the Relational *o* occurs with this Verb to show a direct object. *Teepu o kikimasu.*)
terebi	......N	television; TV set
ototoi	......N	the day before yesterday

tegami	. . . . . . N	letter (correspondence)
-masen deshita	. . .Dv+C	(see 4.4.2)
teepu	. . . . . . N	tape
hirugohan	. . . . . . N	lunch; noon meal
heya	. . . . . . .N	room
asagohan	. . . . . . .N	breakfast; morning meal
rekoodo	. . . . . . .N	record
nihon'go	. . . . . . .N	Japanese language
watakushi	. . . . . . .N	I (The contracted form *watashi* may also be used.) (see 4.4.8)
Itoo	. . . . . . .N	family name
-mashoo	. . . . . .Dv	OO form of *-masu* (see 4.4.11)
ban'gohan	. . . . . . .N	supper; evening meal

4.6 HIRAGANA PRACTICE

4.6.1 Recognize the difference or similarity between two *hiragana* in each of the following pairs:

に……に	は……け	た……た	さ……さ
に……は	は……ほ	た……に	さ……き
に……け	け……け	な……な	き……き
に……ほ	ほ……ほ	な……た	き……も
に……こ	ほ……ま	な……は	も……も
は……は	ま……ま	な……ほ	も……ま

4.6.2 Practice writing the following *hiragana:*

1. に [ni] に に に
2. は [ha] は は は
3. け [ke] け け け
4. ほ [ho] ほ ほ ほ ほ
5. ま [ma] ま ま ま
6. た [ta] た た た た
7. な [na] な な な な
8. さ [sa] さ さ さ
9. き [ki] き き き き
10. も [mo] も も も

4.7 DRILLS

4.7.1 Pronunciation Drill

koohii   sayoonara   Itoo   kinoo   depaato   rekoodo

teepu   biiru   kyoo   Soo desu ka /

4.7.2 Pattern Drill

1. Kinoo dekakemashita ka?

2. Iie, dekakemasen deshita.

3. Uchi de ben'kyoo o shimashita.

4. Depaato de kaimono mo shimashita.

5. Resutoran de shokuji o shimashoo.

6. Kamakura e ikimashoo ka?

7. Ee, ikimashoo.

4.7.3 Transformation Drill (statement ⟶ proposition)

1. Ban'gohan o *tabemasu*. ⟶ Ban'gohan o *tabemashoo*.

2. Gakkoo e ikimasu. ⟶ Gakkoo e ikimashoo.

3. Ocha o nomimasu. ⟶ Ocha o nomimashoo.

4. Jisho o kaimasu. ⟶ Jisho o kaimashoo.

5. Sugu kaerimasu. ⟶ Sugu kaerimashoo.

6. Ashita kaimono o shimasu. ⟶ Ashita kaimono o shimashoo.

7. Issho ni shokuji o shimasu. ⟶ Issho ni shokuji o shimashoo.

8. Kore kara dekakemasu. ⟶ Kore kara dekakemashoo.

9. Issho ni eiga o mimasu. ⟶ Issho ni eiga o mimashoo.

10. Uchi de teepu o kikimasu. ⟶ Uchi de teepu o kikimashoo.

4.7.4 Transformation Drill (proposition ⟶ question)

1. Uchi e kaerimashoo. ⟶ Uchi e kaerimashoo *ka*?

2. Sugu dekakemashoo. ⟶ Sugu dekakemashoo ka?

3. Tegami o kakimashoo. ⟶ Tegami o kakimashoo ka?

4. Issho ni ben'kyoo shimashoo. ⟶ Issho ni ben'kyoo shimashoo ka?

5. Hirugohan o tabemashoo. ⟶ Hirugohan o tabemashoo ka?

6. Asatte Kamakura e ikimashoo. ⟶ Asatte Kamakura e ikimashoo ka?

4.7.5 Transformation Drill (imperfect ⟶ perfect)

1. *Ashita* Shin'juku e *ikimasu*. ⟶ *Kinoo* Shin'juku e *ikimashita*.

2. Ashita eiga o mimasu. ⟶ Kinoo eiga o mimashita.

3. Ashita Amerika e kaerimasu. ⟶ Kinoo Amerika e kaerimashita.

56

4. Ashita taipuraitaa o kaimasu. $\longrightarrow$ Kinoo taipuraitaa o kaimashita.

5. Ashita tegami o kakimasu. $\longrightarrow$ Kinoo tegami o kakimashita.

6. Ashita issho ni kaimono o shimasu. $\longrightarrow$ Kinoo issho ni kaimono o shimashita.

7. Ashita nani o shimasu ka? $\longrightarrow$ Kinoo nani o shimashita ka?

8. Ashita ichinichijuu ben'kyoo shimasu ka? $\longrightarrow$ Kinoo ichinichijuu ben'kyoo shimashita ka?

4.7.6 Transformation Drill (affirmative $\longrightarrow$ negative)

1. Heya de ben'kyoo *shimashita*. $\longrightarrow$ Heya de ben'kyoo *shimasen deshita*.

2. Kinoo dekakemashita. $\longrightarrow$ Kinoo dekakemasen deshita.

3. Yoru uchi e kaerimashita. $\longrightarrow$ Yoru uchi e kaerimasen deshita.

4. Kinoo kurasu ga arimashita. $\longrightarrow$ Kinoo kurasu ga arimasen deshita.

5. Issho ni Kamakura e ikimashita. $\longrightarrow$ Issho ni Kamakura e ikimasen deshita.

6. Ototoi eiga o mimashita. $\longrightarrow$ Ototoi eiga o mimasen deshita.

7. Depaato de kaimashita. $\longrightarrow$ Depaato de kaimasen deshita.

8. Ototoi shiken ga arimashita. $\longrightarrow$ Ototoi shiken ga arimasen deshita.

4.7.7 Substitution Drill

Shin'juku de *kaimono o shimashita.*

1. *shokuji o shimashita* . . . . Shin'juku de *shokuji o shimashita.*

2. uchi . . . . Uchi de shokuji o shimashita.

3. ben'kyoo shimashita . . . . Uchi de ben'kyoo shimashita.

4. gakkoo . . . . Gakkoo de ben'kyoo shimashita.

5. teepu o kikimashita . . . . Gakkoo de teepu o kikimashita.

6. hirugohan o tabemashoo . . . . Gakkoo de hirugohan o tabemashoo.

7. resutoran . . . . Resutoran de hirugohan o tabemashoo.

8. nomimashoo ka . . . . Resutoran de nomimashoo ka?

9. doko . . . . Doko de nomimashoo ka?

10. hon o kaimashoo ka . . . . Doko de hon o kaimashoo ka?

4.7.8 Substitution and Expansion Drill (*o* $\longrightarrow$ *mo*)

1. Kinoo eiga *o* mimashita. . . . . Kinoo eiga *o* mimashita. Terebi *mo* mimashita.
   terebi *mo*

2. Ototoi hon o kaimashita. . . . . Ototoi hon o kaimashita. Jisho mo kaimashita.
   jisho mo

3. Ocha o nomimasen ka?   . . . . Ocha o nomimasen ka? Biiru mo
    biiru mo   nomimasen ka?

4. Issho ni hirugohan o tabemashoo.   . . . . . Issho ni hirugohan o tabemashoo.
    ban'gohan mo   Ban'gohan mo tabemashoo.

5. Mainichi rekoodo o kikimasu.   . . . . Mainichi rekoodo o kikimasu. Teepu
    teepu mo   mo kikimasu.

6. Kaimono o shimashoo.   . . . . Kaimono o shimashoo. Shokuji mo
    shokuji mo   shimashoo.

4.7.9   Expansion Drill

1. Kaimashita.   . . . Kaimashita.

   kamera o   . . . Kamera o kaimashita.

   depaato de   . . . Depaato de kamera o kaimashita.

   ototoi   . . . Ototoi depaato de kamera o kaimashita.

2. Mimashita ka?   . . . Mimashita ka?

   Itoo san o   . . . Itoo san o mimashita ka?

   doko de   . . . Doko de Itoo san o mimashita ka?

   kinoo   . . . Kinoo doko de Itoo san o mimashita ka?

3. Ikimashoo.   . . . Ikimashoo.

   gakkoo e   . . . Gakkoo e ikimashoo.

   issho ni   . . . Issho ni gakkoo e ikimashoo.

   ashita   . . . Ashita issho ni gakkoo e ikimashoo.

4. Tabemashoo ka?   . . . Tabemashoo ka?

   ban'gohan o   . . . Ban'gohan o tabemashoo ka?

   doko de   . . . Doko de ban'gohan o tabemashoo ka?

   kyoo   . . . Kyoo doko de ban'gohan o tabemashoo ka?

5. Kimasen deshita.   . . . Kimasen deshita.

   uchi e   . . . Uchi e kimasen deshita.

   sugu   . . . Sugu uchi e kimasen deshita.

   Itoo san wa   . . . Itoo san wa sugu uchi e kimasen deshita.

6. Kikimashita.   . . . Kikimashita.

   rekoodo o   . . . Rekoodo o kikimashita.

   heya de   . . . Heya de rekoodo o kikimashita.

   yoru   . . . Yoru heya de rekoodo o kikimashita.

4.7.10 Response Drill (short answer)

1. Sugu dekakemashoo ka? /ee   . . . . Ee, dekakemashoo.

2. Ocha o nomimasen ka? / ee   . . . . Ee, nomimashoo.

3. Issho ni Kamakura e ikimashoo. / ee   . . . . Ee, ikimashoo.

4. Kyoo tegami o kakimashita ka? / iie   . . . . Iie, kakimasen deshita.

5. Doko de nomimashoo ka? / kissaten   . . . . Kissaten de nomimashoo.

6. Nani o kaimashita ka? / gyuunyuu   . . . . Gyuunyuu o kaimashita.

7. Issho ni kaerimasen ka? / ee   . . . . Ee, kaerimashoo.

8. Kinoo ichinichijuu ben'kyoo shimashita ka? / iie   . . . . Iie, shimasen deshita.

9. Doko de kaimono o shimashita ka? / Gin'za   . . . . Gin'za de shimashita.

10. Ototoi kurasu e kimashita ka? / hai   . . . . Hai, kimashita.

4.7.11 Combination Drill (sore kara)

1. Sugu uchi e kaerimasu.
   Ban'gohan o tabemasu. ⟶ Sugu uchi e kaerimasu. *Sore kara,* ban'gohan o tabemasu.

2. Terebi o mimashita.
   Nihon'go o ben'kyoo shimashita. ⟶ Terebi o mimashita. Sore kara, nihon'go o ben'kyoo shimashita.

3. Depaato de kaimono o shimashoo.
   Koohii o nomimashoo. ⟶ Depaato de kaimono o shimashoo. Sore kara, koohii o nomimashoo.

4. Yoru tegami o kakimashita.
   Rekoodo o kikimashita. ⟶ Yoru tegami o kakimashita. Sore kara, rekoodo o kikimashita.

5. Uchi de shokuji o shimashoo.
   Dekakemashoo. ⟶ Uchi de shokuji o shimashoo. Sore kara, dekakemashoo.

6. Nihon e kimashita.
   Hawai e ikimashita. ⟶ Nihon e kimashita. Sore kara, Hawai e ikimashita.

4.7.12 Combination Drill (sore de)

1. Ashita shiken ga arimasu.
   Ichinichijuu ben'kyoo shimashita. ⟶ Ashita shiken ga arimasu. *Sore de,* ichinichijuu ben'kyoo shimashita.

2. Ototoi dekakemashita.
   Zen'zen ben'kyoo shimasen deshita. ⟶ Ototoi dekakemashita. Sore de, zen'zen ben'kyoo shimasen deshita.

3. Kinoo kurasu ga arimashita.
   Gakkoo e ikimashita. ⟶ Kinoo kurasu ga arimashita. Sore de, gakkoo e ikimashita.

4. Eiga o mimashita.
   Kaimono o shimasen deshita. ⟶ Eiga o mimashita. Sore de, kaimono o shimasen deshita.

5. Kinoo jisho o kaimasen deshita.   ⎫   Kinoo jisho o kaimasen deshita.
   Kyoo kaimasu.   ⎬ ⟶   Sore de, kyoo kaimasu.

6. Resutoran de gohan o tabemashita.   ⎫   Resutoran de gohan o tabemashita.
   Uchi de tabemasen deshita.   ⎬ ⟶   Sore de, uchi de tabemasen deshita.

4.8 EXERCISES

4.8.1 Apply as many Predicates as possible out of Group B to each of the Group A Predicate Modifiers.

A	B
Shin'juku e	shimashoo ka? *shall we do?*
Yamada san o *Mr. Yamada*	tabemasu ka? *eat!*
Nani o *what*	ikimashoo. *shall we go?*
Depaato de *department store*	kakimasen deshita. *did not write*
Doko de *where*	kaimashita ka? *what are you buying?*
Tegami o *letter*	kimasen ka? *coming?*
Mizu o *water*	mimashita. *I see/look/watch*
Kaimono o *shopping*	shokuji o shimashoo. *to dine shall we?*
	nomimasen deshita. *did not drink*

4.8.2 Insert appropriate words in the blanks; each pair consists of a question and an answer to the question.

1. a. (   ) o kaimashita ka?

   b. Jisho (   ) kaimashita.

2. a. Nani (   ) nomimashita ka?

   b. Koohii (   ) nomimashita. Soshite, mizu (   ) nomimashita.

3. a. (   ) e ikimashoo ka?

   b. Resutoran e (   ). (   ), uchi e (   )mashoo.

4. a. Nani o shimashita (   )?

   b. Eiga o (   ).

5. a. Kinoo ben'kyoo (   ) ka?

   b. (   ), zen'zen shi(   ).

4.8.3 What would you say when:

1. you want to agree to someone's idea?

2. you want to praise someone for his effort?

3. you want to ask someone where he went on the previous day?

4. you want to invite someone to dine at your house together with you?

4.8.4   Answer the following questions on the basis of the Dialog:

1. Itoo san wa kinoo dekakemashita ka?

2. Itoo san wa doko de nani o shimashita ka?

3. Koyama san wa kinoo doko de nani o shimashita ka?

4. Asatte shiken ga arimasu ka?

5. Koyama san wa Kamakura e ikimasu ka?

LESSON 5
ON THE STREET

5.1   USEFUL EXPRESSIONS

Chotto shitsurei.[11]

"Excuse me for a moment." The expression at full length is *Chotto shitsurei shimasu.*

Omachidoo sama[11]

"Sorry to have kept you waiting." The expression at full length is *Omachidoo sama deshita.*

Ojama shimasu.

"I am going to bother you (by visiting)."

5.2   DIALOG

Mr. Tanaka: Suzuki san, kono hen[1] ni[2] den'wa ga[3] arimasu ka /

Mr. Suzuki: Asoko[4] ni arimasu yo[5].

Mr. Tanaka: Jaa, chotto shitsurei[11]. Sugu kimasu.

. . . .

Mr. Tanaka: Omachidoo sama[11]

Mr. Suzuki: Doo itashimashite. Ikimashoo ka.

Mr. Tanaka: Ee. A, soko ni Yamada san ga imasu[6] yo / Yobimashoo ka. . . . . Yamada san

Mr. Yamada: A, kon'nichi wa

Mr. Suzuki: Kon'nichi wa Yamada san, kinoo Shin'juku Eki ni imashita ne /

Mr. Yamada: Ee, eiga e ikimashita. Suzuki san wa[7] /

Mr. Suzuki: Chotto hon'ya[8] to[9] gin'koo e ikimashita. Yamada san, kyoo ohima[10] ga arimasu ka /

Mr. Yamada: Ee, arimasu kedo.

Mr. Suzuki: Ima Tanaka san ga[3] uchi e kimasu. Issho ni kimasen ka /

Mr. Yamada: Ee, arigatoo. Ojama shimasu.

5.3   PATTERN SENTENCES

5.3.1

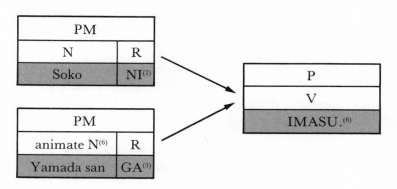

5.3.2

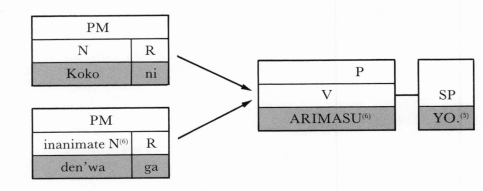

5.4 NOTES

5.4.1 *Kono hen* means "this vicinity," or "this area." The *-hen* is a dependent Noun meaning "area." The use of *kono* "this" will be introduced in Note 8.4.6.

Kono hen ni den'wa ga arimasu ka?   "Is there a telephone in this vicinity?"

Kono hen ni otearai ga arimasu ka?   "Is there a rest room around here?"

Kono hen de shokuji o shimashoo ka? "Shall we eat (our meal) somewhere around here?"

5.4.2 The Relational *ni* used after a place Noun is the Relational of location. A place Noun followed by the Relational *ni* denotes where something or someone is situated or exists, and usually precedes a verbal expression of existence, living, staying, et cetera, that are all inactive.

Verb of existence ⟶ place Noun + *ni* + Verb of existence

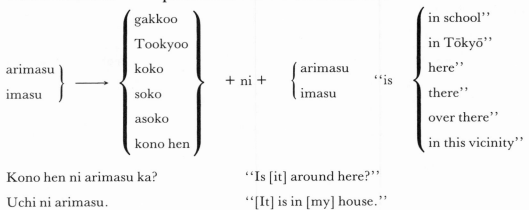

Kono hen ni arimasu ka?   "Is [it] around here?"

Uchi ni arimasu.   "[It] is in [my] house."

Soko ni imasu.   "[Someone] is there."

Doko ni imasu ka?   "Where is [he]?"

See Note 5.4.6 regarding the difference between *arimasu* and *imasu*. Note also that the difference between the Relational *de* introduced in Note 4.4.6 and the Relational *ni* in this lesson does not appear in English equivalents, but they should be used to indicate whether a Verb following a place Noun represents "action" or "existence."

Compare: Soko ni arimasu.   "[It] is there."

               Soko de kaimasu.   "[I] will buy [it] there."

5.4.3   As explained in Note 4.4.3, *ga* is the subject Relational and singles out the Noun as the subject of the following Predicate. Note that the subject followed by *ga* is emphasized.

Predicate ⟶ **Noun (subject) + *ga* + Predicate**

A Predicate can be a Verb, an Adjective, or a Noun plus the Copula.

Den'wa ga arimasu.	"There is a telephone."

The use of *ga* is mandatory when an interrogative Noun such as *nani* is a subject.

interrogative Noun (subject) + *ga* + Predicate + *ka?*

Nani ga arimasu ka?	"What is there?"
Dare ga imasu ka?	"Who is there?"
Donata ga kimashita ka?	"Who came?"
Yamada san ga kimashita.	"Mr. Yamada came."

It can, therefore, be said that when a sentence has the subject followed by *ga,* the sentence is mainly meant to explain "WHO does, or WHAT happens," or "WHO or WHAT is so," et cetera.

5.4.4   *Asoko* is a Noun meaning "that place over there." Here are a group of place Nouns:

koko	"this place" or "here"
soko	"that place" or "there"
asoko	"that place over there" or "over there"
doko	"what place?" or "where?"

Note that these are all Nouns and are often followed by Relationals, such as *de, ni, e,* or other Relationals.

Koko de kaimasu.	"[I] will buy [it] here."
Soko ni imasen.	"[He] is not there."
Asoko e ikimasu ka?	"Are [you] going over there?"
Doko ni arimasu ka?	"Where is [it]?"

Ko, so, a, and *do* as in *koko, soko, asoko,* and *doko* respectively indicate "this ∼," "that ∼," "that ∼ over there," and "wh ∼?" Therefore, *ko, so, a,* and *do* will occur in various series of words of this kind. See Notes 7.4.1, 8.4.6, 8.4.9, and 9.4.12.

   Ko refers to something close to the speaker, *so* refers to something near the hearer or something that has just been mentioned, and *a* to something at a distance from both the speaker and the hearer. Therefore, when someone asks you about something close to him but away from you, he will say *kore,* but you will say *sore.*

   When you compare three things within sight, use *kore* for the thing closest to you, *sore* for the thing next in distance, and *are* for the thing farthest away. See Note 7.4.1.

5.4.5   *Yo* is an emphatic Sentence Particle that occurs at the end of a sentence as does *ka,* and is used to call the hearer's attention to a statement giving warning, new information, assurance, et cetera. It corresponds to English "you know," "I tell you," "say," or "certainly," but sometimes it may not appear in English equivalents and only intonation or stress may imply it.

Asoko ni arimasu yo.	"[It] is over there, [you see]."
Ima Ishii san ga eki ni imasu yo.	"Miss Ishii is now at the station, you know."
Ashita gakkoo e ikimasu ka?	"Are [you] going to school tomorrow?"
Ee, ikimasu yo.	"Yes, [I] certainly will."

Compare *yo* with *ne*. The former is used when the speaker suspects that the listener might have different views, while the latter is used to seek the listener's concurrence.

Soo desu.	"That's right." "(Yes,) it is."
Soo desu ne.	"(Yes,) isn't it?"
Soo desu yo.	"(Yes,) it is. (Didn't you know?)"

5.4.6   *Arimasu* and *imasu* are Verbs meaning "exist." The difference between *arimasu* and *imasu* is that *arimasu* refers to the location of inanimate objects while *imasu* is used with animate objects. In other words, *arimasu* is used to say "(something) is, or is situated (in a place)," and *imasu* is used to say "(someone or an animate object) is (in a place)." Animate objects here include human beings, animals, birds, fish, and insects, but do not include plants.

place Noun + *ni* + { **animate object + *ga* + *imasu*** / **inanimate object + *ga* + *arimasu*** }

eki, uchi, koko, depaato	+ ni +	Suzuki san, otoko no hito, on'na no hito, inu, neko, tori	+ ga + imasu	"Mr. Suzuki, "a man, "a woman, "a dog, "a cat, "a bird	is	in the station" at home" here" in the department store"
		otearai, den'wa, shokudoo	+ ga + arimasu	"the rest room, "a telephone, "a cafeteria		

Koko ni den'wa ga arimasu.	"Here is a telephone."
Koko ni Yamada san ga imasu.	"Here is Mr. Yamada."
Soko ni okane ga arimasu.	"There is some money."
Doko ni inu ga imasu ka?	"Where is the dog?"
Depaato ni nani ga arimasu ka?	"What is in the department store?"

5.4.7   *Suzuki san wa?* means "How about you, Mr. Suzuki?" The complete sentence is *Suzuki san wa doko e ikimashita ka?*, which has been shortened to *Suzuki san wa?* because *doko e ikimashita ka?* is understood.

Jimusho ni Tanaka san ga imasu.	"Mr. Tanaka is in the office."
Suzuki san wa?	"How about Mr. Suzuki?"
Asoko ni posuto ga arimasu yo.	"There is a mailbox over there."
Yuubin'kyoku wa?	"How about the post office?"

5.4.8   *Hon'ya* is a combination of *hon* "book" and *-ya* "-store" or "-shop," and means "bookstore." In the same manner, the words for most of the stores or shops where a certain product is sold, or for the dealers in the product, are formed:

hon'ya	"bookstore or book dealer"
rekoodoya	"record shop or record dealer"
pan'ya	"bakery or baker"

Women often refer to stores or dealers with *-san,* and others often use *-san* when they are thinking specifically of the dealer.

hon'ya san	pan'ya san

5.4.9   The *to* that occurs between Nouns is a Relational. The Relational *to* joins Nouns and is equivalent to "and." When more than two Nouns are listed, *to* appears more than once.

N1 *to* N2 *to* . . . . . . Nn

Jisho to kamera o kaimashita.	"[I] bought a dictionary and a camera."
Gin'za to Shin'juku e ikimashoo.	"Let's go to the Ginza and Shinjuku."
Koko ni inu to neko to tori ga imasu.	"Here are a dog, a cat, and a bird."

Note that *to* is never used to join sentences or predicates. *Soshite* or *sore kara* is used instead.

5.4.10   The normal word for "free time" or "leisure" is *hima.* When the speaker is referring to someone else's free time, the polite prefix *o-* may be attached to the beginning of *hima* in polite speech. Therefore, *ohima* cannot refer to the speaker's. However, some of the *o-* and Noun combinations, such as *ocha* "tea," replace the original Nouns in normal speech. The use of *o* is more common in women's speech.

mizu. . . . . .omizu	"water"
kane . . . . .okane	"money"
tearai . . . . .otearai	"rest room"
Ohima ga arimasu ka?	"Do [you] have (free) time?"
Iie, hima ga arimasen.	"No, [I] don't have free time."

5.4.11 Style and Level

The forms used in this dialog again indicate the relationship existing between the participants. The use of *Omachidoo sama,* and of the *-masu* form such as *arimasu ka* indicates that they are colleagues but not really close. The use of *Jaa, chotto shitsurei* shows that they are more or less equal, as a boss-subordinate relationship does not exist here.

When a person leaves his seat, passes another person, or cuts into a conversation between other people, *Chotto shitsurei* is used. *Omachidoo sama* is the less polite form contrasting with the more polite *Omachidoo sama deshita.* This is also the case with *Chotto shitsurei* as contrasted with the more polite and also more distant *Chotto shitsurei shimasu.*

Shitsurei itself means "losing etiquette." *Rei,* which means etiquette or proper conduct, is an important concept in Japanese relations, and must be strictly observed. Japanese culture contains many more *rei* customs than does American culture.

Chotto and *sugu* are used quite often in Japan. Literally, *chotto* means "for a moment, momentarily, a little bit"; *sugu* means "right away." As used, however, the content of both words is without much meaning. Their function, which is to soften conversation, is much more important. It is in this way that *chotto* functions in the phrase *Chotto shitsurei.* Similar to the English "Excuse me," this phrase could be used when leaving your seat, when passing in front of others, or when joining a conversation already in progress.

Chotto shitsurei, however, cannot be used to mean "Good-bye" as the expression *Shitsurei* is used. *Chotto* is often used as a means of gaining attention in asking someone to come to you. This use of *chotto* is casual and therefore generally only used among peers or toward inferiors.

5.5 VOCABULARY

Dialog

Suzuki	.......N	family name
kono hen	..PN+Nd	this vicinity; this area (see 5.4.1)
ni	.......R	in; at (see 5.4.2)
den'wa	.......N	telephone
ga	.......R	(see 5.4.3)
arimasu	V	is situated (normal form of *aru*) (see 5.4.6)
asoko	.......N	that place over there; over there (see 5.4.4)
yo	......SP	(see 5.4.5)
a	.......SI	oh; ah
soko	.......N	that place; there
imasu	V	exist (normal form of *iru*) (see 5.4.6)
yobimashoo	V	let's call (OO form of *yobimasu←yobu*)
eki	.......N	station
hon'ya	.......N	bookstore (see 5.4.8)
to	.......R	and (see 5.4.9)
gin'koo	.......N	bank
o-	..(prefix)	(see 5.4.10)

hima	. . . . . .Na	free time	
ima	. . . . . .N	now	
Tanaka	. . . . . .N	family name	

Notes

(o)tearai	. . . . . . .N	toilet; rest room
koko	. . . . . . .N	this place; here (see 5.4.4)
dare	. . . . . .Ni	who? (see 5.4.3)
donata	. . . . . .Ni	who? (polite equivalent of *dare*) (see 5.4.3)
otoko no hito	. . . . . . .N	man
on'na no hito	. . . . . .N	woman
inu	. . . . . .N	dog
neko	. . . . . .N	cat
tori	. . . . . . .N	bird; chicken (meat)
shokudoo	. . . . . . .N	dining room (hall); cafeteria; eating place
(o)kane	. . . . . .N	money
jimusho	. . . . . .N	office
posuto	. . . . . . .N	mailbox; postbox
yuubin'kyoku	. . . . . .N	post office
-ya	. . . . . .Nd	-store; -dealer (see 5.4.8)
rekoodoya	. . . . . . .N	musical record shop
pan'ya	. . . . . . .N	bakery

5.6 HIRAGANA PRACTICE

5.6.1   Recognize the difference or similarity between two *hiragana* in each of the following pairs:

ら……ら	え……え	ろ……る	む……む
ら……う	え……そ	そ……そ	む……す
ら……え	ち……ち	そ……る	よ……よ
ら……ち	ち……ろ	る……る	よ……む
う……う	ろ……ろ	る……ら	よ……ま
う……ち	ろ……ら	す……す	
う……ろ	ろ……そ	す……よ	

5.6.2   Practice writing the following *hiragana:*

1. う   [u]   う   う
2. ら   [ra]   ら   ら   ら
3. え   [e]   え   え   え
4. そ   [so]   そ   そ   そ
5. ち   [chi]   ち   ち   ち
6. ろ   [ro]   ろ   ろ
7. る   [ru]   る   る
8. す   [su]   す   す   す
9. よ   [yo]   よ   よ
10. む   [mu]   む   む   む   む

5.6.3   Read and write the following:

ほん   えき   うち   なまえ

よる   にほん   いま   いきます

5.7   DRILLS

5.7.1   Pronunciation Drill

hon   hon'ya   Hon o kaimasu.   Hon'ya de hon o kaimasu.

pan   pan'ya   Pan o kaimasu.   Pan'ya de pan o kaimasu.

kono hen   den'wa   Kono hen ni den'wa ga arimasu.

on'na   on'na no hito   On'na no hito ga imasu.

Kon'nichi wa

5.7.2   Pattern Drill

1. Kono hen ni den'wa ga arimasu ka?

2. Asoko ni arimasu yo.

3. Soko ni Yamada san ga imasu.

4. Kyoo ohima ga arimasu ka?

5. Soko ni nani ga arimasu ka?

6. Asoko ni donata ga imashita ka?

7. Ima Tanaka san ga uchi e kimasu.

8. Hon'ya to gin'koo e ikimashita.

5.7.3   Substitution Drill

Kono hen ni *den'wa* ga arimasu ka?

1. *shokudoo*   . . . . Kono hen ni *shokudoo* ga arimasu ka?

2. otearai   . . . . Kono hen ni otearai ga arimasu ka?

3. hon'ya   . . . . Kono hen ni hon'ya ga arimasu ka?

4. yuubin'kyoku   . . . . Kono hen ni yuubin'kyoku ga arimasu ka?

5. posuto   . . . . Kono hen ni posuto ga arimasu ka?

6. gin'koo   . . . . Kono hen ni gin'koo ga arimasu ka?

7. resutoran   . . . . Kono hen ni resutoran ga arimasu ka?

8. pan'ya   . . . . Kono hen ni pan'ya ga arimasu ka?

5.7.4   Substitution Drill

Asoko ni *Yamada san* ga imasu yo.

1. *otoko no hito*   . . . . Asoko ni *otoko no hito* ga imasu yo.

2. on'na no hito   . . . . Asoko ni on'na no hito ga imasu yo.

3. Suzuki san   . . . . Asoko ni Suzuki san ga imasu yo.

4. tori   . . . . Asoko ni tori ga imasu yo.

5. neko   . . . . Asoko ni neko ga imasu yo.

6. inu   . . . . Asoko ni inu ga imasu yo.

7. inu to neko   . . . . Asoko ni inu to neko ga imasu yo.

8. Koyama san to Ishii san   . . . . Asoko ni Koyama san to Ishii san ga imasu yo.

5.7.5   Expansion Drill

1. Imasu.   . . . . Imasu.

   inu ga   . . . . Inu ga imasu.

   inu to tori ga   . . . . Inu to tori ga imasu.

   uchi ni   . . . . Uchi ni inu to tori ga imasu.

2. Arimasu.   . . . . Arimasu.

   den'wa ga   . . . . Den'wa ga arimasu.

   den'wa to taipuraitaa   . . . . Den'wa to taipuraitaa ga arimasu.

   jimusho ni   . . . . Jimusho ni den'wa to taipuraitaa ga arimasu.

3. Imashita.   . . . . Imashita.

   Yamada san ga   . . . . Yamada san ga imashita.

   eki ni   . . . . Eki ni Yamada san ga imashita.

4. Arimashita yo.   . . . . Arimashita yo.

   gin'koo ga   . . . . Gin'koo ga arimashita yo.

   asoko ni   . . . . Asoko ni gin'koo ga arimashita yo.

5. Arimasu ka?   . . . . Arimasu ka?

   okane ga   . . . . Okane ga arimasu ka?

doko ni	. . . . Doko ni okane ga arimasu ka?
6. Imasu ka?	. . . . Imasu ka?
dare ga	. . . . Dare ga imasu ka?
soko ni	. . . . Soko ni dare ga imasu ka?
7. Arimashita ka?	. . . . Arimashita ka?
nani ga	. . . . Nani ga arimashita ka?
heya ni	. . . . Heya ni nani ga arimashita ka?
8. Imasu ka?	. . . . Imasu ka?
nani ga	. . . . Nani ga imasu ka?
soko ni	. . . . Soko ni nani ga imasu ka?

5.7.6   Substitution Drill

Soko ni *Yamada san* ga *imasu*.
Soko ni *den'wa* ga *arimasu*.

1. *otoko no hito*	. . . . Soko ni *otoko no hito* ga *imasu*.
2. *shokudoo*	. . . . Soko ni *shokudoo* ga *arimasu*.
3. inu	. . . . Soko ni inu ga imasu.
4. jisho	. . . . Soko ni jisho ga arimasu.
5. otearai	. . . . Soko ni otearai ga arimasu.
6. tori	. . . . Soko ni tori ga imasu.
7. tegami	. . . . Soko ni tegami ga arimasu.
8. neko	. . . . Soko ni neko ga imasu.

5.7.7   Substitution Drill

1. Ashita *shiken* ga arimasu.

kurasu	. . . . Ashita *kurasu* ga arimasu.
gakkoo	. . . . Ashita gakkoo ga arimasu.
hima	. . . . Ashita hima ga arimasu.
shiken	. . . . Ashita shiken ga arimasu.

2. Ima *jisho* ga arimasen.

okane	. . . . Ima *okane* ga arimasen.
hima	. . . . Ima hima ga arimasen.
kamera	. . . . Ima kamera ga arimasen.
koohii	. . . . Ima koohii ga arimasen.

5.7.8   Response Drill (short answer)

1. Kono hen ni den'wa ga arimasu ka? / ee   . . . . Ee, arimasu.

2. Ohima ga arimasu ka? / iie   . . . . Iie, arimasen.

3. Doko ni Yamada san ga imashita ka? / eki   . . . . Eki ni imashita.

4. Kinoo shiken ga arimashita ka? / iie   . . . . Iie, arimasen deshita.

5. Jimusho ni dare ga imasu ka? / on'na no hito   . . . . On'na no hito ga imasu.

6. Asoko ni nani ga imasu ka? / inu to neko   . . . . Inu to neko ga imasu.

7. Nani ga arimashita ka? / gyuunyuu   . . . . Gyuunyuu ga arimashita.

8. Gakkoo ni Koyama san ga imashita ka? / iie   . . . . Iie, imasen deshita.

5.7.9   Response Drill

1. Donata *ga* imasu ka? / Yamada san   . . . . Yamada san *ga* imasu.

2. Nani ga imasu ka? / tori   . . . . Tori ga imasu.

3. Dare ga issho ni ikimasu ka? / Itoo san   . . . . Itoo san ga issho ni ikimasu.

4. Nani ga arimashita ka? / gin'koo   . . . . Gin'koo ga arimashita.

5. Donata ga jisho o kaimashita ka? / Koyama san   . . . Koyama san ga jisho o kaimashita.

6. Dare ga uchi e kimashita ka? / on'na no hito   . . . . On'na no hito ga uchi e kimashita.

7. Donata ga biiru o nomimasu ka? / Suzuki san   . . . . Suzuki san ga biiru o nomimasu.

8. Nani ga imashita ka? / neko to inu   . . . . Neko to inu ga imashita.

5.7.10 Substitution Drill (Substitute the italicized word with each of the given words and carry on the conversation.)

A: Kono hen ni *den'wa* ga arimasu ka?

B: Asoko ni arimasu yo.

A: Jaa, chotto shitsurei. Sugu kimasu. . . . . Omachidoo sama.

B: Doo itashimashite.

     1. yuubin'kyoku   2. posuto   3. gin'koo   4. otearai   5. den'wa

5.8   EXERCISES

5.8.1   Rearrange each group of the following words into a good Japanese sentence:

1. imasu	uchi	ga	ni	neko	ne	
2. biiru	ni	to	arimasu	koko	ga	yo	mizu
3. ga	ni	ka	arimasu	hon'ya	kono hen	
4. dare	eki	ka	imashita	ni	ga	

5.8.2   What would you say when:

1. you want to thank someone?

2. you kept someone waiting?

3. someone apologizes to you for having kept you waiting?

4. you greet someone in the afternoon?

5. you want to excuse yourself for a while?

6. you are going to bother someone by visiting him?

5.8.3   Answer the following questions in Japanese:

1. Uchi ni inu ga imasu ka?

2. Kinoo ichinichijuu uchi ni imashita ka?

3. Ashita kurasu ga arimasu ka?

4. Kinoo shiken ga arimashita ka?

LESSON 6
REVIEW AND APPLICATION

6.1 PATTERNS

6.1.1 Place Noun + *e* + motion Verb

a.

```
      (2)
     koko           :    |
     soko           :    |
     asoko          :    |
     kono hen       :    |
     ..............      |
     gin'koo        :    |
     jimusho        :    |
     eki            :    |
     resutoran      :    |
     shokudoo       :    |
     (o)tearai      :    |      (1)
     heya           :    |    ikimasu       |  ka?
     yuubin'kyoku   :  e |    kimasu        |  yo
     gakkoo         :    |    kaerimasu     |  ne
     kissaten       :    |   (dekakemasu)   |  (kedo)
     uchi           :    |
     depaato        :    |
     hon'ya         :    |
     rekoodoya      :    |
     pan'ya         :    |
     ..............      |
     kurasu         :    |
     eiga           :    |
     ..............      |
     Amerika        :    |
     Nihon          :    |
```

```
      (2)                              (1)
     doko        :  e  |  .........  |  ka?
```

b.

```
      (3)                      (2)
     watakushi      :       soko            :
     watashi        :       asoko           :            (1)
     ..............         ..............         ikimasu      |  ka?
                    :  ga                   :  e   kimasu       |  yo
     Yamada san     :       gakkoo          :      kaerimasu    |  ne
                    :       uchi            :     (dekakemasu)  |  (kedo)
     ..............         ..............
     on'na no hito  :                       :
     otoko no hito  :       Hawai           :
```

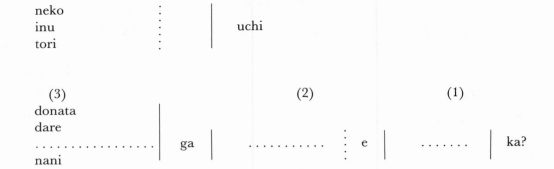

```
neko
inu                :    |    uchi
tori               :    |
```

```
    (3)                        (2)                    (1)
donata             |
dare
.................. | ga |  ..........  : e |  .......  | ka?
nani
```

6.1.2 Noun + *o* + transitive Verb

```
a.      (2)                    (1)
        ocha          :
        koohii        :
        gyuunyuu      :        nomimasu
        biiru         :
        mizu          :
        ..............:        ..............
        gohan         :
        asagohan      :
        hirugohan     :
        ban'gohan     :        tabemasu
        pan           :  o     .              ka?
        bifuteki      :                        yo
        ten'pura      : (mo)   ..............  ne
        tegami        :                       (kedo)
        hon           :        kakimasu
        nihon'go      :
        ..............:        ..............
        teepu         :
        rekoodo       :        kikimasu
        nihon'go      :
        ..............:        ..............
        jisho         :
        hon           :
        taipuraitaa   :        kaimasu
        kamera        :
        ..............:        ..............
        eiga          :
        terebi        :        mimasu
        ..............:        ..............
        Koyama san    :
        on'na no hito :
        inu           :        yobimasu
        neko          :
        ..............:        ..............
```

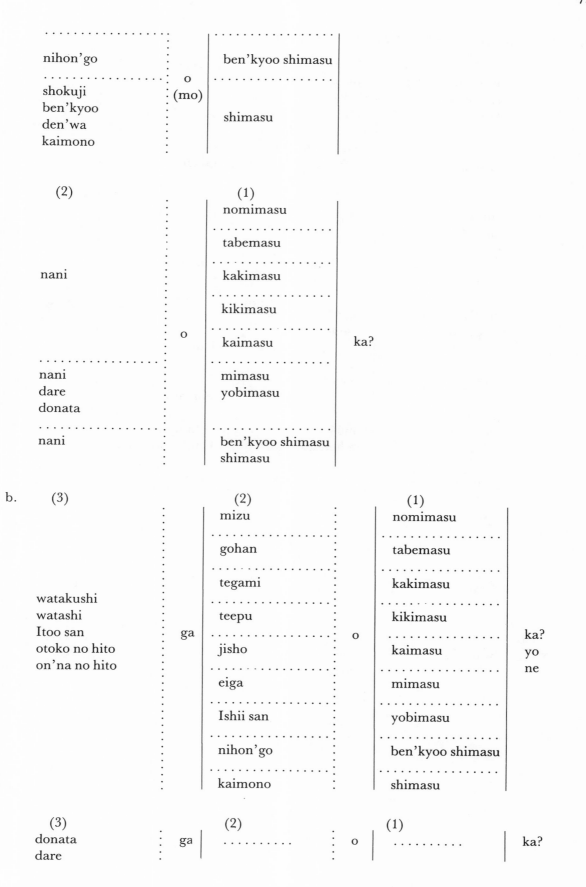

nihon'go	o	ben'kyoo shimasu		
shokuji ben'kyoo den'wa kaimono	(mo)	shimasu		

	(2)		(1)		
	nani	o	nomimasu	ka?	
			tabemasu		
			kakimasu		
			kikimasu		
			kaimasu		
	nani dare donata		mimasu yobimasu		
	nani		ben'kyoo shimasu shimasu		

b.

(3)		(2)		(1)	
watakushi watashi Itoo san otoko no hito on'na no hito	ga	mizu	o	nomimasu	ka? yo ne
		gohan		tabemasu	
		tegami		kakimasu	
		teepu		kikimasu	
		jisho		kaimasu	
		eiga		mimasu	
		Ishii san		yobimasu	
		nihon'go		ben'kyoo shimasu	
		kaimono		shimasu	

(3)		(2)		(1)	
donata dare	ga	....	o	....	ka?

6.1.3 Place Noun + *de* + Noun + *o* + transitive Verb

a.

(3)		(2)		(1)	
resutoran shokudoo koko		mizu ocha biiru		nomimasu	
uchi Gin'za soko		asagohan bifuteki		tabemasu	
heya jimusho		tegami		kakimasu	
uchi heya	de	nihon'go rekoodo	o (mo)	kikimasu	ka? yo ne
hon'ya depaato asoko		hon kamera		kaimasu	
Shin'juku uchi		eiga terebi		mimasu	
eki uchi		inu nihon'go		yobimasu ben'kyoo shimasu	
depaato kono hen		kaimono		shimasu	

(3)		(2)		(1)	
doko	de	....	o	....	ka?

b.

(4)		(3)		(2)		(1)	
watakushi		uchi gin'koo					
Ishii san	ga		de	....	o	....	ka?
		soko					

(4)		(3)		(2)		(1)	
donata dare	ga	....	de	....	o	....	ka?

6.1.4   **Place Noun + *ni* +** { **animate Noun + *ga* + *imasu*** / **inanimate Noun + *ga* + *arimasu*** }

a.

(2)		(1)	
watakushi			ka?
watashi			yo
on'na no hito			ne
otoko no hito	ga	imasu	
Koyama san	(wa)		
. . . .			
inu			
tori			
neko			

(2)		(1)	
donata			
dare	ga	. . . .	ka?
. . . .			
nani			

b.

(2)		(1)	
hon			
jisho			ka?
posuto	ga	arimasu	yo
okane	(wa)		ne
den'wa			
kamera			
koohii			
terebi			
otearai			

(2)		(1)	
nani	ga	. . . .	ka?

c.

(3)		(2)		(1)	
koko					
soko					
asoko					
kono hen		Koyama san	ga	imasu	
depaato	ni	inu	(wa)		ka?
eki		tori			yo
heya		neko			ne
gakkoo		. . . .		. . . .	
Amerika		gyuunyuu			
Hawai		taipuraitaa			
		jisho		arimasu	
		terebi			
		biiru			

(3)	(2)	(1)

```
   (3)                    (2)                              (1)
                      ...............:            : imasu
  doko      :  ni  |..............:  ga  |...............:  ka?
                      ...............:  (wa) | arimasu
```

6.1.5 Noun + *ga* + *arimasu* without a place phrase

```
hima    :
shiken  :  ga   |
kurasu  :  (wa) | arimasu
okane   :  (mo) |
```

6.1.6 Noun + *to* + Noun

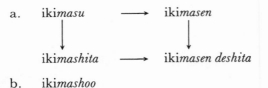

```
toshokan  :        hon'ya     :                  : e ikimashoo
          ............       ............     ............
koohii    :        mizu       :      ———      : o nomimasu
          ............  to   ............  ............
gin'koo   :        yuubin'kyoku :      depaato : ga arimasu
          ............       ............  to  ............
koko      :        soko       :      asoko    : ni imasu
```

6.2 CONJUGATION

6.2.1 Verb

```
a.   ikimasu    ⟶    ikimasen
        │                │
        ▼                ▼
     ikimashita ⟶    ikimasen deshita

b.   ikimashoo
```

6.2.2

	~ e	ikimashita kimasen deshita kaerimasen deshita (dekakemashita)
kinoo ototoi kyoo	~ o	nomimashita tabemashita kakimasen deshita kikimasen deshita kaimashita mimashita yobimasen deshita ben'kyoo shimashita shimasen deshita

	~ ni	imashita arimasen deshita
ima kyoo ashita asatte yoru mainichi	~ e	ikimasu kimashoo kaerimasen ikimasen dekakemasen ka kaerimashoo ka
	~ o	nomimasu tabemasen kakimashoo kikimasen ka kaimashoo ka mimasu yobimashoo ben'kyoo shimasen shimasen ka
	~ ni	imasu imasen imashoo imasen ka arimasu arimasen

6.3   REVIEW DRILLS

6.3.1   Relational Checking Drill *(e, ni, de)*

Tookyoo

1. ikimashoo ka …. Tookyoo *e* ikimashoo ka?
2. imasen …. Tookyoo *ni* imasen.
3. kaimono o shimashita ka …. Tookyoo *de* kaimono o shimashita ka?
4. imashita …. Tookyoo *ni* imashita.
5. kimasen deshita …. Tookyoo *e* kimasen deshita.
6. tabemashita …. Tookyoo *de* tabemashita.
7. arimashita yo …. Tookyoo *ni* arimashita yo.
8. kaimashoo …. Tookyoo *de* kaimashoo.
9. kaerimasu ka …. Tookyoo *e* kaerimasu ka?
10. mimashita …. Tookyoo *de* mimashita.
11. arimasen ne …. Tookyoo *ni* arimasen ne.
12. ikimasen deshita …. Tookyoo *e* ikimasen deshita.

6.3.2 Substitution and Transformation Drill
(Substitute the italicized parts of the dialogs with each of the given words, making necessary changes.)

1. A: Kinoo *dekakemashita* ka?

   B: Iie, *dekakemasen deshita.*

   A: Soo desu ka? Ashita issho ni *dekakemashoo* ka?

   B: Ee, *dekakemashoo.*

       1. kakimasu   2. mimasu   3. kaimasu   4. ikimasu

2. A: Mainichi *koohii* o *nomimasu* ka?

   B: Hai, mainichi *nomimasu.*

   A: *Ocha* mo *nomimasu* ka?

   B: Iie, *nomimasen.*

       1. terebi, mimasu, eiga   2. pan, tabemasu, gohan   3. teepu, kikimasu, rekoodo

6.3.3 Relational Checking Drill *(o, ga)*

1. nani, arimasu ka   . . . . Nani *ga* arimasu ka?

2. taipuraitaa, kaimashita ka   . . . . Taipuraitaa *o* kaimashita ka?

3. nani, mimashoo ka   . . . . Nani *o* mimashoo ka?

4. neko, imashita yo   . . . . Neko *ga* imashita yo.

5. Koyama san, yobimashoo   . . . . Koyama san *o* yobimashoo.

6. okane, arimasen deshita   . . . . Okane *ga* arimasen deshita.

7. rekoodo, kikimasen ka   . . . . Rekoodo *o* kikimasen ka?

8. dare, imasu ka   . . . . Dare *ga* imasu ka?

9. on'na no hito, kimashita   . . . . On'na no hito *ga* kimashita.

10. donata, hanashimashita ka   . . . . Donata *ga* hanashimashita ka?

6.3.4 Substitution Drill
(Substitute *mainichi* with each of the given time words, making necessary changes.)

1. *Mainichi* terebi o mimasu.

       1. ashita   2. kinoo   3. asatte   4. ototoi

2. *Mainichi* teepu o kaimasu.

3. *Mainichi* gakkoo e ikimasen.

4. *Mainichi* kaimono o shimasu.

5. *Mainichi* uchi ni imasen.

6.4 REVIEW EXERCISES

6.4.1   Complete each of the following statements:

1. Ashita shiken ga arimasu. Sore de, _____.

2. Kinoo depaato e ikimashita. Soshite, _____.

3. Hawai e ikimashita. Sore kara, _____.

4. Yoru uchi de rekoodo o kikimashita. Soshite, _____.

5. Okane ga arimasen deshita. Sore de, _____.

6. Kyoo gakkoo e ikimasu. Sore kara, _____.

6.4.2   Ask your friend:

1. where he (she) went today?

2. what he (she) did at school?

3. if there is a typewriter in his (her) house?

4. if he (she) is going to see a movie tomorrow?

5. who was at the bank yesterday?

6. what he (she) drank at night?

7. where he (she) studied the Japanese language?

8. if he (she) often goes shopping in a department store?

9. who is in the office now?

6.4.3   Fill in the blanks with Relationals such as *ga, o, to, e, de, ni, mo.*

1. Nani (   ) shimashoo ka?

   Heya (   ) rekoodo (   ) kikimashoo.

2. Nihon (   ) kimashita. Soshite, gakkoo (   ) nihon'go (   ) ben'kyoo
   shimashita.

3. Koko (   ) den'wa (   ) arimasu ka?

   Iie, arimasen. Asoko (   ) arimasu.

4. Kinoo (   ) kyoo depaato (   ) ikimashita. Soshite, kamera (   ) rekoodo
   (   ) kaimashita. Hon (   ) kaimashita. Sore de, ima zen'zen okane (   )
   arimasen.

5. Kono hen (   ) gin'koo (   ) arimasu ka?

   Hai, arimasu. Yuubin'kyoku (   ) arimasu yo.

6.4.4 Carry on the following dialog:

A: Hello.

B: Hello. Aren't you going to Shinjuku with me?

A: No, I am going home soon.

B: Are you?

A: I am going to have an exam tomorrow. So I will study all day today.

B: Good! Will you be free the day after tomorrow?

A: Yes.

B: Then, shall we go to Shinjuku the day after tomorrow?

A: That's nice. Let's go.

6.5 AURAL COMPREHENSION

6.5.1

やまだ 「おまちどおさま。」
いしい 「いいえ。どこへ いきましょうか。」
やまだ 「ぎんざへ いきましょう。ぎんざで しょくじを しませんか。」
いしい 「いいですね。」
やまだ 「たなかさんも よびましょうか。」
いしい 「いま うちに いませんよ。でかけました。」
やまだ 「どこへ？」
いしい 「かまくらへ いきました。よる かえりますけど。」
やまだ 「そうですか。じゃあ、いきましょう。」

6.5.2

やまだ 「きのう なにを しましたか。」
いしい 「うちで ほんを よみました。それから、てがみを かきました。あなたは？」
やまだ 「しんじゅくへ いきました。」
いしい 「かいもの？」
やまだ 「いいえ、ぎんこうへ いきました。」

6.5.3

　きょう がっこうが ありませんでした。それで、えいがへ いきました。そして、きっさてんで コーヒーを のみました。ケーキも たべました。それから、ほんやへ いきました。ほんやに いしいさんが いました。いっしょに ばんごはんを たべました。
　あした にほんごの クラス* が あります。それで、これから べんきょうを します。テープも ききます。

*nihon'go no kurasu　''Japanese language class''

LESSON 7
A TOUR OF THE CAMPUS

7.1 USEFUL EXPRESSIONS

Hajimemashite[18].

"How do you do?" This expression literally means "It is the first time."

Doozo yoroshiku[18]

This expression is normally used as a reply to *Hajimemashite*, but can be used together with other expressions, or can be used by itself. Literally, this means "Please extend a special favor to me," and may be used in various situations other than introductions.

Sorosoro[17] shitsurei shimasu.

"I'd better be leaving now." This means literally "I am going to commit the rudeness of leaving now."

Mata yukkuri irasshai[18].

"Come again and spend a leisurely time." This expression should not be used to a superior; *Mata (yukkuri) irashite kudasai* is preferred.

7.2 DIALOG

Mr. Smith: Are[1] wa[2] nan desu[3] ka /

Miss Koyama: Toshokan desu.

Mr. Smith: Kirei[4] desu nee[5]. Sore[1] wa /

Miss Koyama: Sore desu ka[6] / Shokudoo desu. Ocha o nomimashoo ka.

Mr. Smith: Ee, nodo ga kawakimashita[7] ne.

. . . .

Prof. Nakamura: Koyama san.

Miss Koyama: A, Nakamura sen'sei[8]. Tomodachi o shookai shimasu.

Sumisu san desu. Kochira[9] wa Nakamura sen'sei desu.

Prof. Nakamura: Hajimemashite.[18]

Mr. Smith: Doozo yoroshiku[18]

Prof. Nakamura: Anata mo[10] koko no[11] gakusei desu ka /

Mr. Smith: Iie, soo ja arimasen[12]. Meriiran'do Daigaku[13] no daigakuin no gakusei desu.

Prof. Nakamura: Sumisu san wa doko de nihon'go[14] o naraimashita ka /

Mr. Smith: Hawai Daigaku de naraimashita. Demo, mada[15] joozu ja arimasen.

Miss Koyama: Sen'sei[8], watashitachi[16] wa sorosoro[17] shitsurei shimasu.

Prof. Nakamura: Soo desu ka / Mata yukkuri irasshai[18].

Mr. Smith: Hai, arigatoo gozaimasu.

7.3 PATTERN SENTENCES

7.3.1

PM		
N	R	
Are	WA(2)	

→

P		SP
Ni	C	
nan	DESU(3)	ka?

7.3.2

PM		
N	R	
Anata	MO(10)	

→

P		SP
N	C	
gakusei	desu	ka?

7.3.3

PM

→

P			
N	R	N	C
Koko	NO(11)	gakusei	desu.

7.3.4

SI
Demo,

PM
Adv.
MADA(15)

→

P			
Na	C	R	E
joozu	JA DE WA		ARIMASEN.(12)

7.4 NOTES

7.4.1   *Are* is a Noun meaning ''that one over there.'' The following are words of this series:

kore   ''this one''

sore   ''that one''

are   ''that one over there''

dore   ''which one?''

Are o kaimashoo.   ''Let's buy that one.''

Kore wa toshokan desu.   ''This is a library.''

Sore o mimashita ka?   ''Did [you] see that one?''

Dore ga shokudoo desu ka?   ''Which is the cafeteria?''

As stated in Note 5.4.4 *kore* refers to something close to the speaker, *sore* refers to something near the hearer or something that has just been mentioned, and *are* to something at a distance from both the speaker and the hearer. Therefore, when someone asks you about something close to him but away from you, he will say *kore,* but you will say *sore.*

7.4.2 *Are wa nan desu ka?* means "What is that?" When an interrogative Noun such as *doko* "where," *dare* "who," or *nani* "what" occurs before the Copula *desu,* thus constituting a part of the Predicate, then the Relational at the end of the Predicate Modifier must not be the subject Relational *ga.* In such a case, the topic Relational *wa* must be used. See Note 7.4.3 for Copula.

Noun (subject) + *wa* + interrogative Noun + *desu ka?*

Koko wa doko desu ka?   "What place is this?" (Sometimes this means "Where am I now?")

Anata wa donata desu ka?   "Who are you?" "What is your name?"

To say "What is this?" *nan,* the contracted form of *nani* "what," will occur before *desu.*

Kore wa nan desu ka?   "What is this?"

Anata no namae wa nan desu ka?   "What is your name?"

7.4.3 The *desu* is the Copula representing the normal imperfect tense. The Copula occurs only after a Noun or an adjectival Noun. The latter will be explained in Note 7.4.4. It is used in the meaning of "A is B," or "A is such and such." The subject of this pattern can be either animate or inanimate. As appeared in Notes 3.4.9 and 4.4.8, the Relational *wa* indicates that the Noun preceding *wa* is the topic. See Note 7.4.12 for the negative form of the Copula *desu.*

Noun (subject) + $\left\{ \begin{array}{c} \textbf{\textit{wa}} \\ \textbf{\textit{ga}} \end{array} \right\}$ **+ Noun +** *desu*

watakushi			gakusei	"I am	a student"
anata		wa	sen'sei	"you are	a teacher"
. . . .	+	ga	. . . .	+ desu	. . . .
Sumisu san				"Mr. Smith is	a friend"
kochira			tomodachi	"this (person) is	

kore		wa	toshokan		a library"
sore	+	ga	heya	"this is	a room"
			Hawai Daigaku	"that is	the University of Hawaii"

Anata wa gakusei desu ka?   "Are you a student?"

Kore wa kamera desu.   "This is a camera."

Kuni wa Amerika desu.   "[I] am from the United States."

Although both *desu* and *arimasu* may be translated "is" in English equivalents, *desu* cannot replace *arimasu* in the sentence *Kamera wa heya ni arimasu* "The camera is in the room."

As indicated in Note 5.4.3, a subject followed by *ga* indicates "WHO does, or WHAT happens," or "WHO or WHAT is so," and so on. The Relational *wa* is used in the place of *ga* when the sentence is meant to describe "how or what something or someone is or does," rather than "WHAT or WHO is so or does."

Compare:

Kore wa toshokan desu.	"This is A LIBRARY."
Kore ga toshokan desu.	"THIS is the library."
Watashi wa Sumisu desu.	"I am SMITH."
Watashi ga Sumisu desu.	"I am Smith. (Not HE or SHE)"

When stressing "WHAT or WHO," the Relational *wa* cannot replace the *ga* and *o* following "WHAT or WHO" even in negation.

Nani ga oishiku arimasen ka?	"What is not tasty?"
Ocha ga oishiku arimasen.	"It is the tea that is not tasty."
Dare ga kimasen ka?	"Who is not coming?"
Sumisu san ga kimasen.	"It is Smith who is not coming."

If the speaker does not need to emphasize the subject or object, the Relational *wa* may take the place of the subject Relational *ga* or the object Relational *o* in an affirmative statement.

Noun (subject) + *ga* + Predicate ⟶ **Noun (subject) + *wa* + Predicate**

Noun (object) + *o* + Verb ⟶ **Noun (object) + *wa* + Verb**

Watakushi *ga* Yamada desu.	⟶	Watakushi *wa* Yamada desu.
Osake *o* nomimasu ka?	⟶	Osake *wa* nomimasu ka?

7.4.4 *Kirei* "pretty," *joozu* "skillful," *heta* "unskillful," *shizuka* "quiet," and *nigiyaka* "lively" are adjectival Nouns. These adjectival Nouns may occur before the Copula *desu, deshita,* et cetera, and usually describe "how something is," or "how someone is," as an Adjective does. In most cases, adjectival Nouns correspond to English adjectives, but since they are Nouns, their behavior is not that of Adjectives; an adjectival Noun does not inflect and the Copula following it does. The subject of the Predicate, which is described by the adjectival Nouns, may be human, animate, or inanimate, and is followed by *ga*.

Noun (subject) + $\left\{ \begin{array}{c} wa \\ ga \end{array} \right\}$ **+ adjectival Noun +** *desu*

kirei desu	"is pretty; is clean"
joozu desu	"is proficient"
heta desu	"is poor (at)"
shizuka desu	"is quiet"
nigiyaka desu	"is lively; is full of people and noise"

hima desu	"is free"
Shokudoo wa kirei desu.	"The cafeteria is clean."
Shin'juku wa nigiyaka desu.	"Shinjuku is (a) busy (town)."
Nanigo ga joozu desu ka?	"What language is [he] good at?"
Eigo ga joozu desu.	"[He] is good at English."

See Note 7.4.12 for the negative of these adjectival Nouns plus *desu*.

7.4.5 *Nee* is a Sentence Particle that stands at the end of a sentence like *ka* and *yo,* and is used to express "admiration," "surprise," or other similar exclamations, usually expecting the hearer's concurrence. *Nee* follows, among others, Predicates of description, such as adjectival Nouns or Adjectives.

Joozu desu nee.	"How proficient [you] are!"

It should be noted, however, that these Particles are used primarily in conversation rather than in written sentences, although young students today have been writing letters and other papers with these words. As a foreigner, try not to use *nee* or *ne* too often. See Note 3.4.12.

7.4.6 By repeating the other party's question, the conversation is continued smoothly. Sometimes this approach will afford more time to answer the question.

7.4.7 *Nodo* means "throat" and *kawakimasu* means "become dry." This expression, which is less direct, is used to indicate that "(someone) is thirsty." Instead of saying "I am hungry," the Japanese usually say *Onaka ga sukimashita* "My stomach is empty."

7.4.8 *Sen'sei* means "teacher." When referring to a person who is a teacher, *sen'sei* may be used instead of *-san*. Physicians, lawyers, and the like may also be called *sen'sei*.

Nakamura sen'sei	"Prof., Dr., or Mr. Nakamura"

Sen'sei can also be used as if it were a pronoun of the second person "you" when speaking to a teacher, a doctor, and so on.

Koyama addressed Professor Nakamura as *sen'sei*. Used here as if it were the second person pronoun, *sen'sei* indicates respect and has the sense of "elder." It is more polite than *anata* and thus, in the context of the dialog, has the effect of conveying to the professor that Koyama understands what is expected socially of her as a student in Japan. As a matter of fact, Japanese students never use *anata* to a teacher. This is displayed, as the conversation progresses, when Professor Nakamura addresses Smith as *anata* rather than *Sumisu san,* and again when in parting he chooses to say *mata irasshai.* He has thus demonstrated that he has gradually ceased to regard Smith as a member of an out-group and therefore the distance implied by his initial greeting is effaced.

Note also that this dialog demonstrates two of the three uses of *sen'sei.* As discussed above, *sen'sei* may be used as if it were a pronoun. In addition, it is a dependent Noun signifying either a professional title specific to teachers and doctors or, less literally, an indication of deserved respect.

Attached to the surname, it is more formal than *-san* (note, however, that *-san* may not be used independently). Incidentally, *sen'sei* as a term of respect has been much abused and is sometimes employed to satisfy or play upon vanity—in the same way a private in the army might, for instance, personally promote his captain to a major, calling him "Major" in order to please him

For centuries the social position of teachers in Japan has been very high. Until recently the superiority of the teacher over the student was unquestioned, and any dialog between them would clearly reflect this. The traditional teacher-student relationship is another example of the vertical orientation in Japanese social group formation, that of superior-inferior. Thus students were obligated to use polite forms of speech in addressing or referring to their teachers, while the latter would normally choose less polite forms or even make no verbal response whatsoever. In the last decade, however, a new trend has emerged. Although most students still address their teachers with customary respect, many of the more radical student groups have insistently objected to the traditional student-teacher relationship. Nevertheless, even though the social gap between student and teacher may be narrowing, it is doubtful whether languagewise it will diminish so soon or to the extent that it has in many Western countries.

7.4.9 *Kochira* is a polite expression meaning "this side." The Japanese usually avoid any expression which may be construed as too direct. *Kore* should never be used when introducing someone to another person. There may be some exceptional cases, but they can be left aside at this stage.

Kochira wa Nakamura sen'sei desu.   "This is Professor Nakamura."

7.4.10 As indicated in Note 4.4.9, the Relational *mo* meaning "also" or "too" may take the place of the Relational *o*. This Relational *mo* may also take the place of the Relationals *wa* and *ga*. See also Notes 8.4.8 and 12.4.5.

$$\text{Noun} + \left\{ \begin{array}{c} ga \\ wa \end{array} \right\} + \text{Predicate} \longrightarrow \text{Noun} + mo + \text{Predicate}$$

Are ga gin'koo desu ka?   "Is that one over there a bank?"

Are *mo* gin'koo desu ka?   "Is that one over there a bank, too?"

Watakushi wa nihon'go o hanashimasu.   "I speak Japanese."

Watakushi *mo* nihon'go o hanashimasu.   "I speak Japanese, too (as well as someone else does)."

Anata "you" is literally "that direction"—that is, although it is considered more direct than *sen'sei*, it nevertheless evades direct confrontation of personalities and illustrates the pervasive Japanese tendency to indirectness of designation. *Anata* is, then, a polite form for second person address. In relation to other forms, *anata* is more polite than *an'ta*, which is quite informal. Women probably use *anata* with greater frequency, especially since Japanese wives have traditionally used this word in addressing their husbands. As a whole, *sen'sei* is used for teachers, *-san* is used for those whose names are known, and *anata* is used broadly except for teachers and superiors.

7.4.11 The Relational *no* occurs between Nouns such as *koko* and *gakusei*. The Noun followed by *no* forms a Noun Modifier and describes the following Noun. Note that it sometimes corresponds to "of," but not always. The meaning of N₁ *no* N₂ will be "N₂ belonging to N₁," "N₂ related to N₁," "N₂ located in N₁," and so on.

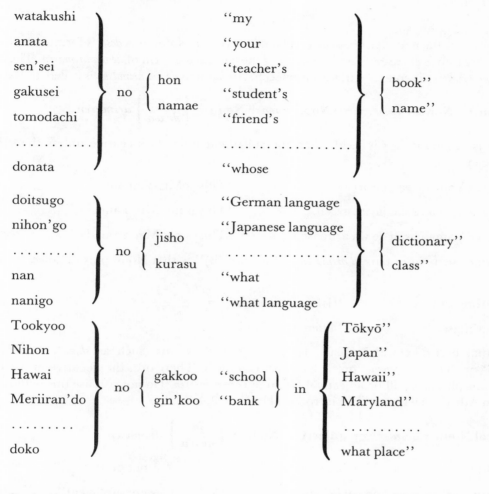

Sen'sei no namae wa Nakamura desu.   "The teacher's name is Nakamura."

Eigo no hon o kaimashita.   "[I] bought a book [written] in English."

Hawai no gakkoo de naraimashita.   "[I] studied it at a school in Hawaii."

When two or more Noun Modifiers, Noun plus *no*, occur, the first Noun Modifier may modify directly the following Noun or both the Modifiers may modify another following Noun. The context usually explains which is the case.

$$
\text{N1 } no + \text{N2 } no + \text{N3} \longrightarrow \begin{cases} \text{N1 } no \\ \text{N2 } no \end{cases} + \quad \text{N3} \\ \text{or} \\ (\text{N1 } no + \text{N2}) \, no \quad + \quad \text{N3}
$$

watakushi no
nihon'go no } sen'sei ⟶ watakushi no nihon'go no sen'sei   "my Japanese language teacher"

(watakushi no tomodachi) no sen'sei ⟶ watakushi no tomodachi no sen'sei "my friend's teacher"

When one of the two or more Noun Modifiers indicates possession, that Modifier of possession usually precedes.

7.4.12 *Soo ja arimasen* is the negative of *Soo desu*. The negative of a Noun plus *desu* is formulated by transforming *desu* into *ja arimasen*. The *ja arimasen* is the contracted form of *de wa arimasen*. The original form *de wa arimasen* is common in formal speech. *Arimasen* in *de wa arimasen* is called an Extender.

Noun + *wa* + **Noun** + *desu* ⟶ **Noun** + *wa* + **Noun** + $\left\{ \begin{array}{c} ja \\ de\ wa \end{array} \right\}$ *arimasen*

Since *ga* is emphatic, *wa* is used when the statement is in the negative unless the subject is emphasized.

Kochira wa Yamada san desu.	"This is Mr. Yamada."
Kochira wa Yamada san ja arimasen.	"This is not Mr. Yamada."
Kochira wa Yamada san de wa arimasen.	"This is not Mr. Yamada."

Do not confuse a Noun plus *ja arimasen* "(A) is not (B)" with a Noun plus *ga arimasen* "there is not."

Hon ja arimasen.	"[It] is not a book."
Hon ga arimasen.	"There is no book."

Nouns that occur before *desu* can also be adjectival Nouns, such as *shizuka* "quiet," *kirei* "pretty" or "clean," *joozu* "proficient," and so forth. Therefore, the negative of these adjectival Nouns plus *desu* will be adjectival Noun plus *ja arimasen*. Do not confuse this with the negative of an Adjective which will be introduced in Note 8.4.5.

adjectival Noun + *desu* ⟶ **adjectival Noun** + $\left\{ \begin{array}{c} ja \\ de\ wa \end{array} \right\}$ *arimasen*

kirei desu	⟶	kirei ja arimasen	"is not pretty"
joozu desu	⟶	joozu ja arimasen	"is not proficient"
heta desu	⟶	heta ja arimasen	"is not poor (at it)"
shizuka desu	⟶	shizuka ja arimasen	"is not quiet"
nigiyaka desu	⟶	nigiyaka ja arimasen	"is not lively"
hima desu	⟶	hima ja arimasen	"is not free"

7.4.13 Names of organizations, such as universities, corporations, et cetera, are always used without *no* "of" as follows:

Meriiran'do Daigaku	"University of Maryland"
Hawai Daigaku	"University of Hawaii"
Tookyoo Gin'koo	"Bank of Tōkyō"
Shin'juku Eki	"Shinjuku Station"

7.4.14 *Nihon'go* is a Noun meaning "the Japanese language." The name of a language is normally formed by adding *-go* to a country's name. *Gaikokugo* "foreign language" is a combination of *gaikoku* "foreign country" and *-go* "language." Similarly, *nihon'jin* means "the Japanese people or nationals." *Gaikokujin* "foreigner" is a combination of *gaikoku* "foreign country" and *-jin* "people."

Nihon	"Japan"	....nihon'go, nihon'jin	"the Japanese language" "a Japanese"
Doitsu	"Germany"	....doitsugo, doitsujin	"the German language" "a German"
Furan'su	"France"	....furan'sugo, furan'sujin	"the French language" "a Frenchman"
Chuugoku	"China"	....chuugokugo, chuugokujin	"the Chinese language" "a Chinese"
gaikoku	"foreign country"	....gaikokugo, gaikokujin	"foreign language" "a foreigner"

Exception: Amerika "U.S.A."   eigo "the English language"

                        ....amerikajin "an American"

      Igirisu   "England"   igirisujin "an Englishman"

Nanigo is used to ask a name of a specific language or "what language?"

Anata wa nanigo o hanashimasu ka?   "What language do you speak?"

7.4.15 *Mada* "(not) yet," like *zen'zen* "(not) at all," is an Adverb used with negative Predicates. Since these Adverbs are used mainly in negation, when they are used alone, they may also carry a negative connotation. Thus, *mada desu* is widely used in giving a negative answer meaning "not yet." See Note 8.4.4.

$$\left. \begin{matrix} mada \\ zen'zen \end{matrix} \right\} + \textbf{negative Predicate}$$

Nihon'go wa mada joozu ja arimasen.   "My Japanese is not good yet."

Tanaka san wa uchi ni kaerimashita ka?   "Did Mr. Tanaka go home?"

Iie, mada desu.   "No, not yet."

Demo, mada joozu ja arimasen. Another typical display of modesty may be seen in this utterance. In America, if one feels that he is not good at something he may well say so. This is also true in Japan. On the other hand, if a person believes that he is good at something, whereas in America he would acknowledge and accept the compliment, such behavior would be embarrassing or awkward *(tereru)*. A Japanese would, in consideration of modesty, disclaim any compliment regardless of the validity of the praise.

  The use of *Joozu ja arimasen* as compared with its American equivalent may be illustrated as follows:

	American	Japanese
Personally feel that you yourself are not deserving of compliment.	No good	*Joozu ja arimasen*
Personally feel that you are good, deserving the compliment.	Thank you	*Joozu ja arimasen*

This exemplifies the characteristic heteronomy of Japanese relations—that is, their non-self-assertion and modesty towards others. In this context, *Joozu ja arimasen* actually means "I'm not really that good."

One exception, however, to the Japanese uniform response of *Joozu ja arimasen* is in the case of a teacher complimenting someone's progress in his course. The Japanese student would not reply with *Mada joozu ja arimasen*. Rather, he would probably accept the compliment.

In considering Japanese groupism, it is useful to consider the intimate groups such as family members or close classmates; the formal groups such as company colleagues or professional association members; and the out-groups, such as *yosomono* or strangers. The degree of in-groupness varies within and among intimate and formal groups, depending on the speakers' views toward closeness and the generally accepted evaluation of closeness. For the members of intimate groups, *en'ryo* (reserve, modesty, and discretion) is required to a lesser degree than among formal group members. But toward out-group members, *en'ryo* actually is not necessary, although polite expressions with distance may be used.

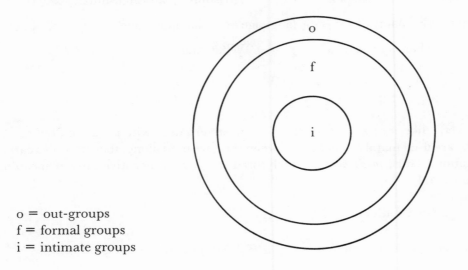

o = out-groups
f = formal groups
i = intimate groups

7.4.16 The *-tachi* in *watakushitachi* is a dependent Noun that turns the word *watakushi* "I" into the plural "we." This is always used with words that indicate animate objects, particularly human beings.

gakusei　　　　　　　"student"　　　. . . . gakuseitachi　　　　　　　"students"

Note that in Japanese the plural form of a word is not mandatory even when you are referring to more than one (being). *Otoko no hito* may refer to "a man" or "men," and *hon* may mean "a book" or "books." The plural forms of words such as *watakushi, anata,* et cetera, however, should be identified with a dependent Noun such as *-tachi*.

wata(ku)shi　　　"I"　　　　. . . . wata(ku)shitachi　　　"we"

anata　　　　　"you"　　　. . . . anatatachi　　　　"you"

Sometimes *-tachi* is used to refer to a group of persons, only one of them being represented.

Yamada san to Itoo san to   ⟶   Yamada san'tachi ga kimashita.
Suzuki san ga kimashita.

"Mr. Yamada, Mr. Itō, and   "Mr. Yamada and some other people came."
Mr. Suzuki came."

7.4.17 Sorosoro

Note the use of *sorosoro* in *Sorosoro shitsurei shimasu*. It may be translated as "slowly" and is a good example of the Japanese tendency to avoid any suggestion of abruptness and lack of modesty or any impact which might be created as a result of taking or suggesting to take a new action. The American equivalent of this softening would be expressed more indirectly, through the use of the participle, as in "I should be going now." Compare this also with the use of *chotto* and *sugu*. These modifiers all serve to minimize something which is felt might offend or inconvenience the listener, and as such demonstrate a distinctive feature of the Japanese attitude toward human relationships. This is once again indicative of the heteronomous tendency in Japanese culture.

Sorosoro ikimashoo ka?   "Shall we go now?"

Sorosoro dekakemasen ka?   "Shall we leave now?"

When used in the imperfect tense, *Shitsurei shimasu* carries the simple meaning of a parting excuse. When used in the perfect tense, *Shitsurei shimashita*, however, the speaker is actually seeking pardon for something he has done. When combined with the Copula *shitsurei desu*, it implies rudeness and takes the form of a reprimand.

7.4.18 Doozo yoroshiku

The expression *Doozo yoroshiku* illustrates the quality of the Japanese attitude toward giving and receiving, which is perhaps most accurately expressed as favoring and appreciating. In humbling oneself by explicitly seeking good or favorable treatment, one hopes to provide a kind of lubrication to facilitate the relationship. *Doozo yoroshiku* is used mainly among peers. Toward a superior, or when it is desirable to maintain a distance, the more formal *Doozo yoroshiku onegai itashimasu* would be used.

Hajimemashite has a much more limited use than its closest English equivalent, "How do you do?" Literally, the term means "It is the first time," and can only be used the first time one meets a person. It cannot be repeated upon subsequent encounters, thus contrasting with the use of its English counterpart, "How do you do?" which can be repeated after the first meeting.

Mata irasshai would never be addressed to a superior; to do so would indicate that the speaker is insensitive to or refuses to differentiate between human relationships. The more polite, and therefore more widely applicable, form is *Mata irashite kudasai*. The *kudasai* ending is preferred in that it softens the air of command in this imperative form. It even implies that the speaker is not requesting but suggesting, especially when the speaker softens his or her voice.

Observe the form of the greetings exchanged between Smith and Professor Nakamura. Normally, if the student were Japanese, this particular version would not occur. The range of possibilities would be as follows:

Japanese student: Hajimemashite.
Prof. Nakamura: Aa.

Japanese student: Hajimemashite. Doozo yoroshiku.
Prof. Nakamura: Aa, yoroshiku.

Japanese student: Hajimemashite. Doozo yoroshiku onegai itashimasu.
Prof. Nakamura: Hajimemashite. Doozo yoroshiku.

Of these, the first would be the most probable. However, since Smith is a foreigner and therefore regarded as a member of an out-group, a more polite form would usually be employed, thus maintaining a distance.

7.5 VOCABULARY

Dialog

are	.......N	that one over there (see 7.4.1)
wa	.......R	(see 7.4.2)
nan	......Ni	what? (see 7.4.2)
desu	C	(see 7.4.3)
toshokan	.......N	(school or public) library
kirei	......Na	pretty; clean (*Kirei* is not an Adjective but an adjectival Noun. Adjectives never end in *-ei.*) (see 7.4.4)
nee	......SP	(see 7.4.5)
sore	.......N	that one (see 7.4.1)
nodo	.......N	throat (see 7.4.7)
kawakimashita	V	got thirsty (see 7.4.7)
Nakamura	.......N	family name
sen'sei	......N	teacher (see 7.4.8)
tomodachi	......N	friend
shookai (o) shimasu	V	introduce (normal form of *shookai (o) suru*)
Sumisu	.......N	Smith
kochira	.......N	this person (direction; one) (see 7.4.9)
anata	.......N	you (see 7.4.10)
no	.......R	(see 7.4.11)
gakusei	.......N	student
soo	....Adv.	in that way; so
ja arimasen	..C+R+E	negative of *desu* (see 7.4.12)
Meriiran'do	.......N	Maryland
daigaku	.......N	university; college
daigakuin	.......N	graduate school
naraimasu	V	study; take lessons; is taught; learn (normal form of *narau*) (Note that *naraimasu* is not always equivalent to ''learn.'')

demo	. . . . . . .SI	but; however
mada	. . . .Adv.	(not) yet; still (see 7.4.15)
joozu	. . . . . .Na	skillful; proficient; good (at) (see 7.4.4)
watashitachi	. . . . . . .N	we (see 7.4.16)
sorosoro	. . . .Adv.	it is about time (see 7.4.17)

Notes

kore	. . . . . . .N	this one (see 7.4.1)
dore	. . . . . .Ni	which one? (see 7.4.1)
namae	. . . . . . .N	name
kuni	. . . . . . .N	country; home (town; country)
heta	. . . . . .Na	unskillful; poor (at)
shizuka	. . . . . .Na	quiet
nigiyaka	. . . . . .Na	lively; cheerful; noisy; bustling
nanigo	. . . . . .Ni	what language? (see 7.4.14)
eigo	. . . . . . .N	English language
onaka	. . . . . . .N	stomach (see 7.4.7)
sukimashita	V	got hungry (see 7.4.7)
amerikajin	. . . . . . .N	an American
hanashimasu	V	speak; talk (normal form of *hanasu*)
doitsugo	. . . . . . .N	German language
arimasen	. . . . . . .E	(see 7.4.12)
de wa arimasen	. .C+R+E	formal equivalent of *ja arimasen* (see 7.4.12)
-go	. . . . . .Nd	language (see 7.4.14)
gaikokugo	. . . . . .N	foreign language
gaikoku	. . . . . . .N	foreign country; abroad
nihon'jin	. . . . . . .N	a Japanese
gaikokujin	. . . . . .N	foreigner
-jin	. . . . . .Nd	(see 7.4.14)
Doitsu	. . . . . . .N	Germany
doitsugo	. . . . . . .N	German language
doitsujin	. . . . . . .N	a German
Furan'su	. . . . . . .N	France
furan'sugo	. . . . . . .N	French language

furan'sujin	.......N	a Frenchman
Chuugoku	.......N	China
chuugokugo	.......N	Chinese language
chuugokujin	.......N	a Chinese
Igirisu	.......N	England
igirisujin	.......N	an Englishman
-tachi	......Nd	(turns the preceding animate Noun into plural) (see 7.4.16)

7.6 HIRAGANA PRACTICE

7.6.1 Recognize the difference or similarity between two *hiragana* in each of the following pairs:

あ……あ	の……の	ね……ぬ	わ……れ
あ……め	の……お	ぬ……ぬ	れ……れ
あ……の	の……つ	ぬ……め	れ……ね
め……め	お……お	ぬ……わ	
め……の	お……あ	わ……わ	
め……ぬ	ね……ね	わ……ね	

7.6.2 Practice writing the following *hiragana*:

1. あ [a] あ あ あ あ
2. め [me] め め め
3. の [no] の の
4. ぬ [nu] ぬ ぬ ぬ
5. お [o] お お お
6. ね [ne] ね ね ね
7. わ [wa] わ わ わ
8. れ [re] れ れ れ

7.6.3 Read and write the following:

これ　それ　あれ　おてあらい　この　ほん　あなた

あの　いぬ　わたくし　ねこ　あめ "rain"

7.7 DRILLS

7.7.1 Pronunciation Drill

nodo   doko   daigaku   daigakuin   shokudoo   mada   demo

tomodachi   dore   dare   Doitsu   Soo desu   Arigatoo

kore   sore   are   kirei   amari   Meriiran'do

7.7.2 Pattern Drill

1. Are wa toshokan desu ka?

2. Iie, toshokan de wa arimasen.

3. Toshokan wa kirei desu ka?

4. Iie, kirei ja arimasen.

5. Are wa nan desu ka?

6. Are wa shokudoo desu.

7. Watashi no tomodachi wa Tookyoo Daigaku no gakusei desu.

8. Ishii san mo koko no gakusei desu.

7.7.3 Substitution Drill

Kore wa *toshokan* desu ka?

1. *gin'koo* . . . . Kore wa *gin'koo* desu ka?

2. doitsugo . . . . Kore wa doitsugo desu ka?

3. namae . . . . Kore wa namae desu ka?

4. yuubin'kyoku . . . . Kore wa yuubin'kyoku desu ka?

5. jisho . . . . Kore wa jisho desu ka?

6. toshokan . . . . Kore wa toshokan desu ka?

7. nanigo . . . . Kore wa nanigo desu ka?

8. nan . . . . Kore wa nan desu ka?

7.7.4 Substitution Drill

Anata wa *Sumisu san* desu ka?

1. *gakusei* . . . . Anata wa *gakusei* desu ka?

2. igirisujin . . . . Anata wa igirisujin desu ka?

3. nihon'jin . . . . Anata wa nihon'jin desu ka?

4. sen'sei . . . . Anata wa sen'sei desu ka?

5. amerikajin . . . . Anata wa amerikajin desu ka?

6. chuugokujin . . . . Anata wa chuugokujin desu ka?

7. Nakamura sen'sei . . . . Anata wa Nakamura sen'sei desu ka?

8. donata . . . . Anata wa donata desu ka?

7.7.5 Substitution Drill

Kore wa *shokudoo* desu.

1. *are, toshokan*   . . . .*Are* wa *toshokan* desu.

2. watakushi, Sumisu   . . . .Watakushi wa Sumisu desu.

3. kochira, Sumisu san   . . . .Kochira wa Sumisu san desu.

4. sore, furan'sugo   . . . .Sore wa furan'sugo desu.

5. Koyama san, tomodachi   . . . .Koyama san wa tomodachi desu.

6. watashitachi, gaikokujin   . . . .Watashitachi wa gaikokujin desu.

7. namae, Suzuki   . . . .Namae wa Suzuki desu.

8. kuni, Amerika   . . . .Kuni wa Amerika desu.

9. daigaku, Tookyoo Daigaku   . . . .Daigaku wa Tookyoo Daigaku desu.

10. anata, doitsujin   . . . .Anata wa doitsujin desu.

11. soko, jimusho   . . . .Soko wa jimusho desu.

12. koko, daigakuin   . . . .Koko wa daigakuin desu.

7.7.6 Transformation Drill

1. Are wa *toshokan desu.*   ⟶ Are wa *toshokan ja arimasen.*

2. Watashi wa gakusei desu.   ⟶ Watashi wa gakusei ja arimasen.

3. Kochira wa Sumisu san desu.   ⟶ Kochira wa Sumisu san ja arimasen.

4. Asoko wa gin'koo desu.   ⟶ Asoko wa gin'koo ja arimasen.

5. Are wa inu desu.   ⟶ Are wa inu ja arimasen.

6. Soko wa kirei desu.   ⟶ Soko wa kirei ja arimasen.

7. Toshokan wa shizuka desu.   ⟶ Toshokan wa shizuka ja arimasen.

8. Kono hen wa nigiyaka desu.   ⟶ Kono hen wa nigiyaka ja arimasen.

9. Joozu desu.   ⟶ Joozu ja arimasen.

10. Heta desu.   ⟶ Heta ja arimasen.

7.7.7 Expansion Drill

1. Hanashimasu ka?   . . . .Hanashimasu ka?

   gaikokugo o   . . . .Gaikokugo o hanashimasu ka?

   Suzuki san wa   . . . .Suzuki san wa gaikokugo o hanashimasu ka?

2. Arimasu yo.   . . . .Arimasu yo.

   koko ni   . . . .Koko ni arimasu yo.

   tegami wa   . . . .Tegami wa koko ni arimasu yo.

3. Naraimashita ka? . . . . Naraimashita ka?

    nanigo o . . . . Nanigo o naraimashita ka?

    anata wa . . . . Anata wa nanigo o naraimashita ka?

4. Imashita. . . . . Imashita.

    eki ni . . . . Eki ni imashita.

    tomodachi wa . . . . Tomodachi wa eki ni imashita.

5. Kaerimasen deshita. . . . . Kaerimasen deshita.

    uchi e . . . . Uchi e kaerimasen deshita.

    watashi wa . . . . Watashi wa uchi e kaerimasen deshita.

6. Kaimono o shimasu. . . . . Kaimono o shimasu.

    kyoo . . . . Kyoo kaimono o shimasu.

    watakushitachi wa . . . . Watakushitachi wa kyoo kaimono o shimasu.

7.7.8 Transformation Drill (ga ⟷ wa)

1. Sumisu san *ga* imasu. ⟷ Sumisu san *wa* imasu.

2. Watashi ga Tanaka desu. ⟷ Watashi wa Tanaka desu.

3. Hima ga arimasen. ⟷ Hima wa arimasen.

4. Okane ga arimasu yo. ⟷ Okane wa arimasu yo.

5. Uchi ga kirei desu. ⟷ Uchi wa kirei desu.

6. Watashi ga ikimasu. ⟷ Watashi wa ikimasu.

7. Tomodachi ga kimashita. ⟷ Tomodachi wa kimashita.

8. Asoko ga Shin'juku Eki desu. ⟷ Asoko wa Shin'juku Eki desu.

7.7.9 Transformation Drill (wa, ga ⟷ mo)

1. Kore *wa* furan'sugo desu. ⟷ Kore wa furan'sugo desu. *Sore mo*
    sore   furan'sugo desu.

2. Hon'ya ga arimasu. ⟷ Hon'ya ga arimasu. Rekoodoya mo
    rekoodoya   arimasu.

3. Nihon'go ga joozu desu. ⟷ Nihon'go ga joozu desu.
    chuugokugo   Chuugokugo mo joozu desu.

4. Sumisu san wa gakusei desu. ⟷ Sumisu san wa gakusei desu. Koyama
    Koyama san   san mo gakusei desu.

5. Inu ga imasu. ⟷ Inu ga imasu. Neko mo imasu.
    neko

6. Koko wa gin'koo desu ka? ⟷ Koko wa gin'koo desu ka? Soko mo
    soko   gin'koo desu ka?

7. Eigo ga heta desu.
   doitsugo

➞ Eigo ga heta desu. Doitsugo mo
   heta desu.

8. Nakamura san wa sen'sei desu.
   kochira

➞ Nakamura san wa sen'sei desu. Kochira
   mo sen'sei desu.

7.7.10 Expansion Drill

1. Kore wa hon desu.
   watakushi no

   . . . . Kore wa *watakushi no* hon desu.

2. Jisho o kaimashita.
   nihon'go no

   . . . . Nihon'go no jisho o kaimashita.

3. Watashitachi wa gakusei desu.
   Hawai Daigaku no

   . . . . Watashitachi wa Hawai Daigaku no
   gakusei desu.

4. Eiga o mimashoo.
   Igirisu no

   . . . . Igirisu no eiga o mimashoo.

5. Namae wa nan desu ka?
   anata no

   . . . . Anata no namae wa nan desu ka?

6. Kochira wa sen'sei desu ka?
   nan no

   . . . . Kochira wa nan no sen'sei desu ka?

7. Are wa heya desu ka?
   donata no

   . . . . Are wa donata no heya desu ka?

8. Anata wa gakusei desu ka?
   doko no

   . . . . Anata wa doko no gakusei desu ka?

9. Kuni wa doko desu ka?
   Sumisu san no

   . . . . Sumisu san no kuni wa doko desu ka?

10. Depaato de kaimono o shimashita.
    Gin'za no

    . . . . Gin'za no depaato de kaimono o
    shimashita.

7.7.11 Expansion Drill

1. Kore wa *watashi no* hon desu.
   nihon'go no

   . . . . Kore wa *watashi no nihon'go no*
   hon desu.

2. Anata no jisho o mimashoo.
   eigo no

   . . . . Anata no eigo no jisho o mimashoo.

3. Are wa dare no hon desu ka?
   doitsugo no

   . . . . Are wa dare no doitsugo no hon
   desu ka?

4. Itoo sen'sei no kurasu e ikimashoo.
   nihon'go no

   . . . . Itoo sen'sei no nihon'go no kurasu
   e ikimashoo.

5. Sumisu sen'sei wa watashitachi
   no sen'sei desu.
   eigo no

   . . . . Sumisu sen'sei wa watashitachi no
   eigo no sen'sei desu.

6. Doko no gakusei ga imasu ka?
   daigakuin no

   . . . . Doko no daigakuin no gakusei ga
   imasu ka?

7.7.12 Response Drill (short answer)

1. Anata wa sen'sei desu ka? / iie   . . . . Iie, sen'sei de wa arimasen.

2. Nanigo o hanashimasu ka? / eigo   . . . . Eigo o hanashimasu.

3. Dore ga anata no heya desu ka? / sore   . . . . Sore ga watakushi no heya desu.

4. Kore wa doko no kamera desu ka?
   / Nihon no kamera   . . . . Nihon no kamera desu.

5. Anata wa daigakuin no gakusei desu ka? / iie   . . . . Iie, daigakuin no gakusei ja arimasen.

6. Kuni wa doko desu ka? / Amerika   . . . . Amerika desu.

7. Kono hen wa nigiyaka desu ka? / iie   . . . . Iie, nigiyaka ja arimasen.

8. Sumisu san wa igirisujin desu ka? / iie   . . . . Iie, igirisujin de wa arimasen.

9. Soko wa nan no gakkoo desu ka? / nihon'go   . . . . Nihon'go no gakkoo desu.

10. Soo desu ka? / iie   . . . . Iie, soo ja arimasen.

7.8 EXERCISES

7.8.1   What would you say when:

     1. you are introduced to someone?

     2. you want to introduce Mr. Koyama to Professor Smith?

     3. you agree with what someone says?

     4. you are about to leave the place where you are?

     5. you got hungry?

     6. you got thirsty?

7.8.2   Choose one of the following Relationals, referring to the given English sentence:

     1. Kore (wa, ga) donata no heya desu ka?   "Whose room is this?"

     2. Dore (wa, ga) anata no jisho desu ka?   "Which is your dictionary?"

     3. Kochira (wa, ga) Yamada san desu.   "This is Mr. Yamada."
            (emphasis on "this")

     4. Nanigo (wa, ga) joozu desu ka?   "What language is [he] good at?"

     5. Kochira (wa, ga) watashi no sen'sei desu.   "This is my teacher."
            (no emphasis on "this")

     6. Anata (wa, ga) doko de naraimashita ka?   "Where did you take lessons?"

     7. Anata (wa, mo) doitsugo (o, mo)
          naraimashita ka?   "Did you study German (as well as something
            else)?"

     8. Sore (wa, ga) nan desu ka?   "What is that?"

     9. Watashi (wa, mo) chuugokugo (o, mo)
          hanashimasu.   "I speak Chinese (as well as Japanese)."

102

7.8.3   Rearrange each group of the following words into a good Japanese sentence:

1. ja arimasen   shokudoo   kirei   no   daigaku   wa

2. donata   wa   are   hon   desu   no   ka

3. desu   nan   wa   are   ka

4. soko   mo   tomodachi   o   nihon'go   naraimashita   de

5. wa   no   Hawai   Daigaku   de wa arimasen   gakusei   watakushi

6. ka   desu   gakkoo   nan   no   namae   wa

7.8.4   Carry on a dialog according to the following English.

A: Whose book is this?

B: That is Professor Smith's book.

A: What book is this?

B: That's a book of the French language. Professor Smith is a teacher of French.

A: Is he? Is that one over there a book of French, too?

B: No, it isn't. That is a book of Japanese.

7.8.5   Answer the following questions on the basis of the Dialog:

1. Sumisu san to Koyama san wa doko ni imasu ka?

2. Sumisu san to Koyama san wa doko de ocha o nomimasu ka?

3. Koyama san wa gakusei desu ka?

4. Nakamura san mo gakusei desu ka?

5. Sumisu san wa doko no gakusei desu ka?

6. Sumisu san wa Nihon no daigaku de nihon'go o naraimashita ka?

LESSON 8
GOING TO A COFFEE SHOP

8.1 USEFUL EXPRESSIONS

Shibaraku.

"I have not seen you for a long time." In polite speech *desu (nee)* may be added to *Shibaraku*.

Ogen'ki desu ka₁₁/

This expression is the most common equivalent for "How are you?" Literally this means "Are you in good spirits?" *Gen'ki desu ka?* may also be used in less formal or polite speech.

Okagesama de₁₂

This expression, which is used in various situations, is often used in reply to the above expression, and means "(Fine), thank you." The literal meaning is "Thanks to you, to God, et cetera." The informal expression, *(Ee,) gen'ki desu* can also be used.

8.2 DIALOG

Yamamoto:	Watanabe san ja arimasen ka₁/
Watanabe:	A, Yamamoto san Shibaraku. Ogen'ki desu ka/
Yamamoto:	Ee. Watanabe san mo/
Watanabe:	Ee, okagesama de
Yamamoto:	Tokoro de₂, ima isogashii₃ desu ka/
Watanabe:	Iie, amari₄ isogashiku arimasen₅ kedo/
Yamamoto:	Chotto sono₆ nen de ocha o nomimasen ka/
Watanabe:	Ii desu ne. . . . Soko ni kissaten ga arimasu yo/ Hairimasu ka/
Yamamoto:	Sono mise wa yoku arimasen. Koohii ga mazui n₃ desu. Sore ni₇, mise mo₈ kirei ja arimasen. Den'en e ikimashoo.
Watanabe:	Soko wa tooi desu ka/
Yamamoto:	Iie, chikai desu yo/ Kotchi₉ desu.
Watanabe:	Yamamoto san wa sono kissaten e yoku ikimasu ka/
Yamamoto:	Ee, yoku ikimasu. Soko no koohii wa totemo₄ oishii n desu. On'gaku mo ii desu.
Watanabe:	Yamamoto san wa₁₀ on'gaku ga₁₀ suki desu nee.
Yamamoto:	Ee, daisuki desu. Saa, kono₆ mise desu. Hairimashoo.

8.3 PATTERN SENTENCES

8.3.1

PM	→	P			SP
Nt		A	PC	C	ka?
Ima		isogashiI[3]	(N)	DESU[3]	

8.3.2

PM	→	P	
Adv.		A	E
Amari		isogashiKU	ARIMASEN.[5]

8.3.3

PM		→	P			
N	R		Na	C	R	E
Mise	MO[8]		kirei	ja		ariMASEN.[8]

8.3.4

PM		→	PM		→	P	
N	R		N	R		Na	C
Yamada san	WA[10]		on'gaku	GA[10]		suki	desu.

8.4 NOTES

8.4.1 *Yamamoto san ja arimasen ka?* is an indirect expression. The traditional Japanese tends to use indirect expressions to avoid giving others any impression that he/she is aggressive, self-confident, self-assertive, or dogmatic. Instead of saying "You are so and so," the more indirect expression "Aren't you so and so?" is more frequently used.

8.4.2 *Tokoro de* means "by the way" and functions as a softener in changing a topic.

8.4.3 *Isogashii* is the imperfect tense form of an Adjective meaning "is busy." The imperfect tense form of any Adjective has one of these endings: *-ai, -ii, -ui,* or *-oi,* and the final *-i* is the inflected part of the Adjective. In the normal spoken style of Japanese, Adjectives are followed by the Copula *desu* or *n desu* when they are in the position of the final Predicate.

tooi desu	"is far"	chikai desu	"is near"
ii desu* (yoi desu)	"is good"	warui desu	"is bad"
ookii desu	"is big"	chiisai desu	"is small"
oishii desu	"is tasty"	mazui desu	"is tasteless"
urusai desu	"is noisy"	isogashii desu	"is busy"
kitanai desu	"is dirty"		

*Note that *ii* is the colloquial alternative of *yoi* meaning "good," and all the inflected forms of this Adjective are based on *yoi*. See Notes 8.4.5, 9.4.9, 11.4.4, and 11.4.7.

The normal pattern of an adjectival Predicate will be:

Adjective + *(n)* + *desu* ⟶ **Noun (subject) +** $\begin{Bmatrix} ga \\ wa \end{Bmatrix}$ **+ (Adverb) + Adjective + *(n)* + *desu***

Kono eiga wa ii desu.	"This movie is good."
Anata no uchi wa tooi desu ka?	"Is your house far?"
Dore ga chiisai desu ka?	"Which is small?"
Bifuteki mo oishii desu.	"Beefsteak is also delicious."
Asoko wa kitanai desu.	"That place is dirty."

The *n* sometimes occurs between an Adjective and the Copula *desu*—*mazui n desu*. In this case *n* is called the Pre-Copula. The difference between *desu* and *n desu* is slight, but it may be said that *n desu* is a little more emphatic, colloquial, and elucidative.

Heya ga ookii n desu.	"The room is big, you know."
Sono eiga wa tsumaranai n desu.	"That movie is dull."

8.4.4   Like *mada*, this word *amari* "(not) very" is an Adverb of degree used with negative Predicates. See Note 7.4.15.

$\left. \begin{matrix} amari \\ mada \end{matrix} \right\}$ **+ negative Predicate**

Doitsugo wa amari joozu de wa arimasen.	"[I] am not very good at the German language."
Amari isogashiku arimasen.	"[I] am not too busy."

On the other hand, *totemo* "very" and *chotto* "a little" are Adverbs of degree used with affirmative Predicates.

Nakamura sen'sei wa totemo isogashii desu.	"Prof. Nakamura is very busy."
Koko wa chotto urusai desu ne.	"This place is a little noisy, isn't it?"

8.4.5   *Isogashiku arimasen* is the negative of *isogashii desu* "is busy." The normal negative imperfect tense form of an Adjective is formed by the KU form of the Adjective plus *arimasen*. The KU form is formed by changing the *-i* ending of an Adjective into *-ku*.

Adjective*(-i)* + *desu* ⟶ **Adjective*(-ku)* + *(wa)* + *arimasen***

isogashii desu	⟶ isogashiku arimasen	"is not busy"
oishii desu	⟶ oishiku arimasen	"is not tasty"
mazui desu	⟶ mazuku arimasen	"is not tasteless"
yoi desu (ii desu)	⟶ yoku arimasen	"is not good"
warui desu	⟶ waruku arimasen	"is not bad"
ookii desu	⟶ ookiku arimasen	"is not big"
chiisai desu	⟶ chiisaku arimasen	"is not small"
tooi desu	⟶ tooku arimasen	"is not far"
chikai desu	⟶ chikaku arimasen	"is not near"
kitanai desu	⟶ kitanaku arimasen	"is not dirty"
urusai desu	⟶ urusaku arimasen	"is not noisy"

The Relational *wa* may occasionally be injected between the KU form and *arimasen*. In this case, *kitanaku wa arimasen,* for example, will be close to the idea "as to 'dirty', it is not so," and this may be used in response to a question asking if something is dirty.

Kitanai desu ka?	"Is [it] dirty?"
Iie, kitanaku wa arimasen.	"No, [it] is not."

Since *wa* does not have any emphatic function beyond indicating prominence, it often takes the place of *ga* or *o* in a negative answer.

On'gaku o kikimasu ka?	"Do [you] listen to music?"
Iie, on'gaku wa kikimasen.	"No, [I] don't listen to music."
On'gaku ga suki desu ka?	"Do [you] like music?"
Iie, on'gaku wa suki ja arimasen.	"No, [I] do not like music."

8.4.6 *Sono* is a Pre-Noun that occurs before a Noun modifying the Noun, and has the meaning of "that," as in "that area." Pre-Nouns are used to show that the speaker is referring to specific things or people as English demonstrative adjectives such as "this," "that," and "which?" do. Here are words of this series:

kono	"this"
sono	"that"
ano	"that over there"
dono	"which?"

Noun ⟶ Pre-Noun + Noun

$$
\left.\begin{matrix} \text{kono} \\ \text{sono} \\ \text{ano} \\ \text{dono} \end{matrix}\right\} + \left\{\begin{matrix} \text{-kata} & \text{``this''} \\ \text{-hen} & \text{``that''} \\ \text{hon} & \text{``that''} \\ \text{gakusei} & \text{``which''} \end{matrix}\right\} + \left\{\begin{matrix} \text{``person''} \\ \text{``area''} \\ \text{``book''} \\ \text{``student''} \end{matrix}\right.
$$

Ano kata wa donata desu ka?	"Who is that person?"
Sono hen de kaimashoo.	"Let's buy it around there."
Dono gin'koo e ikimasu ka?	"Which bank are [you] going to?"
Kono mise e hairimashita.	"[We] went into this store."

Note that each of the Pre-Nouns *kono, sono, ano,* and *dono* modifies the following Noun; and that *kore, sore, are,* and *dore* are Nouns.

Kore wa hon desu ka?	"Is this a book?"
Kono hon wa ii desu ka?	"Is this book good?"

Kono kata means "this person." *-Kata* is a dependent Noun meaning "person," and is a polite equivalent for *hito*. However, *-kata* is always preceded by a word while *hito* can be used by itself.

Kono kata wa Sumisu san desu.	"This person is Mr. Smith."
Kono kata wa donata desu ka?	"Who is this person?" (polite)
Koko ni hito ga imasu.	"Here are [some] people."

8.4.7 *Sore ni* means "besides" or "moreover" and is a Sentence Interjective. This expression reinforces *mo*.

Kono mise wa shizuka desu. Sore ni, koohii mo oishii desu.	"This shop is quiet. Besides, they serve good coffee."

8.4.8 The Relational *mo,* when used in a negative sentence, means "either" in the negative sense.

On'gaku mo yoku arimasen.	"The music is not good, either."
Watakushi mo ikimasu.	"I am going, too."
Watakushi mo ikimasen.	"I am not going, either."
Kono teepu mo kikimasu.	"I will listen to this tape, too."
Kono teepu mo kikimasen.	"I will not listen to this tape either."

Compare with Notes 4.4.9, 7.4.10, 11.4.5, and 12.4.5.

8.4.9 *Kotchi* means "this way" or "this one." Here are words of this series:

kotchi	"this way"	atchi	"that way"
sotchi	"that way"	dotchi	"which way?"

Dotchi e ikimashoo ka?   "Which way shall we go?"

Kotchi e ikimashoo.   "Let's go this way."

8.4.10   *Yamamoto san wa on'gaku ga suki desu* means "Mr. Yamamoto likes music." When it is necessary to identify "about WHOM that description is said," *wa* usually occurs after the person or animate Noun; "WHAT is such and such" is followed by the Relational *ga*.

In order to express the following ideas:

	(a)	(b)
Someone	is good	at something.
	is poor	at something.
	likes	something or someone else.
	dislikes	something or someone else.

(a) is followed by the Relational *wa*, and (b) by the Relational *ga*. When a sentence includes both of the Relationals *wa* and *ga*, *wa* normally precedes *ga*. This may be called "absolute sequence" in contrast with "relative sequence" that has been introduced in Note 4.4.12.

Thus:

Noun + *wa* + Noun + *ga* + Predicate

watakushi		nihon'go		joozu desu
anata		supootsu		heta desu
kono kata	wa	e	ga	. . . .
ano hito		. . . .		suki desu
Suzuki san		on'gaku		daisuki desu
		supootsu		kirai desu
		e		daikirai desu
		ben'kyoo		
		Itoo san		

Anata wa nihon'go ga joozu desu nee.   "You speak Japanese very well."

Watashi wa doitsugo ga heta desu.   "My German is poor."

Yamada san wa Ishii san ga suki desu.   "Mr. Yamada likes Miss Ishii."

Watashi wa ben'kyoo ga kirai desu.   "I dislike studying."

Ano hito wa supootsu ga dame desu.   "He does not excel in sports."

8.4.11   *Ogen'ki desu ka* has been described as the most common equivalent for "How are you?" However, the Japanese expression is not used as a daily greeting, and, when meeting one Japanese, another Japanese does not use *Ogen'ki desu ka?* unless the two of them have not seen each other for some time. The Japanese expression *Ikaga desu ka?* has similar tendencies, as it is not used with those whom you meet often.

8.4.12 Heteronomous Expressions

This lesson contains a number of other-directed expressions which show the moderation, modesty, and self-restraint of the Japanese in their relations—characteristics which we have grouped under the heading "heteronomy."

For example, *sono hen de* is used by the speaker so as not to constrain the listener, so as not to appear to be imposing the speaker's suggestion on the listener. The vague "somewhere" implied by *sono hen de* is much less specific than the English expression, which in fact emphasizes place. Rather, *sono hen de* does not indicate place; in fact, out of context the term is meaningless, and in context, its content is insignificant, allowing the speaker's suggestion to be nonbinding on the other. See Note 5.4.1 for *-hen*.

Okagesama de has no equivalent in American usage. Another typical example of raising the status of the listener and humbling oneself, the thought conveyed by this expression is, "Through your grace, I am well," "Thanks to you, I am well," or "Fortunately I am well, thanks to you."

In the dialog, Watanabe's answer *Iie, amari isogashiku arimasen* illustrates further the characteristic avoidance of any suggestion of self-importance. The word *amari* resembles *chotto* in that it is less important for its content than for its softening effect: to say that one is not busy is to hint that he is not important enough to be busy. *Amari* is used to give a softening effect. A direct negation may sound too direct or even harsh. This softener is frequently used in a negative reply.

In this connection, the traditional Japanese develops a sense of awkwardness *(tereru)* when praised by others. He is inclined to attribute his achievement to others. Among intimate group members such as father and son, however, a son would not use *Okagesama de* to his father in referring to his admission to a college, since his father could not have had anything to do with his admission. But even in this case he could use *Okagesama de* to his friends or formal group members.

8.4.13 Kissaten or Japanese Coffee Shop

Kissaten literally translates as "tea-sipping shop," although "coffee shop" is a closer equivalent. It bears little resemblance to an ordinary American coffee shop.

First of all, the coffee served is a different brew than American coffee, being far stronger and perhaps closer to espresso. Most people add cream and sugar and rarely drink black coffee unless he or she is an unsuspecting foreigner used to the much weaker American type of coffee. Most *kissaten* offer limited menus, with items such as desserts and sandwiches, as well as a variety of nonalcoholic and alcoholic beverages. The sandwiches are similar to American teatime sandwiches or hors d'oeuvres.

Kissaten are popular spots for students, either on dates or in groups. Many feature a particular type of music such as jazz, classical, or popular.

The most striking difference, however, is that the Japanese may spend hours in a *kissaten* after ordering a single cup of coffee, reading, talking, discussing business, or just listening to the music.

8.5 VOCABULARY

Dialog

Watanabe	. . . . . . .N	family name
Yamamoto	. . . . . . .N	family name
gen'ki	. . . . . .Na	healthy; in good spirits
tokoro de	. . . . . . .SI	by the way; incidentally (see 8.4.2)
isogashii	. . . . . . .A	is busy (see 8.4.3)
amari	. . . .Adv.	(not) very much; (not) very often (see 8.4.4)
isogashiku arimasen	. . . . . . .A	is not busy (KU form of *isogashii*—is busy plus *arimasen*) (see 8.4.5)
sono	. . . . . .PN	that (see 8.4.6)
-hen	. . . . . .Nd	area; vicinity (see 5.4.1 and 8.4.6)
ii	. . . . . . .A	is good (see 8.4.3)
hairimasu	V	go in (normal form of *hairu*)
mise	. . . . . . .N	shop; store
yoku (arimasen)	. . . . . . .A	KU form of *yoi*—is good (see 8.4.5)
mazui	. . . . . . .A	is tasteless; does not taste good
n (desu)	. . . . . .PC	(see 8.4.3)
sore ni	. . . . . . .SI	besides; moreover (see 8.4.7)
mo	. . . . . . .R	(not) either (see 8.4.8)
Den'en	. . . . . . .N	name of a coffee shop
tooi	. . . . . . .A	is far
chikai	. . . . . . .A	is near
kotchi	. . . . . . .N	this way; this one (see 8.4.9)
totemo	. . . .Adv.	very (see 8.4.4)
oishii	. . . . . . .A	is tasty; is good; is delicious
on'gaku	. . . . . . .N	music
suki	. . . . . .Na	like; fond of
daisuki	. . . . . .Na	like very much
saa	. . . . . . .SI	now!
kono	. . . . . .PN	this (see 8.4.6)

Notes

yoi	. . . . . . .A	is good (see 8.4.3)
warui	. . . . . . .A	is bad

ookii	.......A	is big; is large
chiisai	.......A	is small; is little (in size)
urusai	.......A	is noisy; is annoying
kitanai	.......A	is dirty; is unclean; is messy
chotto	....Adv.	a little (see 8.4.4)
(-ku) arimasen	.......E	(see 8.4.5)
ano	......PN	that over there (see 8.4.6)
dono	......PN	which? (see 8.4.6)
-kata	......Nd	person (see 8.4.6)
hito	.......N	person
sotchi	.......N	that way; that one (see 8.4.9)
atchi	.......N	that way; that one
dotchi	......Ni	which way?; which one?
supootsu	.......N	sport
e	.......N	painting(s); picture
kirai	......Na	dislike
daikirai	......Na	dislike very much
dame	......Na	no good

8.6   HIRAGANA PRACTICE

8.6.1   Recognize the difference or similarity between two *hiragana* in each of the following pairs:

ふ……ふ	や……や	ゆ……ゆ	を……を
か……か	や……み	ゆ……め	と……を
せ……せ	み……み	ひ……ひ	
せ……や	み……や	と……と	

8.6.2   Practice writing the following *hiragana:*

1. ふ [fu]   ふ   ふ   ふ   ふ
2. か [ka]   か   か   か
3. せ [se]   せ   せ   せ
4. や [ya]   や   や   や
5. み [mi]   み   み   み
6. ゆ [yu]   ゆ   ゆ   ゆ

7. ひ	[hi]	ひ	ひ	ひ	
8. と	[to]	と	と		
9. を	[o]	を	を	を	

8.6.3 Read and write the following:

ほんや　のみます　おかね

やまもとさんも　みせに　いました。

あの　ひとを　みましたよ。

8.7 DRILLS

8.7.1 Pronunciation Drill

hairimasu kirai naraimasu daikirai daisuki urusai

chikai kitanai namae gaikokujin

8.7.2 Pattern Drill

1. Ima isogashii desu ka?

2. Iie, amari isogashiku arimasen.

3. Sono mise wa yoku arimasen.

4. Koohii ga mazui n desu.

5. Kono mise mo kirei ja arimasen.

6. Soko no koohii wa totemo oishii n desu.

7. Yamamoto san wa on'gaku ga suki desu nee.

8.7.3 Substitution Drill

Soko wa *ii* desu.

1. *kitanai*	. . . .	Soko wa *kitanai* desu.
2. chikai	. . . .	Soko wa chikai desu.
3. tooi	. . . .	Soko wa tooi desu.
4. ookii	. . . .	Soko wa ookii desu.
5. urusai	. . . .	Soko wa urusai desu.
6. chiisai	. . . .	Soko wa chiisai desu.
7. *ano hito*	. . . .	*Ano hito* wa chiisai desu.
8. isogashii	. . . .	Ano hito wa isogashii desu.
9. warui	. . . .	Ano hito wa warui desu.
10. sono bifuteki	. . . .	Sono bifuteki wa warui desu.
11. mazui	. . . .	Sono bifuteki wa mazui desu.
12. oishii	. . . .	Sono bifuteki wa oishii desu.

8.7.4   Transformation Drill

1. Soko wa *kitanai desu*. ⟶ Soko wa *kitanaku arimasen*.

2. Ano kissaten wa ii desu. ⟶ Ano kissaten wa yoku arimasen.

3. Asoko wa urusai desu. ⟶ Asoko wa urusaku arimasen.

4. Ano mise no on'gaku wa warui desu. ⟶ Ano mise no on'gaku wa waruku arimasen.

5. Watashi no heya wa chiisai desu. ⟶ Watashi no heya wa chiisaku arimasen.

6. Koko no ocha wa oishii desu. ⟶ Koko no ocha wa oishiku arimasen.

7. Ano e wa ookii desu. ⟶ Ano e wa ookiku arimasen.

8. Eki wa chikai desu. ⟶ Eki wa chikaku arimasen.

9. Kono gohan wa mazui desu. ⟶ Kono gohan wa mazuku arimasen.

10. Gin'koo wa tooi desu. ⟶ Gin'koo wa tooku arimasen.

11. Ano kata wa isogashii desu. ⟶ Ano kata wa isogashiku arimasen.

8.7.5   Transformation Drill

1. Nihon'go ga *joozu desu*. ⟶ Nihon'go ga *joozu ja arimasen*.

2. Eiga wa suki desu. ⟶ Eiga wa suki ja arimasen.

3. Kono teepu wa dame desu. ⟶ Kono teepu wa dame ja arimasen.

4. Watashi wa gen'ki desu. ⟶ Watashi wa gen'ki ja arimasen.

5. Biiru wa kirai desu. ⟶ Biiru wa kirai ja arimasen.

6. Supootsu ga heta desu. ⟶ Supootsu ga heta ja arimasen.

7. Kono hen wa shizuka desu. ⟶ Kono hen wa shizuka ja arimasen.

8. Ano mise wa kirei desu. ⟶ Ano mise wa kirei ja arimasen.

9. Ashita hima desu. ⟶ Ashita hima ja arimasen.

10. Den'en wa nigiyaka desu. ⟶ Den'en wa nigiyaka ja arimasen.

8.7.6   Substitution Drill

1. *Kore* wa ii desu nee.
   on'gaku
   . . . . *Kono on'gaku* wa ii desu nee.

2. Sore wa Nihon no kamera desu.
   kamera
   . . . . Sono kamera wa Nihon no kamera desu.

3. Are wa ookii desu.
   daigaku
   . . . . Ano daigaku wa ookii desu.

4. Sore wa mazui desu.
   koohii
   . . . . Sono koohii wa mazui desu.

5. Dore ga ii desu ka?
   e
   . . . . Dono e ga ii desu ka?

6. Sore o mimashita ka?   . . . . Sono eiga o mimashita ka?
   eiga

7. Are o kaimashoo.   . . . . Ano taipuraitaa o kaimashoo.
   taipuraitaa

8. Dore o shimasu ka?   . . . . Dono supootsu o shimasu ka?
   supootsu

8.7.7 Mixed Response Drill (negative and antonym)

1. Kissaten wa tooi desu ka?   . . . . *Iie,* tooku arimasen. *Chikai* desu.

2. Sono kamera wa ii desu ka?   . . . . Iie, yoku arimasen. Warui desu.

3. Ano toshokan wa ookii desu ka?   . . . . Iie, ookiku arimasen. Chiisai desu.

4. Kono hen wa shizuka desu ka?   . . . . Iie, shizuka ja arimasen. Urusai desu.

5. Inu ga suki desu ka?   . . . . Iie, suki de wa arimasen. Kirai desu.

6. Anata no heya wa kirei desu ka?   . . . . Iie, kirei ja arimasen. Kitanai desu.

7. Ashita isogashii desu ka?   . . . . Iie, isogashiku arimasen. Hima desu.

8. Gaikokugo ga heta desu ka?   . . . . Iie, heta de wa arimasen. Joozu desu.

9. Sono mise no bifuteki wa oishii desu ka?   . . . . Iie, oishiku arimasen. Mazui desu.

10. Asoko wa nigiyaka desu ka?   . . . . Iie, nigiyaka de wa arimasen. Shizuka desu.

8.7.8 Response Drill (Adverb)

1. Anata no uchi wa ookii desu ka? / *totemo*   . . . . Hai, *totemo* ookii desu.

2. Ano mise wa kirei desu ka? / amari   . . . . Iie, amari kirei de wa arimasen.

3. Sono koohii wa oishii desu ka? / zen'zen   . . . . Iie, zen'zen oishiku arimasen.

4. Toshokan wa shizuka desu ka? / amari   . . . . Iie, amari shizuka de wa arimasen.

5. Kyoo isogashii desu ka? / totemo   . . . . Hai, totemo isogashii desu.

6. Kono hon wa ii desu ka? / zen'zen   . . . . Iie, zen'zen yoku arimasen.

7. Terebi ga suki desu ka? / amari   . . . . Iie, amari suki de wa arimasen.

8. E ga joozu desu ka? / zen'zen   . . . . Iie, zen'zen joozu de wa arimasen.

9. Soko wa tooi desu ka? / totemo   . . . . Hai, totemo tooi desu.

10. Eigo wa joozu desu ka? / mada   . . . . Iie, mada joozu ja arimasen.

8.7.9 Transformation Drill (*o, ga, wa* ⟶ *mo*)

1. Watashi wa eiga o mimasen.   ⟶   Watashi wa eiga o mimasen.
   Terebi *o* mimasen.   Terebi *mo* mimasen.

2. Onaka ga sukimashita.   ⟶   Onaka ga sukimashita.
   Nodo ga kawakimashita.   Nodo mo kawakimashita.

3. Watashi wa furan'sugo o naraimasen deshita.   ⟶   Watashi wa furan'sugo o naraimasen deshita.
    Sumisu san wa naraimasen deshita.   Sumisu san mo naraimasen deshita.

4. Soko no koohii wa yoku arimasen.   ⟶   Soko no koohii wa yoku arimasen.
    On'gaku wa yoku arimasen.   On'gaku mo yoku arimasen.

5. Kinoo kaimono o shimasen deshita.   ⟶   Kinoo kaimono o shimasen deshita.
    Ben'kyoo o shimasen deshita.   Ben'kyoo mo shimasen deshita.

6. Watashi wa eiga o mimasen.   ⟶   Watashi wa eiga o mimasen.
    Koyama san wa eiga o mimasen.   Koyama san mo mimasen.

7. Jimusho ni Suzuki san ga imasen.   ⟶   Jimusho ni Suzuki san ga imasen.
    Ishii san ga imasen.   Ishii san mo imasen.

8. Watashi wa asagohan o tabemasen.   ⟶   Watashi wa asagohan o tabemasen.
    Hirugohan o tabemasen.   Hirugohan mo tabemasen.

8.7.10 Expansion Drill (*wa . . . ga* sequence)

1. Daisuki desu.   . . . . Daisuki desu.

   on'gaku   . . . . On'gaku *ga* daisuki desu.

   watashi   . . . . Watashi *wa* on'gaku *ga* daisuki desu.

2. Dame desu.   . . . . Dame desu.

   supootsu   . . . . Supootsu ga dame desu.

   Watanabe san   . . . . Watanabe san wa supootsu ga dame desu.

3. Joozu ja arimasen.   . . . . Joozu ja arimasen.

   gaikokugo   . . . . Gaikokugo ga joozu ja arimasen.

   ano hito   . . . . Ano hito wa gaikokugo ga joozu ja arimasen.

4. Mazui desu.   . . . . Mazui desu.

   koohii   . . . . Koohii ga mazui desu.

   ano kissaten   . . . . Ano kissaten wa koohii ga mazui desu.

5. Yoku arimasen ka?   . . . . Yoku arimasen ka?

   nani   . . . . Nani ga yoku arimasen ka?

   kono mise   . . . . Kono mise wa nani ga yoku arimasen ka?

6. Suki desu ka?   . . . . Suki desu ka?

   dore   . . . . Dore ga suki desu ka?

   anata   . . . . Anata wa dore ga suki desu ka?

7. Heta desu.   . . . . Heta desu.

   nihon'go   . . . . Nihon'go ga heta desu.

   watashitachi   . . . . Watashitachi wa nihon'go ga heta desu.

8. Kirai desu.   . . . . Kirai desu.

   neko   . . . . Neko ga kirai desu.

   Nakamura sen'sei   . . . . Nakamura sen'sei wa neko ga kirai desu.

9. Oishii desu.   . . . . Oishii desu.

   bifuteki   . . . . Bifuteki ga oishii desu.

   kono resutoran   . . . . Kono resutoran wa bifuteki ga oishii desu.

10. Kirai ja arimasen.   . . . . Kirai ja arimasen.

    ben'kyoo   . . . . Ben'kyoo ga kirai ja arimasen.

    watakushi   . . . . Watakushi wa ben'kyoo ga kirai ja arimasen.

8.8   EXERCISES

8.8.1   Connect antonymous expressions with a line:

Kirai desu.	Isogashii desu.
Kirei desu.	Chiisai desu.
Mazui desu.	Chikai desu.
Hima desu.	Yoi desu.
Ookii desu.	Shizuka desu.
Heta desu.	Daikirai desu.
Tooi desu.	Kitanai desu.
Urusai desu.	Ii desu.
Daisuki desu.	Joozu desu.
Warui desu.	Suki desu.
Dame desu.	Oishii desu.

8.8.2   Correct errors, if any:

1. Watakushi wa on'gaku o daisuki desu.

2. Koko wa kireku arimasen nee.

3. Ima amari isogashiku ja arimasen.

4. Koko no koohii wa amari oishii desu.

5. Soko wa amari tooiku arimasen.

6. Ano kissaten de hairimashoo ka?

7. Ano kata ga supootsu wa joozu ja arimasen.

8. Sore mo iku arimasen. Warui desu.

8.8.3   Choose the right word:

1. (Dore) ga anata no jisho desu ka? /dore, dono
2. (Sono) kamera o kaimashita. /sore, sono
3. (Kore) wa watakushi no heya desu. /kore, kono
4. (Ano) hon'ya e hairimashoo. /are, ano
5. (Dono) kuni e ikimashita ka? /dore, dono
6. (Kono) shokudoo de tabemasen ka? /kore, kono

8.8.4   Ask questions that will lead to the following answers:

1. Okagesama de (gen'ki desu).
2. Iie, kono ocha wa oishiku arimasen.
3. Kissaten e hairimashita.
4. Ee, totemo chikai desu yo.
5. Iie, amari suki ja arimasen.
6. Iie, totemo ookii desu.
7. Iie, mada desu.

8.8.5   Answer the following questions:

1. (Anata no) Uchi wa tooi desu ka?
2. (Uchi wa) Doko desu ka?
3. Soko wa shizuka desu ka?
4. (Uchi wa) Ookii desu ka?
5. Sono uchi wa ii desu ka?

LESSON 9
TALKING ABOUT BOOKS AND THINGS

9.1 USEFUL EXPRESSIONS

Ii (n) desu ka⌐   "Is it all right with you?"

Doozo goyukkuri.   "Please take your time." The original meaning of *yukkuri* is "slowly," and *(Doozo) goyukkuri* is also used to mean "Have a leisurely time."

9.2 DIALOG

Ishii: Itoo san wa yoku zasshi ya₁ shin'bun o yomimasu ka⌐

Itō: Iie, zasshi ya shin'bun wa₂ amari yomimasen. Demo, hon wa₂ yoku yomimasu yo⌐

Ishii: Kono goro hon ga takai desu ne⌐

Itō: Hon'too desu ne. Dakara, boku₃ wa itsumo₄ toshokan de karimasu.

Ishii: Watashi mo taitei toshokan de karimasu ga₅, tokidoki kaimasu.

Itō: Sono hon wa Ishii san no₆ desu ka₇, toshokan no desu ka₇.

Ishii: Watashi no desu. Ototoi furuhon'ya de kaimashita. Toshokan de sagashimashita ga,

         nakatta₈ n desu.

Itō: Zuibun rippa desu ne. Takakatta₉ desu ka⌐

Ishii: Iie, takaku arimasen deshita₁₀.

Itō: Moo₁₁ yomimashita ka⌐

Ishii: Ee, yomimashita.

Itō: Doo deshita₁₂ ka⌐

Ishii: Totemo omoshirokatta desu. Itoo san mo yomimasen ka⌐

Itō: Ii n desu ka⌐

Ishii: Ee, doozo goyukkuri

9.3 PATTERN SENTENCES

9.3.1

PM				P				SP
PN	N	R		N	R	N⁽⁶⁾	C	
Sono	hon	wa	→	Ishii san	NO⁽⁶⁾		desu	ka?

9.3.2

PM	
N	R
Toshokan	de

→

P	
V	R
sagashimashita	GA[5],

PM

→

P		
A	PC	C
naKATTA	(N)[8]	DESU.

9.3.3

PM

→

P	
Ni	C
Doo	deshiTA[12]

SP
ka?

9.3.4

SI
Iie,

P		
A	E	C
takaKU	ARIMASEN	DESHITA[10].

9.3.5

SI
Iie,

P				
N	C	R	E	C
Ishii san	JA DE WA		ARIMASEN	DESHITA[12],

9.3.6

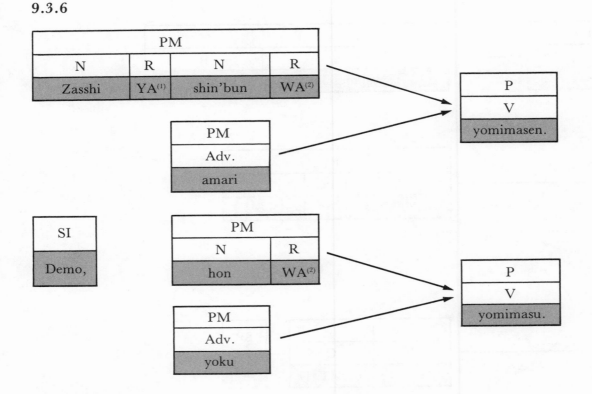

9.4 NOTES

9.4.1 The *ya* between Nouns is a Relational, and is used like the Relational *to* "and," which has been introduced in Note 5.4.9. Both *to* and *ya* may correspond to "and" in English, but *ya* is used merely to pick up some of the things in a group and mention them, while *to* functions to list all the things to be mentioned.

Eiga ya terebi ga suki desu ka?	"Do [you] like movies, television, and the like?"
Byooin to gin'koo e ikimashita.	"[I] went to the hospital and the bank."
Byooin ya gin'koo e ikimashita.	"[I] went to the hospital, the bank, and some other place(s)."

9.4.2 *Shin'bun wa yomimasen. Demo, hon wa yomimasu* means "[I] don't read newspapers. But, [I] read books," and *shin'bun* and *hon* are in contrast. The Relational *wa* thus has a function to contrast one with other(s).

Watashi wa hon o karimasu ga, *Sumisu san* wa karimasen.	"I am going to borrow books, but Mr. Smith is not."
Watashi wa *jisho* wa kaimashita ga, *hon* wa karimashita.	"I bought the dictionary, but I borrowed the books."
Ima wa daisuki desu ga, *mae* wa kirai deshita.	"[I] like [it] very much now, but [I] didn't like [it] before."

Sometimes only the first part of the above sentence occurs, and the second may not be expressed. But, even in that case, the Relational *wa* is that of contrast.

Ishii san to Sumisu san ga imashita ka?	"Were Mr. Ishii and Mr. Smith [there]?"
Sumisu san wa imashita.	"Mr. Smith was [there]." (implies "Mr. Ishii wasn't.")

9.4.3 *Boku* is a less formal equivalent of *watakushi* "I" or "me," and *kimi* is that of *anata* "you." They are used almost exclusively by men and may be used to intimate friends or inferiors. A woman in the same circumstances would choose *watashi* or *atashi* for the first person and *anata* for the second person.

9.4.4 *Itsumo* "always" or "usually," *taitei* "generally," *sugu* "soon," *totemo* "very," *tokidoki* "sometimes," *chotto* "a little," *zuibun* "extremely," and *moo* "already" are Adverbs. They usually occur immediately before Predicates or in any other place except after Predicates, and form Predicate Modifiers.

Predicate ⟶ Adverb + Predicate

Watakushi wa itsumo uchi de hirugohan o tabemasu.	"I always have lunch at home."
Nihon no hito wa taitei koohii ga suki desu.	"Japanese people generally like coffee."
Tokidoki depaato e ikimasu.	"[I] sometimes go to department stores."
Totemo ii desu.	"[It] is very good."
Chotto takai desu.	"[It] is a little expensive."
Sugu tabemasu.	"[I] will eat [it] right now."
Moo jisho o kaimashita ka?	"Did [you] already buy a dictionary?"

When *zuibun* is used with an Adjective or an adjectival Noun, the Sentence Particles *nee, ne,* and *yo* are used.

Zuibun joozu desu nee.	"How skillful!"
Zuibun ookii desu nee.	"It's extremely big!"

9.4.5 *Ga* that occurs at the end of a nonfinal clause, or before a comma, is the clause Relational corresponding to "but," "although," et cetera. The Relational *ga* is used to connect two sentences, like a conjunction in English. See Notes 4.4.10 and 12.4.7.

Sentence 1 ⎫
Sentence 2 ⎭ ⟶ **Sentence 1 + *ga*, + Sentence 2**

Tooi desu. ⎫ Ii desu. ⎭	⟶ Tooi desu ga, ii desu.	"[It] is far, but [it] is good."
Ookii desu. ⎫ Yasui desu. ⎭	⟶ Ookii desu ga, yasui desu.	"[The house] is large, but [it] is inexpensive."

In Japanese *ga* sometimes may be used less strictly than "but" in English. In that case, *ga* may be used merely to connect two sentences as if it were "and" in English.

Watakushi mo sono eiga o mimashita ga,
  omoshirokatta desu.   "I saw that movie too, and it was interesting."

The clause Relational *ga* is often used with the pattern of "would like to (do)," to soften the directness of the desire.

Uchi e kaeritai n desu ga . . .   "I want to go home, but may I?"

Koohii o nomitai n desu ga . . .   "I would like to have some coffee."

"I would like to do such and such, but will that be all right with you?" or "I want to do this, but do you mind it?" is the idea of using *ga*.

9.4.6   *Ishii san no desu* means "It is Mr. Ishii's." A Noun *hon* after *no* has been omitted because it is understood. When the implication is clear, a Noun following *no* may be omitted.

watashi no (hon)	⟶ watashi no	"mine"
anata no (hon)	⟶ anata no	"yours"
kimi no (hon)	⟶ kimi no	"yours"
ano kata no (hon)	⟶ ano kata no	"his; hers"
Yamamoto san no (hon)	⟶ Yamamoto san no	"Mr. Yamamoto's"
gakkoo no (hon)	⟶ gakkoo no	"the school's"

9.4.7   *Ishii san no desu ka, toshokan no desu ka?* is called an "alternate question," meaning "Is that book Mr. Ishii's or the library's?" An alternate question is one in which the listener is given two or more choices for an answer. When the original sentences share one or more Predicate Modifiers (abbr. PM), the Predicate Modifier may be deleted except in the first choice. Predicates in an alternate question may be identical or different.

$$PM_1 + PM_2 + \text{Predicate 1} + ka?$$
$$PM_1 + PM_3 + \text{Predicate 2} + ka?$$
$$\Big\} \quad PM_1 + PM_2 + \text{Predicate 1} + ka, PM_3 + \text{Predicate 2} + ka?$$

Kono jisho wa ii desu ka, warui desu ka?   "Is this dictionary good or bad?"

Kore wa anata no desu ka, Nakamura san no   "Is this yours or Mr. Nakamura's?"
  desu ka?

Anata wa itsumo Asahi Shin'bun o yomimasu   "Do you always read the Asahi newspaper,
  ka, Yomiuri Shin'bun o yomimasu ka,   or the Yomiuri newspaper,
  Mainichi Shin'bun o yomimasu ka?   or the Mainichi newspaper?"

9.4.8   *Nakatta* is the plain perfect tense form or TA form of *nai* which is an Adjective meaning "non-existent," and is an equivalent of *arimasen*. When the plain equivalent of *arimasen* is required, *nai* should be used. *Nai* inflects like other Adjectives. The Copula *desu* coming after *nai* or *nakatta* formulates the normal spoken style. See Note 9.4.9.

9.4.9   *Takakatta* is the TA form or the perfect tense form of the Adjective *takai* and means "was expensive." The plain perfect tense form—the TA form—of an Adjective is formulated by inflecting the -*i* ending of the imperfect tense form into -*katta*. The Copula *desu* will also follow this form in the normal spoken style. This text does not consider *takai deshita* as good usage, but prefers *takakatta desu*.

Adjective(-i) + (n) + desu ⟶ Adjective(-katta) + (n) + desu

tooi desu	⟶ tookatta desu	"was far"
chikai desu	⟶ chikakatta desu	"was near"
ii desu* (yoi desu)	⟶ yokatta desu	"was good"
warui desu	⟶ warukatta desu	"was bad"
takai desu	⟶ takakatta desu	"was expensive"
yasui desu	⟶ yasukatta desu	"was inexpensive"
ookii desu	⟶ ookikatta desu	"was big"
chiisai desu	⟶ chiisakatta desu	"was small"
omoshiroi desu	⟶ omoshirokatta desu	"was interesting"
tsumaranai desu	⟶ tsumaranakatta desu	"was dull"
muzukashii desu	⟶ muzukashikatta desu	"was difficult"
yasashii desu	⟶ yasashikatta desu	"was easy"
oishii desu	⟶ oishikatta desu	"was delicious"
mazui desu	⟶ mazukatta desu	"was tasteless"
urusai desu	⟶ urusakatta desu	"was noisy"
kitanai desu	⟶ kitanakatta desu	"was dirty"
isogashii desu	⟶ isogashikatta desu	"was busy"
nai desu	⟶ nakatta desu	"was nonexistent"

* The perfect tense form of *ii desu* is *yokatta desu*. See Notes 8.4.5 and 11.4.7.

Shiken wa muzukashikatta desu.	"The examination was difficult."
Sono kissaten wa ii desu ka?	"Is that coffee shop good?"
Mae wa yokatta n desu ga, ima wa yoku arimasen.	"It was good before, but it is not good now."

9.4.10 *Takaku arimasen deshita* is the perfect tense form of *takaku arimasen* "is not expensive," or the negative perfect tense form of *takai desu* "is expensive." The negative perfect tense form of an Adjective is formulated by the negative imperfect form—the KU form of the Adjective plus *arimasen*—plus *deshita*. See Note 8.4.5.

Adjective(-ku) + arimasen ⟶ Adjective(-ku) + arimasen + deshita

muzukashiku arimasen	⟶ muzukashiku arimasen deshita	"was not hard"
yasashiku arimasen	⟶ yasashiku arimasen deshita	"was not easy"
yasuku arimasen	⟶ yasuku arimasen deshita	"was not cheap"

takaku arimasen	⟶ takaku arimasen deshita	"was not expensive"
omoshiroku arimasen	⟶ omoshiroku arimasen deshita	"was not interesting"
tsumaranaku arimasen	⟶ tsumaranaku arimasen deshita	"was not dull"

Eiga wa omoshirokatta desu ka?   "Was the movie interesting?"

Iie, zen'zen omoshiroku arimasen deshita.   "No, it wasn't interesting at all."

Byooin wa tookatta desu ka?   "Was the hospital far?"

Iie, tooku arimasen deshita.   "No, it was not far."

9.4.11 *Moo* "already" is an Adverb. It usually occurs immediately before Predicates or in any other place except after Predicates, and forms a Predicate Modifier. The function of *moo* is opposite that of *mada* "not yet." See Note 9.4.4.

Moo yomimashita ka?   "Did [you] already read [it]?"

Ee, moo yomimashita.   "Yes, [I] already did."

Iie, mada desu.   "No, not yet."

9.4.12 *Deshita* is the TA form or the perfect tense form of the Copula *desu*. *Deshita* may be used to mean "A was B."

As indicated in Note 7.4.4, Nouns that occur before *desu* can also be an adjectival Noun such as *suki* "is fond of."

$$\text{Noun (subject)} + \left\{ \begin{array}{c} ga \\ wa \end{array} \right\} + \left\{ \begin{array}{c} \text{Noun} \\ \text{adjectival Noun} \end{array} \right\} + desu \longrightarrow$$

$$\text{Noun (subject)} + \left\{ \begin{array}{c} ga \\ wa \end{array} \right\} + \left\{ \begin{array}{c} \text{Noun} \\ \text{adjectival Noun} \end{array} \right\} + deshita$$

Doo deshita ka? means "How was [it]?"

Doo is an interrogative Noun meaning "how?" Here are the Nouns of this series:

koo	"this way"
soo	"that way" or "so"
aa	"that way"
doo	"what way?" or "how?"

Ano hon wa doo desu ka?   "How is that book?"

Shiken wa doo deshita ka?   "How was the exam?"

The negative of a Noun or an adjectival Noun plus *desu* is formulated by changing *desu* to *ja arimasen*. Similarly, the negative of the Noun or the adjectival Noun plus *deshita* is formulated by changing *deshita* to *ja arimasen deshita*.

$$\text{Noun (subject)} + \left\{ \begin{array}{c} wa \\ ga \end{array} \right\} + \left\{ \begin{array}{c} \textbf{Noun} \\ \textbf{adjectival Noun} \end{array} \right\} + \left\{ \begin{array}{c} ja \\ de\ wa \end{array} \right\} arimasen \longrightarrow$$

$$\text{Noun (subject)} + \left\{ \begin{array}{c} wa \\ ga \end{array} \right\} + \left\{ \begin{array}{c} \textbf{Noun} \\ \textbf{adjectival Noun} \end{array} \right\} + \left\{ \begin{array}{c} ja \\ de\ wa \end{array} \right\} arimasen\ deshita$$

soo ja arimasen	$\longrightarrow$ soo ja arimasen deshita	"was not so"
gakusei ja arimasen	$\longrightarrow$ gakusei ja arimasen deshita	"was not a student"
gen'ki ja arimasen	$\longrightarrow$ gen'ki ja arimasen deshita	"was not fine"
rippa ja arimasen	$\longrightarrow$ rippa ja arimasen deshita	"was not splendid"
hon'too ja arimasen	$\longrightarrow$ hon'too ja arimasen deshita	"was not true"

Toshokan wa shizuka ja arimasen deshita.   "The library was not quiet."

Sen'sei wa nihon'jin de wa arimasen deshita.   "The teacher was not a Japanese."

9.4.13 Japanese Newspapers and Books

The foreigner in Japan might be surprised at the popularity of reading among the population. The literacy rate in Japan is one of the highest in the world, considerably higher than that of the United States. In 1968, 99.9 percent of the Japanese population within the appropriate age group attended secondary schools.

Asahi Shin'bun, which has one of the largest circulations in the world, is published in Tōkyō and Ōsaka. In addition to claiming a daily circulation of over eleven million copies each for the morning and evening editions for the year 1981, *Asahi Shin'bun* also publishes an English language edition. Another newspaper *Yomiuri Shin'bun* claimed a daily circulation of thirteen million copies in 1981.

The Japanese are avid readers of books and magazines as well as newspapers. In 1980, 27,891 book titles and 3,325 annual, monthly, and weekly magazines were published. That reading is almost a national way of life for the Japanese is evidenced in the large numbers of persons absorbed in their reading that one is certain to see on trains, in coffee shops, and in parks. Many habitually carry reading material with them so that they can read when they have a few minutes to spare.

Another interesting aspect of Japanese culture is the emphasis placed on one's personal library. Status is connected with ownership of books, and thus, although the library system is readily available to the public, there is an abundance of bookstores.

Beginning with the Meiji period Japanese culture has often been termed a "translation culture," due to the extensiveness of translation activities. Hundreds of books covering a diversity of topics such as social science, literature, law, politics, and education have been translated. There are Japanese editions of the works of such writers as Somerset Maugham, William Faulkner, Andre Gide, Anatole France, Leo Tolstoy, and many others as well as novels of contemporary China and the Soviet Union. During 1980, as many as 2,650 foreign language books were translated and published in Japan.

9.5   VOCABULARY

Dialog

zasshi	. . . . . . .N	magazine	
ya	. . . . . . .R	and (selective) (see 9.4.1)	

shin'bun	.......N	newspaper
yomimasu	V	read (normal form of *yomu*)
wa	......R	(see 9.4.2)
kono goro	......N	these days
takai	......A	is expensive
hon'too	......N	true; real
dakara	......SI	so; therefore
boku	......N	I (used by men) (see 9.4.3)
itsumo	....Adv.	always; usually
karimasu	V	borrow (normal form of *kariru*)
taitei	....Adv.	generally; in most cases
ga	......Rc	but; although (see 9.4.5)
tokidoki	....Adv.	sometimes; once in a while
furuhon'ya	......N	secondhand bookstore
sagashimashita	V	looked for (TA form of *sagashimasu*←*sagasu*) (*Sagashimasu* is a transitive Verb; it follows the direct object Relational *o*.)
nakatta	......A	there was not; was nonexistent (TA form of *nai*) (see 9.4.8)
zuibun	....Adv.	extremely; quite
rippa	......Na	fine; magnificent
takakatta	......A	was expensive (TA form of *takai*) (see 9.4.9)
takaku arimasen deshita	......A	was not expensive (negative perfect tense form of *takai*) (see 9.4.10)
moo	....Adv.	already (see 9.4.11)
doo	......N	how? (see 9.4.12)
deshita	C	TA form of *desu* (see 9.4.12)
omoshirokatta	......A	was interesting (TA form of *omoshiroi*) (see 9.4.9)
doozo	......SI	please

Notes

byooin	......N	hospital
mae	......N	before
koo	......N	in this way
soo	......N	in that way; so
aa	......N	in that way
atashi	......N	I (used by women) (see 9.4.3)

kimi	......N	you (used by men)
yasui	......A	is inexpensive
Asahi	......N	Asahi (Newspaper)
Yomiuri	......N	Yomiuri (Newspaper)
Mainichi	......N	Mainichi (Newspaper)
nai	......A	there is not; is nonexistent (see 9.4.8)
muzukashii	......A	is difficult
yasashii	......A	is easy
tsumaranai	......A	is uninteresting; is dull; is unimportant
(-ku) arimasen deshita	......E	perfect tense form of *arimasen* (see 9.4.10)
ja arimasen deshita	C	perfect tense form of *ja arimasen* (see 9.4.12)
de wa arimasen deshita	C	negative perfect tense form of *desu* (see 9.4.12)

Drills

| tatemono | ......N | building |

9.6 HIRAGANA PRACTICE

9.6.1 Recognize the difference or similarity between two *hiragana* in each of the following pairs:

か……が	す……ず	と……ど	ひ……ぴ
き……ぎ	せ……ぜ	は……ば	ふ……ぶ
く……ぐ	そ……ぞ	ひ……び	へ……ぺ
け……げ	た……だ	ふ……ぶ	ほ……ぼ
こ……ご	ち……ぢ	へ……べ	
さ……ざ	つ……づ	ほ……ぼ	
し……じ	て……で	は……ぱ	

9.6.2 Read and write the following:

がいこく　ぼく　ぎんざ　すばらしい　えんぴつ
しんぶん　みず
わたなべさんが　います。　どこですか。
まいにち　てんぷらを　たべました。
ずいぶん　げんきですね。
でんわが　ありません。

128

9.7 DRILLS

9.7.1 Pronunciation Drill

Ookikatta desu.   Nakatta desu.   Yokatta desu.   Chiisakatta desu.   Tookatta desu.

Yasashikatta desu.   Warukatta desu.   Omoshirokatta desu.   Takakatta desu.

Muzukashikatta desu.   Chikakatta desu.   Tsumaranakatta desu.   Yasukatta desu.

9.7.2 Pattern Drill

1. Takakatta desu ka?

2. Iie, takaku arimasen deshita.

3. Suzuki san wa gen'ki deshita ka?

4. Iie, amari gen'ki ja arimasen deshita.

5. Doo deshita ka?

6. Totemo omoshirokatta desu.

7. Sono hon wa Ishii san no desu ka, toshokan no desu ka?

8. Watashi no desu.

9. Toshokan ni nai n desu ka?

10. Watashi wa zasshi ya shin'bun o yomimasen.

11. Shin'bun wa yomimasu ga, zasshi wa yomimasen.

9.7.3 Transformation Drill

1. Watanabe san wa gakusei *desu.* ⟶ Watanabe san wa gakusei *deshita.*

2. Kono kata wa sen'sei desu. ⟶ Kono kata wa sen'sei deshita.

3. Soko wa kirei desu. ⟶ Soko wa kirei deshita.

4. Koko wa gin'koo desu. ⟶ Koko wa gin'koo deshita.

5. Eiga ga suki desu. ⟶ Eiga ga suki deshita.

6. Nihon'go ga heta desu. ⟶ Nihon'go ga heta deshita.

7. Kono hen wa shizuka desu. ⟶ Kono hen wa shizuka deshita.

8. Sore wa hon'too desu. ⟶ Sore wa hon'too deshita.

9. Soo desu ka? ⟶ Soo deshita ka?

10. Are wa nan desu ka? ⟶ Are wa nan deshita ka?

11. Sen'sei wa donata desu ka? ⟶ Sen'sei wa donata deshita ka?

12. Shiken wa doo desu ka? ⟶ Shiken wa doo deshita ka?

9.7.4 Transformation Drill

1. Sore wa hon'too *de wa arimasen.* ⟶ Sore wa hon'too *de wa arimasen deshita.*

2. Amari gen'ki ja arimasen. ⟶ Amari gen'ki ja arimasen deshita.

3. Byooin wa rippa ja arimasen. ⟶ Byooin wa rippa ja arimasen deshita.

4. Ano on'na no hito wa sen'sei ja arimasen. ⟶ Ano on'na no hito wa sen'sei ja arimasen deshita.

5. Soko wa furuhon'ya de wa arimasen. ⟶ Soko wa furuhon'ya de wa arimasen deshita.

6. E wa joozu ja arimasen. ⟶ E wa joozu ja arimasen deshita.

7. Are wa Nihon no zasshi de wa arimasen. ⟶ Are wa Nihon no zasshi de wa arimasen deshita.

8. Daigaku no toshokan wa kirei ja arimasen. ⟶ Daigaku no toshokan wa kirei ja arimasen deshita.

9. Are wa Asahi Shin'bun de wa arimasen. ⟶ Are wa Asahi Shin'bun de wa arimasen deshita.

10. Ano mise wa hon'ya ja arimasen. ⟶ Ano mise wa hon'ya ja arimasen deshita.

9.7.5 Transformation Drill

1. Kono hon wa taka*i desu.* ⟶ Kono hon wa taka*katta desu.*

2. Eiga wa tsumaranai desu. ⟶ Eiga wa tsumaranakatta desu.

3. Okane ga nai desu. ⟶ Okane ga nakatta desu.

4. Boku no inu wa ookii desu. ⟶ Boku no inu wa ookikatta desu.

5. Kono zasshi wa omoshiroi desu. ⟶ Kono zasshi wa omoshirokatta desu.

6. Ano hon'ya wa chiisai desu. ⟶ Ano hon'ya wa chiisakatta desu.

7. Kono hon wa ii desu. ⟶ Kono hon wa yokatta desu.

8. Shiken wa muzukashii desu. ⟶ Shiken wa muzukashikatta desu.

9. Tomodachi no uchi wa chikai desu. ⟶ Tomodachi no uchi wa chikakatta desu.

10. Kono jisho wa yasui desu. ⟶ Kono jisho wa yasukatta desu.

11. Nihon'go no shin'bun wa yasashii desu. ⟶ Nihon'go no shin'bun wa yasashikatta desu.

12. Ishii san no shiken wa warui desu. ⟶ Ishii san no shiken wa warukatta desu.

9.7.6 Transformation Drill

1. Shiken wa yasashi*ku arimasen.* ⟶ Shiken wa yasashi*ku arimasen deshita.*

2. Heya wa kitanaku arimasen. ⟶ Heya wa kitanaku arimasen deshita.

3. Sono zasshi wa omoshiroku arimasen. ⟶ Sono zasshi wa omoshiroku arimasen deshita.

4. Bifuteki wa yasuku arimasen. ⟶ Bifuteki wa yasuku arimasen deshita.

5. Kyoo wa zen'zen isogashiku arimasen. ⟶ Kyoo wa zen'zen isogashiku arimasen deshita.

6. Furuhon'ya wa tooku arimasen. ⟶ Furuhon'ya wa tooku arimasen deshita.

7. Ano mise wa yoku arimasen. ⟶ Ano mise wa yoku arimasen deshita.

8. Kono mise no pan wa amari takaku arimasen. ⟶ Kono mise no pan wa amari takaku arimasen deshita.

9. Nihon'go wa muzukashiku arimasen. ⟶ Nihon'go wa muzukashiku arimasen deshita.

10. Toshokan wa ookiku arimasen. ⟶ Toshokan wa ookiku arimasen deshita.

9.7.7 Transformation Drill

1. Sono hon wa *toshokan no hon* desu.   ⟶   Sono hon wa *toshokan no* desu.

2. Anata no hon wa takakatta desu ka?   ⟶   Anata no wa takakatta desu ka?

3. Ishii san no jisho o karimashoo.   ⟶   Ishii san no o karimashoo.

4. Kotchi no mise wa yasui desu.   ⟶   Kotchi no wa yasui desu.

5. Watashi no shiken wa yoku arimasen deshita.   ⟶   Watashi no wa yoku arimasen deshita.

6. Tomodachi no namae o kakimashita.   ⟶   Tomodachi no o kakimashita.

7. Ano hito no teepu ga arimasu yo.   ⟶   Ano hito no ga arimasu yo.

8. Doitsu no kamera wa nai desu ka?   ⟶   Doitsu no wa nai desu ka?

9.7.8 Substitution Drill

1. *Taitei* toshokan de hon o karimasu.

   tokidoki   . . . . *Tokidoki* toshokan de hon o karimasu.

   itsumo   . . . . Itsumo toshokan de hon o karimasu.

   yoku   . . . . Yoku toshokan de hon o karimasu.

2. Hon wa *itsumo* takai desu.

   taitei   . . . . Hon wa taitei takai desu.

   tokidoki   . . . . Hon wa tokidoki takai desu.

3. *Taitei* uchi de ban'gohan o tabemasu.

   itsumo   . . . . Itsumo uchi de ban'gohan o tabemasu.

   yoku   . . . . Yoku uchi de ban'gohan o tabemasu.

4. *Itsumo* Yomiuri Shin'bun o yomimasu.

   taitei   . . . . Taitei Yomiuri Shin'bun o yomimasu.

   yoku   . . . . Yoku Yomiuri Shin'bun o yomimasu.

   tokidoki   . . . . Tokidoki Yomiuri Shin'bun o yomimasu.

9.7.9 Combination Drill

1. Zasshi wa yasui desu.
Hon wa takai desu.   ⟶   Zasshi wa yasui desu *ga,* hon wa takai desu.

2. Chotto tooi desu.
Totemo ii desu.   ⟶   Chotto tooi desu ga, totemo ii desu.

3. Boku wa gakusei desu.
Tomodachi wa sen'sei desu.   ⟶   Boku wa gakusei desu ga, tomodachi wa sen'sei desu.

4. Kono jisho wa chiisai desu.
Kono jisho wa takakatta desu.   ⟶   Kono jisho wa chiisai desu ga, takakatta desu.

5. Sono hon o yomimashita.
   Totemo muzukashikatta desu.
   → Sono hon o yomimashita ga, totemo
   muzukashikatta desu.

6. Tokidoki hon o kaimasu.
   Taitei toshokan de karimasu.
   → Tokidoki hon o kaimasu ga, taitei
   toshokan de karimasu.

7. Sono hon o sagashimashita.
   Toshokan ni arimasen deshita.
   → Sono hon o sagashimashita ga,
   toshokan ni arimasen deshita.

9.7.10 Combination Drill (alternate question)

1. Sono hon wa Ishii san no desu ka?
   Sono hon wa toshokan no desu ka?
   → Sono hon wa Ishii san no desu ka,
   toshokan no desu ka?

2. Nihon'go wa yasashii desu ka?
   Nihon'go wa muzukashii desu ka?
   → Nihon'go wa yasashii desu ka,
   muzukashii desu ka?

3. Itsumo Asahi Shin'bun o yomimasu ka?
   Itsumo Mainichi Shin'bun o yomimasu ka?
   → Itsumo Asahi Shin'bun o yomimasu ka,
   Mainichi Shin'bun o yomimasu ka?

4. Anata wa furan'sugo o naraimashita ka?
   Anata wa doitsugo o naraimashita ka?
   → Anata wa furan'sugo o naraimashita ka,
   doitsugo o naraimashita ka?

5. Shiken wa yokatta desu ka?
   Shiken wa warukatta desu ka?
   → Shiken wa yokatta desu ka,
   warukatta desu ka?

6. Itoo san wa kaimono ga kirai desu ka?
   Itoo san wa kaimono ga suki desu ka?
   → Itoo san wa kaimono ga kirai desu ka,
   suki desu ka?

7. Ashita eiga o mimashoo ka?
   Ashita uchi ni imashoo ka?
   → Ashita eiga o mimashoo ka,
   uchi ni imashoo ka?

9.7.11 Response Drill (o ——→ wa)

1. Itsumo Asahi Shin'bun o yomimasu ka?   . . . . Iie, Asahi Shin'bun wa yomimasen.

2. Toshokan de teepu o karimashita ka?   . . . . Iie, teepu wa karimasen deshita.

3. Mainichi gyuunyuu o nomimasu ka?   . . . . Iie, gyuunyuu wa nomimasen.

4. Anata wa chuugokugo o hanashimasu ka?   . . . . Iie, chuugokugo wa hanashimasen.

5. Kinoo kamera o kaimashita ka?   . . . . Iie, kamera wa kaimasen deshita.

6. Yoku terebi o mimasu ka?   . . . . Iie, terebi wa mimasen.

7. Supootsu o shimasu ka?   . . . . Iie, supootsu wa shimasen.

8. Mae chuugokugo o naraimashita ka?   . . . . Iie, chuugokugo wa naraimasen deshita.

9.7.12 Expansion Drill (wa . . . wa contrast)

1. Yomimasu.
   hon, zasshi
   . . . . Hon wa yomimasu ga, zasshi wa yomimasen.

2. Omoshiroi desu.
   eiga, terebi
   . . . . Eiga wa omoshiroi desu ga, terebi wa omoshiroku
   arimasen.

3. Arimasu.
kissaten, shokudoo

. . . . Kissaten wa arimasu ga, shokudoo wa arimasen.

4. Hanashimasu.
nihon'go, chuugokugo

. . . . Nihon'go wa hanashimasu ga, chuugokugo wa hanashimasen.

5. Suki desu.
koohii, ocha

. . . . Koohii wa suki desu ga, ocha wa suki de wa arimasen.

6. Imashita.
otoko no hito, on'na no hito

. . . . Otoko no hito wa imashita ga, on'na no hito wa imasen deshita.

7. Yokatta desu.
kono hon, sono hon

. . . . Kono hon wa yokatta desu ga, sono hon wa yoku arimasen deshita.

8. Isogashikatta desu.
kinoo, ototoi

. . . . Kinoo wa isogashikatta desu ga, ototoi wa isogashiku arimasen deshita.

9.8 EXERCISES

9.8.1 Transform the following into the perfect tense form:

1. Okane ga ~~nai n desu~~. *nakatta desu.*
2. Doo ~~desu ka?~~ *deshita ka?*
3. Totemo ~~omoshiroi desu~~. *omoshiro katta desu.*
4. Ano hito wa suki ja arimasen. *deshita*
5. Ano hon wa yasashiku arimasen ~~yo~~. *deshita*
6. Watakushi no sen'sei wa furan'sujin ~~desu~~. *deshita*
7. Are wa watashi no de wa arimasen. *deshita*
8. Shiken wa waruku arimasen ~~yo~~. *deshita*
9. Hon'too ~~desu ka?~~ *deshita ka?*
10. Ten'pura wa ~~oishii desu~~. *oishi katta desu.*

9.8.2 Insert a Relational or a Sentence Particle in each blank, and give an English equivalent for each sentence:

1. Mainichi koohii (と) ocha (を) nomimasu.
2. Kono shin'bun wa Yamada san (の) desu.
3. Sono kamera (は) takai desu (か), yasui desu (か)?
4. Hirugohan (を) tabemashita (が), ban'gohan (を) mada desu.
5. Sono jisho wa daigaku (の) desu (か), anata (の) desu (か)?

9.8.3   Answer the following questions:

1. Iie, yoku arimasen deshita.

2. Amari omoshiroku arimasen deshita.

3. Iie, mada desu.

4. Iie, tsumaranakatta desu.

5. Suzuki san no desu.

6. Iie, shizuka ja arimasen deshita.

7. Ee, totemo kirei deshita.

9.8.4   Answer the following questions on the basis of the Dialog:

1. Itoo san wa tokidoki hon o kaimasu ka?

2. Dare ga ototoi hon o kaimashita ka?

3. Takakatta desu ka, yasukatta desu ka?

4. Sono hon wa doo deshita ka?

5. Dare ga sono hon o karimasu ka?

LESSON 10
REVIEW AND APPLICATION

10.1 CONJUGATION

10.1.1 Noun
Adjectival Noun ⎬ + Copula

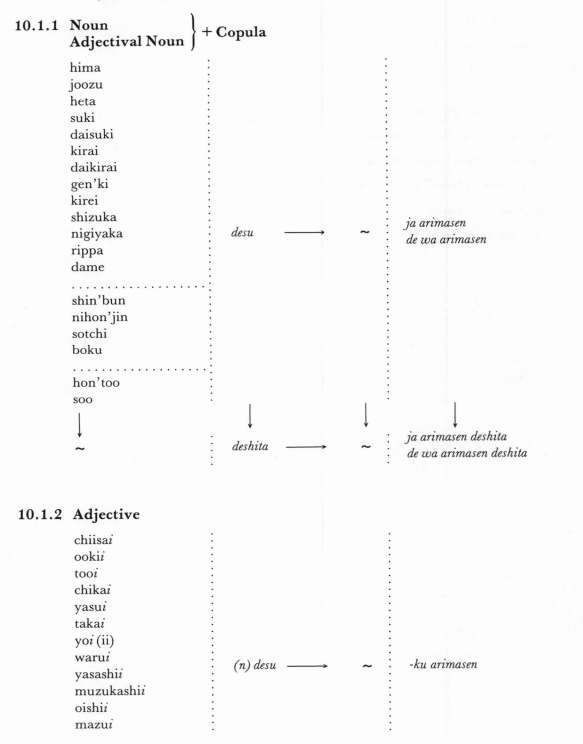

hima
joozu
heta
suki
daisuki
kirai
daikirai
gen'ki
kirei
shizuka
nigiyaka · · · · · · · · · · desu ⟶ ~ · · · · · · · · · · *ja arimasen*
rippa *de wa arimasen*
dame

· · · · · · · · · · · · · · · · · ·
shin'bun
nihon'jin
sotchi
boku
· · · · · · · · · · · · · · · · · ·
hon'too
soo

~ · · · · · · · · · · *deshita* ⟶ ~ · · · · · · · · · · *ja arimasen deshita*
de wa arimasen deshita

10.1.2 Adjective

chiisa*i*
ooki*i*
too*i*
chika*i*
yasu*i*
taka*i*
yo*i* (ii)
waru*i*
yasashi*i* · · · · · · · · · · *(n) desu* ⟶ ~ · · · · · · · · · · *-ku arimasen*
muzukashi*i*
oishi*i*
mazu*i*

omoshiro*i*
tsumarana*i*
kitana*i*
urusa*i*
isogashi*i*

↓   ↓   ↓   ↓

~   *-katta*   *(n) desu* ⟶ ~ : *-ku arimasen deshita*

10.2 PATTERNS

10.2.1 Noun + { *wa* / *mo* / *ga* } + Noun + *desu*

a.   inanimate Noun

(2)		(1)		
kore		zasshi		
sore		byooin		ka?
are	wa	furuhon'ya	desu	yo
kono tatemono	mo	toshokan		ne
	ga	daigaku		nee
		daigakuin		

(2)		(1)		
dore	ga	. . . .	desu	ka?

(2)		(1)		
sen'sei no uchi				
byooin		dore		
toshokan				
. . . .	wa	. . . .	desu	ka?
sono mise				
ano e		nan		
namae				

b.   animate Noun

(2)		(1)		
watakushi		amerikajin		
watashi		chuugokujin		
atashi		gaikokujin		
boku		gakusei		
anata		Sumisu		ka?
ano hito	wa			yo
kono kata	mo		desu	ne
watashitachi	ga			nee
kochira				
. . . .		. . . .		
Sumisu san		gakusei		
		sen'sei		
		tomodachi		
		igirisujin		

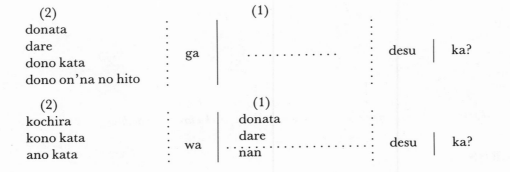

(2)		(1)		
donata				
dare	ga	.....	desu	ka?
dono kata				
dono on'na no hito				

(2)		(1)		
kochira		donata		
kono kata	wa	dare	desu	ka?
ano kata		nan		

10.2.2 Noun + { wa / mo / ga } + adjectival Noun + *desu*

(2)		(1)		
ben'kyoo		suki		
on'gaku		kirai		
eiga		daisuki		
kaimono		daikirai		
ten'pura				
eigo		joozu		
nihon'go		heta		
furan'sugo				
doitsugo				ka?
gaikokugo				yo
e			desu	ne
supootsu	ga			nee
	(wa)			
toshokan	(mo)	rippa		
		kirei		
		nigiyaka		
		shizuka		
ano hito		gen'ki		
		kirei		
		hima		
		shizuka		
		nigiyaka		
		rippa		
		dame		

↓

(2)		(1)		
......	wa	doo	desu	ka?

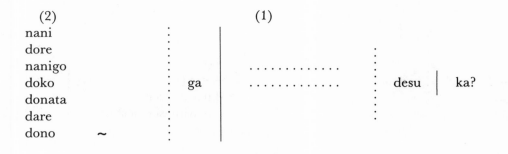

(2)			(1)			
nani	:			:		
dore	:			:		
nanigo	:		. . . .	:		
doko	:	ga	. . . .	:	desu	ka?
donata	:			:		
dare	:			:		
dono	~	:			:		

10.2.3 Noun + $\begin{Bmatrix} \textbf{\textit{wa}} \\ \textbf{\textit{mo}} \\ \textbf{\textit{ga}} \end{Bmatrix}$ + Adjective + *(n) desu*

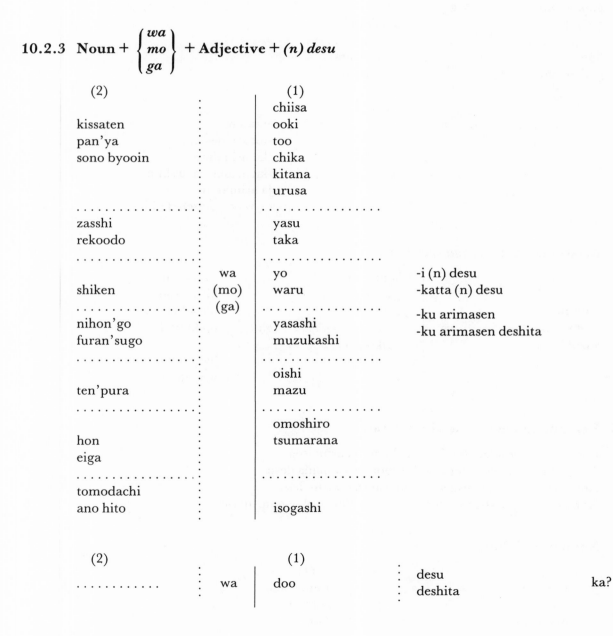

(2)		(1)	
	:	chiisa	
kissaten	:	ooki	
pan'ya	:	too	
sono byooin	:	chika	
	:	kitana	
	:	urusa	
. . . .	:	. . . .	
zasshi	:	yasu	
rekoodo	:	taka	
. . . .	:	. . . .	
	wa	yo	-i (n) desu
shiken	(mo)	waru	-katta (n) desu
. . . .	(ga)	. . . .	-ku arimasen
nihon'go	:	yasashi	-ku arimasen deshita
furan'sugo	:	muzukashi	
. . . .	:	. . . .	
	:	oishi	
ten'pura	:	mazu	
. . . .	:		
	:	omoshiro	
hon	:	tsumarana	
eiga	:		
. . . .	:	. . . .	
tomodachi	:		
ano hito	:	isogashi	

(2)		(1)			
. . . .	:	wa	doo	:	desu
				:	deshita	ka?

(2)		(1)	
doko			
nani			
dore		-i (n) desu	
dono ~	ga	-katta (n) desu	ka?
donata		-ku arimasen	
dare		-ku arimasen deshita	

10.2.4 Relationals *wa* and *mo* replacing *ga* or *o* in negative sentences

(2)		(1)
Yamada san		kimashita
gaikokujin	ga	imasu
on'gaku		suki desu
hon	o	karimashita
gaikokugo		naraimasu

(2)		(1)	
....	wa		-masen
....	mo	~	-masen deshita
			-ku arimasen
			-ku arimasen deshita
			ja arimasen
			de wa arimasen deshita

10.2.5 Relationals *wa* . . . *ga* sequence

		supootsu		suki desu
		gyuunyuu		kirai desu
watashi		koohii		daisuki desu
anata	wa	....	ga	daikirai desu
Suzuki san		gaikokugo		....
		e		joozu desu
		kaimono		heta desu

10.2.6 Relationals *wa* . . . *wa* in contrast

Eiga *wa* suki desu ga, terebi *wa* suki de wa arimasen.
Asagohan *wa* tabemashita ga, hirugohan *wa* mada desu.
Kono jisho *wa* takai desu ga, sono jisho *wa* yasui desu.
Kono hen ni gin'koo *wa* arimasu ga, yuubin'kyoku *wa* arimasen.

10.2.7 Noun + *no* + Noun

a.

(2)		(1)
watashi		tomodachi
anata	no	sen'sei
ano kata		kuni
....		....

kuni	:	namae
sen'sei	:	
....	:	....
gaikoku	:	toshokan
Doitsu	:	gakusei
Meriiran'do Daigaku	no	
koko	:	
....	:	....
Furan'su	:	
hon'ya	:	hon
furuhon'ya	:	

(2)		(1)
donata	:	
dare	:	
....	no	....
doko	:	

(2)		(1)
nihon'go	:	kurasu
eigo	no	shiken
gaikokugo	:	gakkoo
		hon

(2)		(1)
nanigo	:	
nan	no	....

(2)		(1)
Amerika	:	depaato
Nihon	no	daigaku
gaikoku	:	shin'bun
Shin'juku	:	

(2)		(1)
doko	no	....

b. Watashi no (jisho) wa doko ni arimasu ka?

Eigo no (jisho) o kaimashita.

Amerika no (depaato) wa chiisai desu.

Kore wa donata no (kamera) desu ka?

10.2.8 Pre-Noun

	:	kata
kono	:	hito
sono	:	hen
ano	:	kuni
	:	sen'sei
↓		↓
dono	.	....

10.2.9 *ko-, so-, a-,* and *do-*

kore	koo	kono	~	koko	kotchi
sore	soo	sono	~	soko	sotchi
are	aa	ano	~	asoko	atchi
dore	doo	dono	~	doko	dotchi

10.3 REVIEW DRILLS (Lessons 7, 8, and 9)

10.3.1 Substitution and Transformation Drill

A: Yoku *biiru* o *nomimasu* ka?

B: Iie, zen'zen *nomimasen.*

A: Soo desu ka? *Biiru* wa kirai desu ka?

B: Ee, daikirai desu.

    1.   *terebi, mimasu*   3.   *supootsu, shimasu*

    2.   *koohii, nomimasu*   4.   *ben'kyoo, shimasu*

10.3.2 Substitution and Transformation Drill

A: Moo *hon o yomimashita* ka?

B: Ee, *yomimashita. Anata* wa?

A: Mada desu kedo. Doo deshita ka?

B: Totemo *yokatta desu.*

    1.   *hirugohan o tabemasu, oishii desu*   4.   *sono eiga o mimasu, omoshiroi desu*

    2.   *sono kissaten e ikimasu, kirei desu*   5.   *ano tatemono o mimasu, rippa desu*

    3.   *kamera o kaimasu, yasui desu*

10.3.3 Transformation Drill (→perfect tense)

1. Shiken wa muzukashi*i desu.*   ⟶   Shiken wa muzukashi*katta desu.*

2. Ano shokudoo wa kirei *desu.*   ⟶   Ano shokudoo wa kirei *deshita.*

3. Sore wa hon'too desu.   ⟶

4. Shiken wa dame desu.   ⟶

5. Kyoo isogashii desu.   ⟶

6. Toshokan wa shizuka desu.   ⟶

7. Ano hon'ya wa ii desu.   ⟶

8. Doitsugo no ben'kyoo wa yasashii desu.   ⟶

9. Gyuunyuu wa kirai desu.   ⟶

10. Ano neko wa chiisai desu.   ⟶

10.4   REVIEW EXERCISES

10.4.1   Complete each of the following:

    1. Watakushi wa eiga ga suki desu. *Demo*, _____.

       Watakushi wa eiga ga suki desu. *Dakara*, _____.

       Watakushi wa eiga ga suki desu. *Sore ni*, _____ *mo* _____.

    2. Kono mise wa on'gaku ga ii desu. *Demo*, _____.

       Kono mise wa on'gaku ga ii desu. *Dakara*, _____.

       Kono mise wa on'gaku ga ii desu. *Sore ni*, _____ *mo* _____.

    3. Kinoo eiga o mimashita. *Demo*, _____.

       Kinoo eiga o mimashita. *Dakara*, _____.

       Kinoo eiga o mimashita. *Sore ni*, _____ *mo* _____.

10.4.2   Fill in each of the blanks with the most appropriate of the following words:

donata, nan, nani, dono, doo, dore, doko

    1. Toshokan ni _____ no zasshi ga arimashita ka?

       Nihon no zasshi ga arimashita.

    2. Kore wa _____ no rekoodo desu ka?

       Sumisu san no desu.

    3. _____ kissaten e hairimashoo ka?

       Sono kissaten e hairimashoo.

    4. _____ no teepu o kikimasu ka?

       Furan'sugo no teepu o kikimasu.

    5. Ashita _____ o shimasu ka?

       Uchi de hon o yomimasu.

    6. Shin'bun wa _____ ni arimasu ka?

       Asoko desu yo.

    7. _____ ga anata no kamera desu ka?

       Kore desu.

    8. Shiken wa _____ deshita ka?

       Totemo warukatta desu.

9. Are wa _____ desu ka?

Are desu ka? Byooin desu yo.

10. _____ tatemono ga gin'koo desu ka?

Are desu.

10.4.3 Choose the correct Relational:

1. Anata (wa, ga) gakusei desu ka?

Hai, soo desu. Tanaka san (wa, ga, mo) gakusei desu.

2. Anata (wa, ga) on'gaku (wa, ga, o) suki desu ka?

Hai, daisuki desu. E (wa, ga, o, mo) suki desu.

3. Anata (wa, ga) on'gaku (wa, ga, o) suki desu ka?

Hai, daisuki desu. Ishii san (wa, ga, mo) on'gaku (wa, ga, o, mo) suki desu.

4. Nihon'go (ga, no) jisho (wa, o) takai desu ka?

Iie, takaku arimasen. Chuugokugo (ga, no, mo) jisho (wa, o, mo) takaku arimasen.

5. Yamada san (ga, o) yobimashoo ka?

Ee, yobimashoo. Suzuki san (ga, o, mo) yobimashoo.

6. Yamamoto san (wa, ga) yoku zasshi (ya, no) hon (ga, o) yomimasu ka?

Zasshi (wa, ga, o) yomimasu ga, hon (wa, ga, o) yomimasen.

7. Kyoo eiga o mimasu ka?

Iie, eiga (wa, ga) mimasen. Terebi (mo, o) mimasu.

10.4.4 Substitute the italicized word with each of the given words, making necessary changes:

1. Ano kata no uchi wa *totemo* tooi desu.

   1. *amari*   2. *chotto*   3. *zen'zen*   4. *zuibun* . . . *nee*

2. *Yoku* Asahi Shin'bun o yomimasu.

   1. *itsumo*   2. *tokidoki*   3. *taitei*   4. *moo*

10.4.5 Carry on the following dialog in Japanese:

A: Do you like sports?

B: Yes, I do.

A: Do you play tennis?

B: Yes, but I am not good at it.

A: Won't you play tennis with me?

B: How nice!

A: Will you be free tomorrow?

B: Tomorrow? No, I am not free tomorrow.

A: Then, how about the day after tomorrow?

B: I won't be busy.

A: Then, let's play tennis the day after tomorrow.

10.4.6 Carry on dialogs according to the following situations:

1.   You meet a friend whom you have not seen for a long time.

2.   You are introduced to someone.

10.5   AURAL COMPREHENSION

10.5.1 こやま 「あれは　なんですか。」
いとう 「どれですか。」
こやま 「あの　たてものです。」
いとう 「ああ、あれですか。あれは　びょういんです。」

10.5.2 スミス 「はじめまして。スミスです。」
やまだ 「やまだです。どうぞ　よろしく。」
スミス 「こちらこそ。やまださん、しごと*　は　なんですか。」
やまだ 「がくせいです。」
スミス 「そうですか。この　だいがくの　がくせいですか。」
やまだ 「いいえ、とうきょうだいがくの　がくせいです。スミスさんは？」
スミス 「わたしは　サラリーマン† です。」

*shigoto ''job''
†sarariiman ''company worker''

10.5.3 やまだ 「もう　ひるごはんを　たべましたか。」
いしい 「はい、たべました。あなたは？」
やまだ 「まだです。おなかが　すきました。」
いしい 「れいぞうこ*　に　サンドイッチ† が　ありますよ。わたしも　たべましたが、とても
　　　　　おいしかったです。あなたも　たべませんか。」
やまだ 「ええ、ありがとう。」

*reizooko ''refrigerator''
†san'doitchi ''sandwiches''

144

10.5.4 スミス 「これは なんですか。」
こやま 「コンピューター・ゲーム* です。」
スミス 「ゲームですか。どこのですか。」
こやま 「にほんのです。」
スミス 「あなたの？」
こやま 「ええ。あなたも しませんか。」
スミス 「でも、いいんですか。」
こやま 「ええ、どうぞ。おもしろいですよ。」

*kon'pyuutaa geemu ''computer game''

10.5.5 おととい いとうさんと あたしは まるぜんへ いきました。まるぜんは ほんやです。とても
おおきいです。いとうさんは がいこくの ほんを かいました。あたしは おんがくの ほんを
さがしましたが、ありませんでした。それから、ぎんざへ いきました。ぎんざは とても
にぎやかでした。ちょっと かいものを しました。そして、ビフテキやへ はいりました。
あたしたちは ビフテキや サラダ* や デザート† を たべました。おいしかったですが、とても
たかかったです。

*sarada ''salad''
†dezaato ''dessert''

10.5.6 スミスさんは だいがくいんの がくせいです。カナダ* じんです。いま にほんに います。
カナダで ちょっと にほんごを ならいましたが、まだ あまり じょうずではありません。
こやまさんは スミスさんの ともだちです。こやまさんと スミスさんは よく いっしょに
でかけます。こやまさんは おんがくが だいすきです。スミスさんも だいすきです。きょう
こやまさんと スミスさんは コンサート† へ いきました。

*Kanada ''Canada''
†kon'saato ''concert''

LESSON 11
SUZUKI VISITS MINORU

11.1 USEFUL EXPRESSIONS

Doozo ohairi kudasai.$_{15}$

"Please come in." This expression is a polite equivalent of *(Doozo) haitte kudasai.*

Ashita wa doo desu ka$_{15}$/

"How about tomorrow?" ~ *wa doo desu ka?* is often used to ask if something is all right with the listener or if someone would like to have something. The more polite equivalent would be ~ *wa ikaga desu ka?*

11.2 DIALOG

Suzuki: Minoru kun$_1$, imasu ka/

Minoru: A, Suzuki san   Doozo ohairi kudasai.

Suzuki: Ojama shimasu.

Minoru: Yoku furimasu$_2$ nee. Soto wa mushiatsukatta deshoo$_3$.

Suzuki: Iie, amari mushiatsuku nakatta$_4$ desu yo. Ashita$_5$ mo ame desu ka/

Minoru: Ashita wa ten'ki ga ii deshoo$_6$. Rajio de soo iimashita yo/

Suzuki: Sore wa yokatta$_7$. Minoru kun wa oyogi ga suki deshoo$_8$, Umi ka$_9$, puuru de issho

 ni oyogimasen ka/

Minoru: Itsu$_5$ desu ka/

Suzuki: Ashita wa doo desu ka/

Minoru: Ashita desu ka/ Kono shuumatsu wa tsugoo$_{10}$ ga warui n desu. Jitsu wa, ashita kuni$_{11}$ e

 kaerimasu.

Suzuki: Kuni e/ Minoru kun no uchi wa Tookyoo deshoo$_{11}$/

Minoru: Iie, Hokkaidoo desu.

Suzuki: Oya, soo desu ka. Jaa, gokazoku$_{12}$ wa minasan$_{13}$ Hokkaidoo desu ka/

Minoru: Chichi$_{14}$ to haha wa Sapporo ni imasu ga, ani to ane wa Tookyoo desu.

Suzuki: Sapporo no natsu wa suzushii n deshoo/

Minoru: Amari suzushiku nai n desu. Ima goro wa moo tabun atsui deshoo.

11.3 PATTERN SENTENCES

11.3.1

PM	
N	R
Ten'ki	ga

→

P	
A	C
iI	DESHOO.[6]

11.3.2

PM	
N	R
Soto	wa

→

P	
A	C
mushiatsuKATTA	DESHOO.[3]

11.3.3

PM	
N	R
Ten'ki	ga

→

P		
A	E	C
yoKU	NAI[4]	DESHOO.[6]

11.3.4

PM
Adv.
Amari

→

P			
A	E	PC	C
mushiatsuKU	NAKATTA[4]	(N)	DESHOO.[4]

11.3.5

PM	
N	R
Oyogi	ga

→

P	
Na[8]	C
suki	DESHOO?[8]

11.4 NOTES

11.4.1 *-Kun* in *Minoru kun* is a dependent Noun that is used in the same way as *-san* in *Yamada san*. The *-kun*, however, is used normally by men, while *-san* can be used by both men and women. *-Kun* may not be used with the name of a person who is superior to the speaker. It is commonly used among friends, classmates, and such.

In the dialog, Minoru is addressed by Suzuki as *Minoru kun,* indicating that Suzuki is an older friend. By replying with *Suzuki san,* Minoru shows that Suzuki is his superior, at least in Minoru's eyes. Thus the way in which people address each other serves to show their relative positions. Notice that Minoru is the first name.

11.4.2 Here, the subject *ame* is omitted since it is understood. This Verb *furimasu* usually refers to *ame* "rain" or *yuki* "snow."

11.4.3 As explained in Notes 8.4.3 and 9.4.9, an Adjective may occur before the Copula *desu*. An Adjective may also occur before *deshoo* which is the OO form of *desu*. When the perfect tense form or the TA form of an Adjective occurs with *deshoo*, it is the presumptive to the past: "something or someone must have been such and such." See Note 11.4.6 for *deshoo* form. *Mushiatsukatta* is the TA form of *mushiatsui* "hot and humid" and means "[It] must have been hot and humid" when it occurs with *deshoo*. As indicated in Note 11.4.4, *(n) desu* may follow the *nakatta* form. Similarly, *(n) deshoo* may also follow the *nakatta* form.

Adjective *(-katta)* + *(n)* + *desu* ⟶ **Adjective *(-katta)* + *(n)* + *deshoo***

Adjective *(-ku)* + *nakatta* + *(n)* + *desu* ⟶ **Adjective *(-ku)* + *nakatta* + *(n)* + *deshoo***

Yoru wa samukatta deshoo.	"It must have been cold in the evening."
Ano mise no koohii wa oishikatta deshoo.	"The coffee of that shop must have been good."
Kinoo wa ten'ki ga yokatta deshoo.	"The weather must have been good yesterday."
Kono mizu wa tsumetakatta deshoo.	"I suppose this water was cold."
Samuku nakatta deshoo.	"I suppose it was not cold."

11.4.4 The plain negative form of an Adjective is the combination of the KU form of an Adjective plus the Extender *nai* and its plain perfect tense form or TA form *nakatta*. *Desu* may follow *nai* or *nakatta* to make the statement more polite. They are more or less similar to the normal polite forms in politeness and are more spoken style in their flavor.

yoku { arimasen / arimasen deshita } ⟶ yoku { nai / nakatta } desu   "It { is / was } not good."

muzukashiku { arimasen / arimasen deshita } ⟶ muzukashiku { nai / nakatta } desu   "It { is / was } not difficult."

atsuku { arimasen / arimasen deshita } ⟶ atsuku { nai / nakatta } desu   "It { is / was } not hot."

atatakaku { arimasen / arimasen deshita } ⟶ atatakaku { nai / nakatta } desu   "It { is / was } not warm."

suzushiku { arimasen / arimasen deshita } ⟶ suzushiku { nai / nakatta } desu.   "It { is / was } not cool."

Adjective *(-i)* + *(n)* + *desu* ⟶ **Adjective** *(-ku)* + *nai* + *(n)* + *desu*

Adjective *(-katta)* + *(n)* + *desu* ⟶ **Adjective** *(-ku)* + *nakatta* + *(n)* + *desu*

Anata no uchi wa tooi desu ka?	"Is your house far?"
Iie, tooku nai desu.	"No, it is not far."
Hokkaidoo wa samukatta desu ka?	"Was it cold in Hokkaidō?"
Iie, amari samuku nakatta desu yo.	"No, it was not very cold."

All the above forms have been introduced in the following Notes:

Adjective *(-i)* + *(n)* + *desu*	Note 8.4.3
Adjective *(-ku)* + *arimasen*	Note 8.4.5
Adjective *(-katta)* + *(n)* + *desu*	Note 9.4.9
Adjective *(-ku)* + *arimasen deshita*	Note 9.4.10
Adjective *(-ku)* + *nai* + *(n)* + *desu*	Note 11.4.4
Adjective *(-ku)* + *nakatta* + *(n)* + *desu*	Note 11.4.4

11.4.5 The time Nouns such as *ashita* "tomorrow," *kinoo* "yesterday," *ima* "now," *mae* "before," et cetera, may be used adverbially without any Relational following. Usually a time word phrase precedes another Predicate Modifier.

Ototoi ikimashita.	"He went [there] the day before yesterday."
Asatte no asa uchi ni imasu.	"[I] will be at home in the morning of the day after tomorrow."

Here are more time expressions.

ashita	kyoo	kinoo
"tomorrow"	"today"	"yesterday"
ashita no asa	kesa	kinoo no asa
"tomorrow morning"	"this morning"	"yesterday morning"
ashita no hiru	kyoo no hiru	kinoo no hiru
"tomorrow noon"	"this noon"	"yesterday noon"
ashita no yoru	kyoo no yoru	kinoo no yoru
ashita no ban	kon'ban	kinoo no ban
"tomorrow night"	"tonight"	"last night"

The interrogative time Noun to ask "when?" is *itsu*.

Itsu dekakemashita ka?	"When did [he] go out?"
Shiken wa itsu desu ka?	"When will the exam be?"

The Relational of topic *wa* or the Relational *mo* "also, or (not) either" may occasionally be placed after these time Nouns. Their function is the same as that of substituting *ga* or *o*.

Kinoo oyogimashita.	"[I] swam yesterday."
Kinoo wa oyogimashita.	"As for yesterday, [I] swam."
Kinoo wa oyogimasen deshita.	"As for yesterday, [I] didn't swim."
Kinoo mo oyogimashita.	"[I] swam yesterday, too."
Kinoo mo oyogimasen deshita.	"[I] did not swim yesterday, either."

Natsu is a Noun meaning "summer." Like *kyoo* "today," *kon'getsu* "this month," *natsu* "summer," and the other names of seasons can be used without any Relational following. Here are the names of the four seasons:

haru "spring"	natsu "summer"	aki "fall"	fuyu "winter"

Natsu doko e ikimashoo ka?	"Where shall we go in the summer?"
Yama ka umi e ikimashoo.	"Let's go to the mountains or the seaside."
Fuyu yasumi nani o shimasu ka?	"What are [you] going to do during the winter vacation?"

11.4.6 *Deshoo* is the OO form of the Copula *desu*, as introduced already in Note 11.4.3. While *desu* makes a statement definite or confirmative, *deshoo* functions to make it suppositional, presumptive, uncertain, less confirmative, et cetera, and is often expressed as "I suppose," "will (probably) be."

Deshoo follows an Adjective, a Noun, an adjectival Noun or a Verb. Only the Adjective plus *deshoo* construction will be summarized here.

Adjective *(-i)* + *deshoo*	Note 11.4.6
Adjective *(-katta)* + *deshoo*	Note 11.4.3
Adjective *(-ku)* + *nai deshoo*	Note 11.4.6
Adjective *(-ku)* + *nakatta deshoo*	Note 11.4.3

Adjective + *(n)* + *desu* ⟶ Adjective + *(n)* + *deshoo*

Atsui desu.	"It's hot."
Atsui deshoo.	"It must be hot."
Ten'ki ga ii deshoo.	"The weather will be fine."
Ten'ki ga yoku nai deshoo.	"The weather will not be fine."
Ten'ki ga yokatta deshoo.	"The weather must have been fine."
Ten'ki ga yoku nakatta deshoo.	"The weather must not have been fine."
Ano eiga wa omoshiroi deshoo.	"That movie will (probably) be interesting."
Ano eiga wa omoshiroku nai deshoo.	"That movie will not be interesting."

Ano eiga wa omoshirokatta deshoo.   "That movie must have been interesting."

Ano eiga wa omoshiroku nakatta deshoo.   "That movie must not have been interesting."

Deshoo and *desu yo* are often confused by foreigners because of the similarity of sounds. However, there is a difference in intonation and juncture. Train yourself to be able to distinguish them.

Samukatta desu <u>yo</u> /

Samukatta deshoo.

11.4.7 As explained before, *yokatta desu* is the perfect tense form of *ii desu*. (See Note 9.4.9.) However, since this expression *Sore wa yokatta* was the speaker's own monologue, undirected to anybody, the more polite version *Sore wa yokatta desu* was not used.

11.4.8 *Deshoo* also follows a Noun or an adjectival Noun.

$$\left\{ \begin{array}{l} \textbf{Noun} \\ \textbf{adjectival Noun} \end{array} \right\} + \textbf{\textit{desu}} \longrightarrow \left\{ \begin{array}{l} \textbf{Noun} \\ \textbf{adjectival Noun} \end{array} \right\} + \textbf{\textit{deshoo}}$$

Oyogi ga suki deshoo.   "[He] will (probably) like swimming."

Yamada san wa gakusei deshoo.   "I presume that Mr. Yamada is a student."

Sore wa hon'too deshoo.   "That must be true."

Toshokan wa itsumo shizuka deshoo.   "The library will (probably) be quiet all the time."

When the *deshoo* as in *suki deshoo?* is said with a rising intonation, it is a question asking for the hearer's agreement to the statement like *desu ne?*. But *deshoo?* bears a little more uncertainty.

Compare:

Anata wa oyogi ga suki desu ka?   "Do you like swimming?" (genuine question)

Anata wa oyogi ga suki desu ne?   "You like swimming, don't you?" (for confirmation)

Anata wa oyogi ga suki deshoo?   "You probably like swimming, don't you?" (for confirmation but less certain)

Ashita wa yasumi deshoo?   "Isn't tomorrow a holiday?
  Nani o shimasu ka?   What are you going to do?"

Sono hon wa takai deshoo?   "That book is probably expensive.
Don't you think so?"

11.4.9 *Ka* between Nouns is a Relational, and is used like the Relationals *to* and *ya*. *Ka*, however, is used as an equivalent of "or" as in "A or B."

Ashita ka asatte ikimasu.   "[I] will go [there] tomorrow or the day after tomorrow."

Hon ka zasshi o kaimasu.   "[I] will buy a book or a magazine."

Sumisu san wa kissaten ka shokudoo ni   "Mr. Smith was in a coffee shop or a cafeteria."
  imashita yo.

11.4.10 *Tsugoo ga warui (n desu)* is used idiomatically to mean "circumstances do not permit (one's doing such and such)." The opposite expression *tsugoo ga ii (n desu)* is "circumstances permit (one's doing such and such)," or "something suits one's convenience." As indicated in 8.4.3, the *n* after *warui* and before *desu* is called the Pre-Copula and makes this expression a little more emphatic, colloquial and elucidative.

Gotsugoo wa doo desu ka?	"Are you available?"
Ee, ii desu.	"Yes, I am."
Chotto tsugoo ga warui n desu.	"I am not available."

11.4.11 *Minoru kun no uchi wa Tookyoo deshoo?* means "Minoru's home is in Tōkyō, isn't it?" In expressing "something or someone is in a place," ~ *ni arimasu* or ~ *ni imasu* may be replaced by *desu*, and the Copula *desu* is common when referring to locations of buildings, houses, et cetera.

$$\text{Noun} + wa + \text{place Noun} + \begin{Bmatrix} ni\ arimasu \\ ni\ imasu \end{Bmatrix} \longrightarrow \text{Noun} + wa + \text{place Noun} + desu$$

Eki wa doko ni arimasu ka?   ⟶   Eki wa doko desu ka?
                                         "Where is the station?"

Boku no uchi wa Tookyoo ni arimasu.   ⟶   Boku no uchi wa Tookyoo desu.
                                           "My house is in Tōkyō."

Itoo san wa ima gakkoo ni imasu.   ⟶   Itoo san wa ima gakkoo desu.
                                           "Mr. Itō is at school now."

Shujin wa kyoo uchi ni imasu.   ⟶   Shujin wa kyoo uchi desu.
                                           "My husband is home today."

Kuni covers three meanings: nation, native place, and locality. An American might refer to his country (nation), or to going to the country (locality), but "country" does not carry the meaning of "native place." An American, therefore, would not say, "Where is your *kuni* (native place)?", but this meaning is strongly present in the Japanese term. One's native place is extremely important because that is where one's ancestors lived. With the emphasis on the family in Japan, and respect for the traditional, it follows that where one's family came from and where one's ancestors lived would carry great importance.

11.4.12 Like *o-* as in *ohima* "leisure time," the prefix *go-* may occur at the beginning of some Nouns to show politeness. In normal-style speech, the use of this word is conventionally limited. Both *o-* and *go-* are common in women's speech.

Compare:

kazoku	....	plain word for "family," so you can use *kazoku* either to refer to someone else's family in less formal or ordinary speech or to your own

gokazoku*	. . . .	this word may be used only to refer to someone else's family
shujin	. . . .	(my) husband; (my) master
goshujin	. . . .	(someone else's) husband; (someone else's) master: *go-* is mandatory

*The prefixes *o-* and *go-* may be attached to a word in three instances:

1) In showing respect towards others; kazoku ⟶ gokazoku "family"

2) *-o* and *-go* may sometimes be added to show that what is being discussed is either the third or second person's view, thought, behavior, or belongings.

    yukkuri ⟶ goyukkuri "leisurely"

    tsugoo ⟶ gotsugoo "convenience"

The above two meanings, therefore, demonstrate that *o-* and *go-* are used for the second or third person, rather than for the first person.

3) Whether in reference to the first, second, or third person, *o-* and *go-* may be attached to give elegance and flavor to a particular word. For example: *kane—okane; mizu—omizu; tearai— otearai; hiru—ohiru; mise—omise; cha—ocha.* Terms such as these became so frequently used in Japan that the word with the attached affix has become the common, accepted term. However, outside of the regularly used combinations, such usages occur more frequently in women's and children's conversation.

11.4.13 *Minasan* means "everybody." In this case, *minasan* refers to everyone in the second person's family. This word is more polite than *min'na. Minasan* is not used in reference to the speaker's own family.

Minasan ogen'ki desu ka?	"Is everyone [in your family] fine?"
Hai, min'na gen'ki desu.	"Yes, [we] are all fine."

11.4.14 *Chichi* "father," *haha* "mother," *ani* "older brother," *ane* "older sister," et cetera are used to refer to the speaker's own family members. As partly explained in Note 11.4.12, depending upon whether you are referring to your own family members or to someone else's, different terms will be used in Japanese. Here are some more examples:

When referring to your family members:		When referring to someone else's family members:
chichi	"father"	otoosan
haha	"mother"	okaasan
ani	"older brother"	oniisan
ane	"older sister"	oneesan
otooto	"younger brother"	otootosan
imooto	"younger sister"	imootosan
kodomo	"child"	kodomosan *or* okosan

shujin	"husband"	goshujin
kanai	"wife"	okusan
kazoku	"family"	(go)kazoku

Otoosan wa ogen'ki desu ka?   "How is your father?"

Hai, chichi wa gen'ki desu.   "Yes, my father is fine."

Goshujin wa sen'sei deshoo?   "Isn't your husband a teacher?"

Ee, shujin wa sen'sei desu.   "Yes, he is a teacher."

Ane wa gakusei desu ga, oneesan wa?   "My older sister is a student, but what about your older sister?"

11.4.15 Speech Level

Using different forms of the expressions *Doozo ohairi kudasai* and *Doo desu ka* signify different degrees of politeness toward another person. This is illustrated in the following examples. Expressions on the left side of the sign (>) indicate a greater degree of politeness than the expressions on the right side.

1) Enter!

   Doozo ohairi kudasai. > Doozo haitte kudasai. > Ohairi nasai. > Doozo ohairi. > Ohairi. > Haire.

2) How is it?

   Ikaga desu ka? > Doo desu ka? > Doo?

11.5 VOCABULARY

Dialog

Minoru	. . . . . . .N	boy's first name
-kun	. . . . . .Nd	equivalent of *-san* (used by men) (see 11.4.1)
furimasu	V	(rain or snow) fall (normal form of *furu*) (see 11.4.2)
soto	. . . . . . .N	outside
mushiatsukatta	. . . . . . .A	was hot and humid (TA form of *mushiatsui*)
deshoo	C	OO form of *desu* (see 11.4.3, 11.4.6, and 11.4.8)
mushiatsuku nakatta	. . . .A+E	was not hot and humid (plain equivalent of *mushiatsuku arimasen deshita*) (see 11.4.4 and 11.4.6)
ame	. . . . . . .N	rain
ten'ki	. . . . . . .N	weather
rajio	. . . . . . .N	radio
de	. . . . . . .R	by means of (see 12.4.6)
iimashita	V	said (TA form of *iimasu* ⟵ *iu*)

oyogi	.......N	swimming
umi	.......N	sea; seaside
ka	.......R	or (see 11.4.9)
puuru	.......N	swimming pool
oyogimasu	V	swim (normal form of *oyogu*)
itsu	.......Ni	when? (see 11.4.5)
shuumatsu	.......N	weekend
tsugoo	.......N	convenience (see 11.4.10)
jitsu wa	.......SI	the fact is; in fact
Hokkaidoo	.......N	Hokkaidō Prefecture (northern island of Japan)
oya	.......SI	oh!; oh?; my!
go-	..(prefix)	(see 11.4.12)
kazoku	.......N	family (see 11.4.12 and 11.4.14)
minasan	.......N	everyone (see 11.4.13)
chichi	.......N	(my) father (see 11.4.14)
haha	.......N	(my) mother
Sapporo	.......N	capital city of Hokkaidō
ani	.......N	(my) older brother
ane	.......N	(my) older sister
natsu	.......N	summer
suzushii	.......A	is cool
suzushiku nai	.....A+E	is not cool (plain equivalent of *suzushiku arimasen*) (see 11.4.4 and 11.4.6)
ima goro	.......N	about this time; at this time
tabun	....Adv.	probably; perhaps
atsui	.......A	is hot

Notes

yuki	.......N	snow
samui	.......A	is cold (weather)
tsumetai	.......A	is cold (thing)
(-ku) nai	.......E	(see 11.4.4 and 11.4.6)
(-ku) nakatta	.......E	(see 11.4.4 and 11.4.6)
atatakai	.......A	is warm (sometimes *attakai*)

asa	.......N	morning
hiru	.......N	noon (it sometimes means ''lunch'')
ban	.......N	evening; night
kesa	.......N	this morning
kon'ban	.......N	tonight
haru	.......N	spring
aki	.......N	autumn; fall
fuyu	.......N	winter
yama	.......N	mountain
yasumi	.......N	vacation; holiday; closed; absent
shujin	.......N	(my) husband
goshujin	.......N	someone else's husband
min'na	.......N	all; everyone (see 11.4.13)
otoosan	.......N	(someone else's) father (see 11.4.14)
okaasan	.......N	(someone else's) mother
oniisan	.......N	(someone else's) older brother
oneesan	.......N	(someone else's) older sister
otooto	.......N	(my) younger brother
imooto	.......N	(my) younger sister
kodomo	.......N	child
okosan	.......N	(someone else's) child
kanai	.......N	my wife
okusan	.......N	(someone else's) wife

11.6 HIRAGANA PRACTICE

11.6.1 Recognize the difference or similarity between the two *hiragana* in each of the following pairs:

きや……きゃ	みゆ……みゅ	りよ……りょ
きゆ……きゅ	みよ……みょ	ぎや……ぎゃ
きよ……きょ	りや……りゃ	ぎゆ……ぎゅ
しや……しゃ	しゆ……しゅ	ぎよ……ぎょ
ひや……ひゃ	しよ……しょ	じや……じゃ
ひゆ……ひゅ	ちや……ちゃ	じゆ……じゅ
ひよ……ひょ	ちゆ……ちゅ	ちよ……ちょ
みや……みゃ	りゆ……りゅ	にや……にゃ

にゆ……にゅ	びや……びゃ	ぴや……ぴゃ
にょ……にょ	びゅ……びゅ	ぴゅ……ぴゅ
じょ……じょ	びょ……びょ	ぴょ……ぴょ

11.6.2 Read and write the following:

しょくじ	しゅじん	じゃあ
としょかん	じむしょ	おちゃ

11.7 DRILLS

11.7.1 Pronunciation Drill

Ii deshoo. Ii desu yo. Soo deshoo. Soo desu yo.

Hon'too deshoo. Hon'too desu yo. Suzushii deshoo. Suzushii desu yo.

Oyogi ga suki deshoo. Oyogi ga suki desu yo.

Natsu wa atsui deshoo. Natsu wa atsui desu yo.

Shuumatsu wa hima deshoo. Shuumatsu wa hima desu yo.

11.7.2 Pattern Drill

1. Ashita wa ten'ki ga ii deshoo.

2. Kyoo wa ten'ki ga yoku nai deshoo.

3. Soko no natsu wa suzushii n deshoo?

4. Iie, amari suzushiku nai n desu.

5. Soto wa mushiatsukatta deshoo?

6. Iie, mushiatsuku nakatta desu yo.

7. Minoru kun wa oyogi ga suki deshoo.

8. Minoru kun no uchi wa doko desu ka?

9. Tabun Tookyoo deshoo.

11.7.3 Transformation Drill

1. Kyoo wa mushiatsui *desu*. ⟶ Kyoo wa mushiatsui *deshoo*.

2. Asatte wa yasumi desu. ⟶ Asatte wa yasumi deshoo.

3. Minoru san wa gakusei desu. ⟶ Minoru san wa gakusei deshoo.

4. Ashita ten'ki ga warui desu. ⟶ Ashita ten'ki ga warui deshoo.

5. Hokkaidoo wa natsu suzushii desu. ⟶ Hokkaidoo wa natsu suzushii deshoo.

6. Tsugoo ga ii desu. ⟶ Tsugoo ga ii deshoo.

7. Chichi ya haha wa gen'ki desu. ⟶ Chichi ya haha wa gen'ki deshoo.

8. Kodomo wa yuki ga suki desu. ⟶ Kodomo wa yuki ga suki deshoo.

9. Ashita atatakai desu. ⟶ Ashita atatakai deshoo.

10. Sapporo no fuyu wa samui desu. ⟶ Sapporo no fuyu wa samui deshoo.

11.7.4 Transformation Drill

1. Kinoo wa samukatta *desu*.   ⟶   Kinoo wa samukatta *deshoo*.

2. Yoru suzushikatta desu.   ⟶   Yoru suzushikatta deshoo.

3. Ototoi ten'ki ga yokatta desu.   ⟶   Ototoi ten'ki ga yokatta deshoo.

4. Kono rajio wa yasukatta desu.   ⟶   Kono rajio wa yasukatta deshoo.

5. Kono natsu wa atsukatta desu.   ⟶   Kono natsu wa atsukatta deshoo.

6. Tsugoo ga warukatta desu.   ⟶   Tsugoo ga warukatta deshoo.

7. Shiken wa muzukashikatta desu.   ⟶   Shiken wa muzukashikatta deshoo.

8. Ano eiga wa omoshirokatta desu.   ⟶   Ano eiga wa omoshirokatta deshoo.

11.7.5 Transformation Drill

1. Ten'ki ga *yoku arimasen*.   ⟶   Ten'ki ga *yoku nai deshoo*.

2. Ashita atatakaku arimasen.   ⟶   Ashita atatakaku nai deshoo.

3. Sono hon wa muzukashiku arimasen.   ⟶   Sono hon wa muzukashiku nai deshoo.

4. Soko no aki wa samuku arimasen.   ⟶   Soko no aki wa samuku nai deshoo.

5. Heya wa mushiatsuku arimasen.   ⟶   Heya wa mushiatsuku nai deshoo.

6. Kono puuru wa kitanaku arimasen.   ⟶   Kono puuru wa kitanaku nai deshoo.

7. Shuumatsu wa isogashiku arimasen.   ⟶   Shuumatsu wa isogashiku nai deshoo.

8. Ano mise no koohii wa oishiku arimasen.   ⟶   Ano mise no koohii wa oishiku nai deshoo.

11.7.6 Transformation Drill

1. Anata wa oyogi ga suki *desu ne?*   ⟶   Anata wa oyogi ga suki *deshoo?*

2. Tsugoo wa ii desu ne?   ⟶   Tsugoo wa ii deshoo?

3. Soo desu ne?   ⟶   Soo deshoo?

4. Hawai no umi wa kirei desu ne?   ⟶   Hawai no umi wa kirei deshoo?

5. Ashita ten'ki ga yoku nai desu ne?   ⟶   Ashita ten'ki ga yoku nai deshoo?

6. Kuni wa Sapporo desu ne?   ⟶   Kuni wa Sapporo deshoo?

7. Shin'bun wa takaku nai desu ne?   ⟶   Shin'bun wa takaku nai deshoo?

8. Ano kata wa amerikajin desu ne?   ⟶   Ano kata wa amerikajin deshoo?

11.7.7 Response Drill

1. Tsugoo wa doo desu ka? / warui   . . . . Warui *n desu*.

2. Ashita hima desu ka? / iie, isogashii   . . . . Iie, isogashii n desu.

3. Koko no bifuteki wa oishii desu ka?
    / iie, oishiku nai   . . . . Iie, oishiku nai n desu.

4. Shiken wa doo deshita ka? / muzukashikatta .... Muzukashikatta n desu.

5. Ten'ki wa yokatta desu ka? / iie, warukatta .... Iie, warukatta n desu.

6. Byooin wa tooi desu ka? / iie, chikai .... Iie, chikai n desu.

7. Anata no uchi wa ookii desu ka?
   / iie, amari ookiku nai .... Iie, amari ookiku nai n desu.

8. Tookyoo no natsu wa atsui desu ka?
   / iie, amari atsuku nai .... Iie, amari atsuku nai n desu.

11.7.8 Transformation Drill

1. Anata no uchi wa Tookyoo *ni arimasu* ka? ⟶ Anata no uchi wa Tookyoo *desu* ka?

2. Kazoku wa min'na Sapporo *ni imasu.* ⟶ Kazoku wa min'na Sapporo *desu.*

3. Eki wa doko ni arimasu ka? ⟶ Eki wa doko desu ka?

4. Chichi wa uchi ni imasu. ⟶ Chichi wa uchi desu.

5. Shujin wa ima kuni ni imasu. ⟶ Shujin wa ima kuni desu.

6. Jisho wa toshokan ni arimasu. ⟶ Jisho wa toshokan desu.

7. Den'wa wa koko ni arimasu yo. ⟶ Den'wa wa koko desu yo.

8. Rajio wa watashi no heya ni arimasu. ⟶ Rajio wa watashi no heya desu.

9. Okusan wa doko ni imasu ka? ⟶ Okusan wa doko desu ka?

10. Otearai wa doko ni arimasu ka? ⟶ Otearai wa doko desu ka?

11.7.9 Response Drill (family words)

1. *Otoosan* wa ogen'ki desu ka? / hai, *chichi* .... Hai, *chichi* wa gen'ki desu.

2. Gokazoku wa Nihon desu ka? / hai, kazoku .... Hai, kazoku wa Nihon desu.

3. Okusan wa nihon'jin desu ka? / iie, kanai .... Iie, kanai wa nihon'jin ja arimasen.

4. Oniisan wa gakusei desu ka? / ee, ani .... Ee, ani wa gakusei desu.

5. Goshujin wa ima doko desu ka?
   / shujin, jimusho .... Shujin wa ima jimusho desu.

6. Oneesan mo issho ni oyogimasu ka?
   / hai, ane .... Hai, ane mo issho ni oyogimasu.

7. Imootosan wa on'gaku ga suki desu ka?
   / hai, imooto .... Hai, imooto wa on'gaku ga suki desu.

8. Okaasan o yobimashita ka? / iie, haha .... Iie, haha o yobimasen deshita.

9. Okosan wa soo iimashita ka? / iie, kodomo .... Iie, kodomo wa soo iimasen deshita.

10. Otootosan no namae wa nan desu ka?
   / otooto, Minoru .... Otooto no namae wa Minoru desu.

11.7.10 Mixed Transformation Drill

1. *Kyoo* yama e ikimasu.

   ashita mo   ⟶   *Ashita mo* ikimasu.

   asatte wa   ⟶   *Asatte wa* ikimasen.

2. Kyoo gakkoo wa yasumi de wa arimasen.

   ashita mo   ⟶   Ashita mo yasumi de wa arimasen.

   asatte wa   ⟶   Asatte wa yasumi desu.

3. Kinoo ame ga furimashita.

   ototoi mo   ⟶   Ototoi mo furimashita.

   kyoo wa   ⟶   Kyoo wa furimasen deshita.

4. Natsu yoku oyogimasu.

   haru mo   ⟶   Haru mo oyogimasu.

   fuyu wa   ⟶   Fuyu wa oyogimasen.

5. Kinoo atsukatta desu.

   ototoi mo   ⟶   Ototoi mo atsukatta desu.

   ima wa   ⟶   Ima wa atsuku arimasen.

6. Fuyu yuki ga furimasu.

   aki mo   ⟶   Aki mo furimasu.

   haru wa   ⟶   Haru wa furimasen.

7. Kono goro isogashii desu.

   ima mo   ⟶   Ima mo isogashii desu.

   mae wa   ⟶   Mae wa isogashiku arimasen deshita.

11.8 EXERCISES

11.8.1 Connect the contrasting words with a line:

aki	oniisan
ane	okosan
suzushii	oneesan
fuyu	okaasan
atsui	haru
haha	otoosan
ani	atatakai
kanai	natsu
kodomo	goshujin

shujin   okusan

chichi   samui

11.8.2 Express the following ideas using *deshoo:*

1. The weather will probably be good tomorrow.

2. It will not be cold this winter.

3. Mr. Smith must be good at the Chinese language.

4. I suppose that Mr. Suzuki's house will be in Tōkyō.

5. The examination of English will probably not be easy.

11.8.3 Carry on the following conversations in Japanese:

—Are you in (at home), Mr. Ishii?

—Yes. . . . Oh, please come in.

—Thank you. I am going to bother you. It's cold today, isn't it?

—Yes, it is. How about coffee?

—Thank you.

11.8.4 Answer the following questions in Japanese:

1. Anata no kuni wa doko desu ka?

2. Soko wa fuyu mo atatakai desu ka?

3. Ame ya yuki ga yoku furimasu ka?

4. Itsu ame ga furimasu ka?

5. Gokazoku wa minasan soko ni imasu ka?

LESSON 12
SIGHTSEEING

12.1 USEFUL EXPRESSIONS

Dooshite gozon'ji desu ka₁₃ /

"How do you know (it)?" *Gozon'ji desu ka?* is a polite equivalent for *Shitte imasu ka?*

Sore wa sumimasen deshita₁₃.

"I am sorry for what I have done." This expression is used to apologize for what you have done or the trouble that you have caused. *Sore wa* can be omitted.

Nani ka goyoo desu ka /

"Is there anything you want to talk to me about?" *Yoo* means "matter to attend to."

Sore wa zan'nen deshita ne₁₃.

This expression is used to express "regret," "pity," "disappointment," et cetera. This will correspond to "What a pity (that you could not enjoy it fully)," or "That was too bad (that you could not enjoy much because of the bad weather)." The opposite expression would be *(Sore wa) yokatta desu ne* "How lucky you were!" or "I am glad to hear (that you have enjoyed)," et cetera.

12.2 DIALOG

Takada: Buraun san, kinoo wa rusu deshita ne /

Brown: Ee, Nikkoo e ikimashita. Demo, dooshite₁ gozon'ji desu ka /

Takada: Kinoo nido₂ den'wa shimashita.

Brown: Soo, sore wa sumimasen deshita. Nani ka goyoo desu ka /

Takada: Iie, betsu ni₃ Chotto hanashi o shitakatta₄ n desu. Nikkoo e wa₅ den'sha de₆ /

Brown: Ee. Den'sha de ikitaku nakatta₄ n desu kedo₇, Asakusa Eki kara₈ Toobu de ikimashita.

Takada: Nikkoo wa yokatta deshoo.

Brown: Ee, totemo kirei deshita. Demo, hito ga oozei₉ imashita.

Takada: Mizuumi e mo₅ ikimashita ka /

Brown: Ee, ikimashita kedo, ten'ki ga yoku nakatta n desu.

Takada: Sore wa zan'nen deshita ne / Watashi wa sen'getsu₁₀ Kyooto₁₁ ken'butsu o shimashita.

Brown: Ryooan'ji no ishi no niwa o mimashita ka / Are wa subarashii desu ne /

Takada: Ryooan'ji e wa ikimasen deshita. Demo, kon'do₁₂ ikitai₄ desu.

Brown: Watashi mo mata Kyooto ken'butsu o shitai₄ n desu kedo, hima ga nai n desu.

12.3 PATTERN SENTENCES

12.3.1

PM
N
Kon'do

→

P			
V	Da	PC	C
ikI	TAI	(N)	DESU.[4]

12.3.2

PM	
N	R
Hanashi	o

→

P			
V	Da	PC	C
shI	TAKATTA	(N)	DESU.[4]

12.3.3

SI	
Iie,	

P				
V	Da	E	PC	C
shI	TAKU	NAI	(N)	DESU.[4]

12.3.4

PM	
N	R
Den'sha	DE[6]

→

P				
V	Da	E	PC	C
ikI	TAKU	NAKATTA	(N)	DESU.[4]

12.3.5

PM		
N	R	R
Mizuumi	E	MO[5]

→

P
V
ikimashita

SP
ka?

12.3.6

PM		
N	R	R
Mizuumi	E	WA[5]

→

P	
V	C
ikimasen	deshita.

12.4 NOTES

12.4.1 *Dooshite* is an interrogative Adverb meaning "why?" or "how?" The connotation of a sentence usually determines which is the case.

Dooshite gozon'ji desu ka?   "How do you happen to know it?"

Dooshite kimasen deshita ka?   "Why didn't [you] come?"

Dooshite desu ka?   "Why is [it]?"

12.4.2 *Ni* in *nido* is the numeral meaning "two." Here is a list of the ordinary numerals:

0	.... rei; zero		40	.... yon'juu; shijuu
1	.... ichi		50	.... gojuu
2	.... ni		60	.... rokujuu
3	.... san		70	.... shichijuu; nanajuu
4	.... shi; yon; (yo-)*		80	.... hachijuu
5	.... go		90	.... kyuujuu; kujuu
6	.... roku		100	.... hyaku
7	.... shichi; nana		200	.... nihyaku
8	.... hachi		300	.... san'byaku†
9	.... ku; kyuu		400	.... yon'hyaku
10	.... juu		500	.... gohyaku
11	.... juuichi		600	.... roppyaku†
12	.... juuni		700	.... nanahyaku
13	.... juusan		800	.... happyaku†
14	.... juushi; juuyon; (juuyo-)*		900	.... kyuuhyaku
15	.... juugo		1,000	.... sen
16	.... juuroku		2,000	.... nisen
17	.... juushichi; juunana		3,000	.... san'zen†
18	.... juuhachi		4,000	.... yon'sen
19	.... juuku; juukyuu		5,000	.... gosen
20	.... nijuu		6,000	.... rokusen
21	.... nijuuichi		7,000	.... nanasen
:	:		8,000	.... hassen†
30	.... san'juu		9,000	.... kyuusen

Yo- for "four" is never used independently. It is always followed by a counter.
†Phonetic changes or irregular combinations.

10,000	.... ichiman		70,000	.... nanaman
20,000	.... niman		80,000	.... hachiman
30,000	.... san'man		90,000	.... kyuuman
40,000	.... yon'man		100,000	.... juuman
50,000	.... goman		⋮	⋮
60,000	.... rokuman		1,000,000	.... hyakuman

The -do in nido is the counter for frequency or number of times. When nan is followed by -do as in nan'do, it means "how many times." More numbers will be introduced in Lesson 13.

12.4.3 The full sentence may be *Betsu ni yoo wa arimasen* "nothing particular." *Yoo wa arimasen* is omitted because *betsu ni* is always used in negation, and the previous question has made the context quite clear.

12.4.4 *Shitakatta* means "wanted to do" and is the combination of the *shi* portion (which is called the Stem form or Pre-Masu form) of the Verb *shimasu* "do" and the TA form of the adjectival Derivative *-tai* "want to" or "would like to." Like Adjectives, *-tai* is followed by the Copula *desu, n desu, deshoo,* or *n deshoo* in normal style, and conjugates in the following manner.

(Predicate Modifier) + Verb(Stem form) +
- *-tai (n) desu*
- *-taku arimasen* or *-taku nai (n) desu*
- *-takatta (n) desu*
- *-taku arimasen deshita* or *-taku nakatta (n) desu*

(shi)tai (n) desu	"want to (do)"
(shi)taku arimasen *or* (shi)taku nai (n) desu	"do not want to (do)"
(shi)takatta (n) desu	"wanted to (do)"
(shi)taku arimasen deshita *or* (shi)taku nakatta (n) desu	"did not want to (do)"

The less formal way of expressing "do not want to (do)" is *(shi)taku nai (n) desu* and "did not want to (do)" is *(shi)taku nakatta n desu.* See Note 11.4.4.

The *-tai desu* normally represents the speaker's desire to do such and such, and, when used as the second person's desire or the third person's, there is limitation in use. When the Verb before *-tai* requires a direct object, the Relational *o* following the direct object may be replaced by the Relational *ga.* At this stage, however, try to use *o.*

Ashita dekaketai desu ka?	"Do [you] want to go out tomorrow?"

Iie, dekaketaku arimasen.
    Uchi ni itai desu.
	"No, [I] do not want to go out.
	    [I] want to stay home."

Depaato de nani o kaitakatta n desu ka?	"What did [you] want to buy in the department store?"
Kamera o kaitakatta n desu kedo, takakatta n desu.	"[I] wanted to buy a camera, but cameras were expensive there."
Onaka ga sukimashita ka?	"Are [you] hungry?"
Iie. Demo, koohii o nomitai desu.	"No. But [I] would like to have a coffee."

Such expressions of invitation as "Would you like to do such and such?" or "Do you want to do such and such?" normally should not be expressed by using the *-tai desu ka?* These connotations are expressed in negation as follows:

Issho ni eiga o mimasen ka?	"Would [you] like to see a movie with [me]?"
Koohii o nomimasen ka?	"Wouldn't [you] like to drink coffee?"

12.4.5 *Nikkoo e wa* means "to Nikkō." Some Relationals, such as *wa* and *mo,* can take the places of the Relationals *ga* and *o,* as introduced in Notes 4.4.9, 7.4.2, 7.4.3, 7.4.10, 8.4.5, 8.4.8, 9.4.2, and 11.4.5. With other Relationals, such as *de, ni, e, kara,* the *wa* or *mo* occurs immediately after another Relational. This combination of Relationals will be called "multiple Relationals." The function of *wa* and *mo* in multiple Relationals is the same as that of *wa* and *mo* substituting for *ga* and *o.*

$$
\left.\begin{array}{l} \sim\ e \\ \sim\ kara \\ \sim\ ni \\ \sim\ de \end{array}\right\} \longrightarrow \left\{\begin{array}{l} \sim\ e\ wa \\ \sim\ kara\ wa \\ \sim\ ni\ wa \\ \sim\ de\ wa \end{array}\right. \ \ or \ \ \left\{\begin{array}{l} \sim\ e\ mo \\ \sim\ kara\ mo \\ \sim\ ni\ mo \\ \sim\ de\ mo \end{array}\right.
$$

Kyooto e ryokoo shimashita.	"[I] traveled to Kyōto."
Kyooto e wa ryokoo shimasen deshita.	"[I] did not travel to Kyōto."
Kyooto e mo ryokoo shimashita.	"[I] traveled to Kyōto, too."
Hokkaidoo ni mo mizuumi ga takusan arimasu.	"There are many lakes in Hokkaidō, too."
Furuhon'ya de wa kaimashita ga, kono hon'ya de wa kaimasen deshita.	"[I] bought [some books] at a secondhand bookstore, but [I] did not buy [any] at this bookstore."

Nikkō is one of the most famous tourist attractions in Japan. Located north of Tōkyō, Nikkō has both historical and scenic interest. It is the site of the Tōshōgū shrine, built in honor of Ieyasu Tokugawa, the first of the Tokugawa shoguns. The famous carving of the San-saru or "Three Monkeys"—which most Americans will recognize as symbolizing "See no evil, hear no evil, and speak no evil"—also is found at Tōshōgū.

12.4.6 The *de* in *den'sha de ikimashita* means "by electric train." The Relational *de,* used after a Noun that represents "a tool," means "using," "by means of," "with (a tool)," et cetera.

kuruma					car"
den'sha		ikimasu	"go		train"
hikooki	de	kimasu	"come	by	plane"
fune		kaerimasu	"go back		boat"
takushii		ryokoo shimasu	"travel		taxi"
basu					bus"

en'pitsu				with a pencil"
nihon'go	de	kakimasu	"write	in Japanese"
pen				with a pen"

nihon'go	de	hanashimasu	"talk	in Japanese"
den'wa				on the phone"

hashi	de	tabemasu	"eat	with chopsticks"
fooku				with a fork"

rajio	de	kikimasu	"hear	on the radio"
den'wa				on the phone"

Nan de is used to ask "by what (means)?" "with what?" et cetera.

Nan de Nikkoo e ikimashita ka?	"How (by what) did [you] go to Nikkō?"
Kuruma de ikimashita.	"[I] went by car."
Fune de ryokoo shimasu ka, hikooki de ryokoo shimasu ka?	"Are [you] going to travel by boat or by plane?"
Uchi de wa nanigo de hanashimasu ka?	"In what language do [you] speak at home?"
Hashi de tabetai desu ka, fooku de tabetai desu ka?	"Do [you] want to eat with chopsticks or with a fork?"

12.4.7 As introduced in Note 4.4.10, *kedo* is a clause Relational meaning "although." The clause followed by *kedo* is a subordinate clause. *Kedo* is more colloquial than *ga* which was introduced in Note 9.4.5.

Koko wa mushiatsui desu kedo, soto wa suzushii deshoo.	"It is hot and humid here, but it must be cool outside."
Kyooto e wa ikimashita kedo, Ryooan'ji wa ken'butsu shimasen deshita.	"[I] went to Kyōto, but [I] did not visit the Ryōanji Temple."

12.4.8 *Kara* that occurs after a place Noun is a Relational meaning "from." This Relational occurs, like *e*, with motion Verbs, such as *ikimasu, kimasu,* and *kaerimasu.*

motion Verb $\begin{cases} ikimasu \\ kimasu \\ kaerimasu \end{cases}$ ⟶ place Noun + *kara* + motion Verb $\begin{cases} ikimasu \\ kimasu \\ kaerimasu \end{cases}$

Asakusa kara den'sha de ikimashita.	"[I] went by train from Asakusa."
Kesa Nikkoo kara kaerimashita.	"[I] came back from Nikkō this morning."
Itsu gakkoo kara kaerimasu ka?	"When are [you] coming back from school?"
Doko kara kimashita ka?	"Where did [you] come from?"
Watashi no uchi wa gakkoo kara tooi desu.	"My home is far away from the school."

Tōkyō, like most large cities, is divided into a number of districts. Probably among the best known of these, for Americans, are Asakusa, Shinjuku, and Ginza.

12.4.9 *Oozei* is a quantity Adverb meaning "many people." *Takusan* "many" or "much" and *sukoshi* "a few" or "a little" are opposites. Their function is similar to *oozei*'s, but they are also used for inanimate objects.

Tomodachi ga oozei uchi e kimashita.	"Many of my friends came to my house."
Yuki ga takusan furimashita.	"It snowed a lot."
Kuruma ga takusan arimasu.	"There are many cars."
Koohii o sukoshi nomitai desu.	"I want to drink a little coffee."

12.4.10 *Sen'getsu* is the Noun meaning "last month" and occurs in a sentence like other time Nouns introduced in Note 11.4.5. *Sen-* means "the previous." Similarly, *kon-* in *kon'getsu* means "this [month]," and *rai-* in *raigetsu* means "next [month]." *Sen-, kon-,* and *rai-* may be followed by *-getsu* "month" and *-shuu* "week," but they are not as systematic for other cases such as *nen* "year."

raigetsu	"next month"	kon'getsu	"this month"	sen'getsu	"last month"
raishuu	"next week"	kon'shuu	"this week"	sen'shuu	"last week"
rainen	"next year"	kotoshi	"this year"	kyonen	"last year"

The *mai-* as in *mainichi* "every day" may be attached to *asa, ban, -shuu* "week," *-getsu* "month," *-nen* "year," and the combination means "every ∼ ."

maigetsu	"every month"	mainen	"every year"	maishuu	"every week"
maiasa	"every morning"	maiban	"every night"	mainichi	"every day"

Kon'getsu mata Yooroppa e ikimasu.	"[I] am going to Europe again this month."
Sen'shuu ryokoo shimashita. Tanoshikatta desu.	"[I] travelled last week. [I] had a good time."
Maiban ben'kyoo shimasu ka?	"Do [you] study every night?"

These time Nouns are used without any Relationals following except *wa* and *mo*.

Kyonen Hokkaidoo e ryokoo shimashita.   "[I] took a trip to Hokkaidō last year."

Rainen mo Yooroppa e ikimasu.   "[I] am going to Europe next year, also."

12.4.11 *Kyōto* was the political capital of Japan for over a thousand years during the Heian period (A.D. 794–1192). There are few places in Kyōto without temples representing every sect of Japanese Buddhism as well as numerous shrines. Kyōto claims 1,598 Buddhist temples and 253 Shinto shrines. One of the best known is the Ryōanji Temple, famed for its garden.

12.4.12 *Kon'do* means "this time." But *kon'do* is used quite vaguely depending on the context. It may refer to the present, the future, or the past.

Kon'do Furan'su e ikitai desu.   "[I] would like to go to France this time."

Kon'do no shiken wa dame deshita.   "[I] did not do well in this [last] examination."

12.4.13 *Dooshite gozon'ji desu ka?* is a polite form of *Dooshite shitte imasu ka?* "How do you know it?" It provides another example of language form changing according to the relative social status of speaker and listener. *Gozon'ji desu ka?* would be addressed either to a superior or to a peer when the speaker wishes to maintain some distance between himself and the listener. *Dooshite* means "how."

Sore wa sumimasen deshita has been translated as "I'm sorry for what I have done," but the Japanese term carries connotations not present in the American usage of "I'm sorry." It could mean distress of mind or feeling regretful, sad, or pitiful. In this particular instance, Miss Brown uses *Sumimasen deshita* to express "I'm sorry because I caused you the trouble and the disappointment of telephoning me when I was not at home," and not the American meaning "I'm sorry we could not get together." Thus, the term is distinctively other-directed, or an example of heteronomy. Similarly, if a visitor calls while you are not at home—even though no appointment has previously been made—the Japanese usually apologize for causing the visitor trouble by their absence.

In the same way, Mr. Takada states, *Sore wa zan'nen deshita ne,* expressing his regret that the weather was bad. The sentiment here is much stronger than that of the American "That was too bad." Mr. Takada's regret is genuine, for he places himself in the position of Miss Brown, sympathizing and empathizing with her situation. To Americans, the expression of such deep regret over the bad weather which someone else has experienced would appear trivial, if not merely superficial. However, this is a characteristic heteronomous reaction whereby the Japanese shares the feelings of the person actually experiencing something.

12.4.14 Sightseeing

The Japanese tourist in his own country is usually motivated by somewhat different considerations than his American counterpart. Probably the most striking difference is that traditional Japanese seldom travel alone or with their families, but are more likely to join a tour group. These groups are numerous and easily identified by their tour guides, each carrying a flag so that his group members will be able to recognize him from a distance.

Traditionally the Japanese have preferred places known either for scenic beauty or for historical interest. It is only in recent years that they have begun to choose destinations offering various forms of recreation. Even the time-honored custom of visiting hot springs to take mineral or sand baths sprang from health rather than recreational reasons. Skiing, which has become a very popular winter sport in Japan, now attracts more tourists than many other forms of recreation.

12.5 VOCABULARY

Dialog

Buraun	.......N	Brown
rusu	.......N	is out; is not at home
Nikkoo	.......N	city in Tochigi Prefecture (famous for the Tōshōgū Shrine)
dooshite	....Adv.	how?; why? (see 12.4.1)
ni	.......N	two (see 12.4.2)
-do	......Nd	time(s) (see 12.4.2)
den'wa (o) shimasu	V	make a phone call (normal form of *den'wa (o) suru*)
betsu ni	....Adv.	nothing particular (see 12.4.3)
hanashi	.......N	a talk; tale
shitakatta	...V+Da	wanted to do (see 12.4.4)
den'sha	.......N	electric train; streetcar
de	.......R	by means of (see 12.4.6)
ikitaku nakatta	.V+Da+E	did not want to go (see 12.4.4)
Asakusa	.......N	an amusement center in downtown Tōkyō
kara	.......R	from (a place) (see 12.4.8)
Toobu	.......N	the Tōbu rail line
oozei	....Adv.	a lot of people (see 12.4.9)
mizuumi	.......N	lake
sen'getsu	.......N	last month (see 12.4.10)
Kyooto	.......N	old capital of Japan; city in Kyōto Prefecture
ken'butsu	.......N	sightseeing
ken'butsu (o) shimasu	V	see the sights of; visit (normal form of *ken'butsu (o) suru*)
Ryooan'ji	.......N	Ryōanji Temple in Kyōto (famous for its stone garden)
ishi	.......N	stone
niwa	.......N	garden
subarashii	.......A	is wonderful

kon'do	.......N	this time (in the future or in the past) (see 12.4.12)
ikitai	...V+Da	want to go (see 12.4.4)
mata	....Adv.	again

Notes

-tai	......Da	want to (do) (see 12.4.4)
-taku	......Da	KU form of -tai, want to (do) (see 12.4.4)
-takatta	......Da	wanted to (do) (TA form of -tai) (see 12.4.4)
ryokoo	.......N	trip
ryokoo (o) shimasu	V	travel; take a trip (normal form of ryokoo (o) suru)
takusan	....Adv.	a lot (see 12.4.9)
kuruma	.......N	car
hikooki	.......N	airplane
fune	.......N	boat; ship
takushii	.......N	taxi
basu	.......N	bus
en'pitsu	.......N	pencil
pen	.......N	pen
hashi	.......N	chopsticks
fooku	.......N	fork
sukoshi	....Adv.	a little (see 12.4.9)
raigetsu	.......N	next month
kon'getsu	.......N	this month
rainen	.......N	next year
kotoshi	.......N	this year
kyonen	.......N	last year
raishuu	.......N	next week
kon'shuu	.......N	this week
sen'shuu	.......N	last week
-getsu	......Nd	month (see 12.4.10)
-nen	......Nd	year
-shuu	......Nd	week
mai-	..(prefix)	every ~ (see 12.4.10)
maigetsu	.......N	every month

mainen	.......N	every year	
maishuu	.......N	every week	
maiasa	.......N	every morning	
maiban	.......N	every night	
Yooroppa	.......N	Europe	
tanoshii	.......A	is pleasant	

12.6 HIRAGANA PRACTICE

12.6.1 Recognize the difference in each of the following pairs:

いち [ichi] ……いっち [itchi]   もと [moto] ……もっと [motto]

かた [kata] ……かった [katta]   きと [kito] ……きっと [kitto]

また [mata] ……まった [matta]   そと [soto] ……そっと [sotto]

まて [mate] ……まって [matte]   さき [saki] ……さっき [sakki]

12.6.2 Read and write the following:

さっぽろ　ざっし　あつかった　あさって　あっち　どっち

いっしょに　りっぱ　いそがしかったです。　ちょっと　まってください。

12.7 DRILLS

12.7.1 Pronunciation Drill

raigetsu　　rainen　　raishuu　　ryokoo shimasu　　subarashii　　rusu

kuruma　　kara　　Ryooan'ji　　kirei　　Buraun

12.7.2 Pattern Drill

1. Mata Kyooto ken'butsu o shitai n desu ka?

2. Iie, shitaku arimasen.

3. Iie, shitaku nai n desu.

4. Den'sha de ikitakatta n desu ka?

5. Iie, den'sha de wa ikitaku arimasen deshita.

6. Iie, den'sha de wa ikitaku nakatta n desu.

7. Asakusa kara den'sha de ikimashita.

8. Mizuumi e mo ikimashita ka?

9. Iie, mizuumi e wa ikimasen deshita.

12.7.3 Transformation Drill

1. Ashita dekake*masu*.　　⟶　Ashita dekake*tai desu*.

2. Kyooto o ken'butsu shimasu.　　⟶　Kyooto o ken'butsu shitai desu.

3. Kon'do gaikoku e ryokoo shimasu.　　⟶　Kon'do gaikoku e ryokoo shitai desu.

4. Toshokan de hon o karimasu.　　⟶　Toshokan de hon o karitai desu.

5. Natsu kuni e kaerimasu.   ⟶   Natsu kuni e kaeritai desu.

6. Nihon'go de iimasu.   ⟶   Nihon'go de iitai desu.

7. Kissaten e hairimasu.   ⟶   Kissaten e hairitai desu.

8. Kon'ban eiga o mimasu.   ⟶   Kon'ban eiga o mitai desu.

9. Mata Kyooto e ikimasu.   ⟶   Mata Kyooto e ikitai desu.

10. Umi ka puuru de oyogimasu.   ⟶   Umi ka puuru de oyogitai desu.

12.7.4 Response Drill (negative)

1. Sugu dekake*tai desu* ka?   . . . .*Iie,* dekake*taku arimasen.*

2. Furan'sugo o naraitai desu ka?   . . . .Iie, naraitaku arimasen.

3. Mainichi terebi o mitai desu ka?   . . . .Iie, mitaku arimasen.

4. Ima on'gaku o kikitai desu ka?   . . . .Iie, kikitaku arimasen.

5. Kuruma o karitai desu ka?   . . . .Iie, karitaku arimasen.

6. Hikooki de ikitai desu ka?   . . . .Iie, ikitaku arimasen.

7. Natsu ryokoo shitai desu ka?   . . . .Iie, shitaku arimasen.

8. Kon'ban resutoran de shokuji o shitai desu ka?   . . . .Iie, shitaku arimasen.

12.7.5 Transformation Drill

1. *Ashita* ryokoo shi*tai* n desu.
   kinoo   ⟶   Kinoo ryokoo shi*takatta* n desu.

2. Kyoo niwa o mitai n desu.
   ototoi   ⟶   Ototoi niwa o mitakatta n desu.

3. Raigetsu kuni e kaeritai n desu.
   sen'getsu   ⟶   Sen'getsu kuni e kaeritakatta n desu.

4. Kyoo tomodachi o shookai shitai n desu.
   kinoo   ⟶   Kinoo tomodachi o shookai shitakatta n desu.

5. Rainen daigaku e hairitai n desu.
   kyonen   ⟶   Kyonen daigaku e hairitakatta n desu.

6. Kotoshi hon o kakitai n desu.
   kyonen   ⟶   Kyonen hon o kakitakatta n desu.

7. Kon'getsu kuruma o kaitai n desu.
   sen'getsu   ⟶   Sen'getsu kuruma o kaitakatta n desu.

8. Raishuu Nikkoo e ikitai n desu.
   sen'shuu   ⟶   Sen'shuu Nikkoo e ikitakatta n desu.

12.7.6 Transformation Drill

1. Kinoo no hiru dekake*takatta n desu.*   ⟶   Kinoo no hiru dekake*taku arimasen deshita.*

2. Hikooki de ikitakatta n desu.   ⟶   Hikooki de ikitaku arimasen deshita.

3. Kinoo wa oyogitakatta n desu.   ⟶   Kinoo wa oyogitaku arimasen deshita.

4. Ano eiga o mitakatta n desu.   ⟶   Ano eiga o mitaku arimasen deshita.

5. Biiru o nomitakatta n desu.   ⟶   Biiru o nomitaku arimasen deshita.

6. Sen'shuu ryokoo shitakatta n desu.   ⟶   Sen'shuu ryokoo shitaku arimasen deshita.

12.7.7 Transformation Drill

1. Sono zasshi wa yomi*taku arimasen.*   ⟶   Sono zasshi wa yomi*taku nai n desu.*

2. Mizuumi de oyogi*taku arimasen deshita.*   ⟶   Mizuumi de oyogi*taku nakatta n desu.*

3. Sugu uchi e kaeritaku arimasen.   ⟶   Sugu uchi e kaeritaku nai n desu.

4. Eigo de den'wa shitaku arimasen deshita.   ⟶   Eigo de den'wa shitaku nakatta n desu.

5. Amari tabetaku arimasen.   ⟶   Amari tabetaku nai n desu.

6. Basu de kaeritaku arimasen deshita.   ⟶   Basu de kaeritaku nakatta n desu.

12.7.8 Response Drill

1. Ashita ten'ki ga *ii* desu ka?   . . . . *Tabun yoku nai deshoo.*

2. Takushii wa yasui desu ka?   . . . . Tabun yasuku nai deshoo.

3. Ryokoo wa tanoshikatta desu ka?   . . . . Tabun tanoshiku nakatta deshoo.

4. Ashita atsui desu ka?   . . . . Tabun atsuku nai deshoo.

5. Tsugoo ga warui desu ka?   . . . . Tabun waruku nai deshoo.

6. Oniisan wa sen'shuu isogashikatta desu ka?   . . . . Tabun isogashiku nakatta deshoo.

7. Nikkoo wa suzushikatta desu ka?   . . . . Tabun suzushiku nakatta deshoo.

8. Nikkoo wa koko kara chikai desu ka?   . . . . Tabun chikaku nai deshoo.

12.7.9 Expansion and Substitution Drill

1. Ten'ki ga yoku arimasen deshita.   . . . . Ten'ki ga yoku arimasen deshita.

    kinoo   . . . . *Kinoo* ten'ki ga yoku arimasen deshita.

    kinoo no asa   . . . . Kinoo no asa ten'ki ga yoku arimasen deshita.

    kinoo no asa wa   . . . . Kinoo no asa wa ten'ki ga yoku arimasen deshita.

    kinoo no asa mo   . . . . Kinoo no asa mo ten'ki ga yoku arimasen deshita.

2. Nihon'go o ben'kyoo shitai n desu.   . . . . Nihon'go o ben'kyoo shitai n desu.

    kon'ban   . . . . Kon'ban nihon'go o ben'kyoo shitai n desu.

| kon'ban wa | . . . . Kon'ban wa nihon'go o ben'kyoo shitai n desu. |
| kon'ban mo | . . . . Kon'ban mo nihon'go o ben'kyoo shitai n desu. |

3. Gaikoku e ryokoo shimasu.   . . . . Gaikoku e ryokoo shimasu.

raigetsu	. . . . Raigetsu gaikoku e ryokoo shimasu.
raigetsu wa	. . . . Raigetsu wa gaikoku e ryokoo shimasu.
raigetsu mo	. . . . Raigetsu mo gaikoku e ryokoo shimasu.

4. Uchi ni itai desu.   . . . . Uchi ni itai desu.

ashita no ban	. . . . Ashita no ban uchi ni itai desu.
ashita no ban wa	. . . . Ashita no ban wa uchi ni itai desu.
ashita no ban mo	. . . . Ashita no ban mo uchi ni itai desu.

5. Otoosan wa rusu deshita ne.   . . . . Otoosan wa rusu deshita ne.

kesa	. . . . Kesa otoosan wa rusu deshita ne.
kesa wa	. . . . Kesa wa otoosan wa rusu deshita ne.
kesa mo	. . . . Kesa mo otoosan wa rusu deshita ne.

12.7.10 Substitution Drill

Kuruma de *ikimasu ka?*

1. den'sha	. . . . Den'sha de ikimasu ka?
2. kaerimasu ka?	. . . . Den'sha de kaerimasu ka?
3. nan	. . . . Nan de kaerimasu ka?
4. hanashimasu ka?	. . . . Nan de hanashimasu ka?
5. den'wa	. . . . Den'wa de hanashimasu ka?
6. iimashita ka?	. . . . Den'wa de iimashita ka?
7. nanigo	. . . . Nanigo de iimashita ka?
8. kakitai desu ka?	. . . . Nanigo de kakitai desu ka?
9. nihon'go	. . . . Nihon'go de kakitai desu ka?
10. en'pitsu	. . . . En'pitsu de kakitai desu ka?
11. nan	. . . . Nan de kakitai desu ka?
12. ryokoo shimashita ka?	. . . . Nan de ryokoo shimashita ka?
13. fune	. . . . Fune de ryokoo shimashita ka?
14. hikooki	. . . . Hikooki de ryokoo shimashita ka?
15. nan	. . . . Nan de ryokoo shimashita ka?

16. tabemasu ka? . . . . Nan de tabemasu ka?

17. hashi . . . . Hashi de tabemasu ka?

18. fooku . . . . Fooku de tabemasu ka?

12.7.11 Expansion Drill

1. Imashita. . . . . Imashita.

   oozei . . . . Oozei imashita.

   hito ga . . . . Hito ga oozei imashita.

   niwa ni . . . . Niwa ni hito ga oozei imashita.

2. Nomimasu. . . . . Nomimasu.

   takusan . . . . Takusan nomimasu.

   koohii o . . . . Koohii o takusan nomimasu.

   mainichi . . . . Mainichi koohii o takusan nomimasu.

3. Ben'kyoo shimashita. . . . . Ben'kyoo shimashita.

   sukoshi . . . . Sukoshi ben'kyoo shimashita.

   nihon'go o . . . . Nihon'go o sukoshi ben'kyoo shimashita.

   kinoo no ban . . . . Kinoo no ban nihon'go o sukoshi ben'kyoo shimashita.

4. Tanoshikatta desu. . . . . Tanoshikatta desu.

   ryokoo wa . . . . Ryokoo wa tanoshikatta desu.

   ame ga furimashita kedo . . . . Ame ga furimashita kedo, ryokoo wa tanoshikatta desu.

5. Ikimashita. . . . . Ikimashita.

   den'sha de . . . . Den'sha de ikimashita.

   takushii de ikitakatta n desu kedo . . . . Takushii de ikitakatta n desu kedo, den'sha de ikimashita.

6. Hanashimasu ka? . . . . Hanashimasu ka?

   nihon'go de . . . . Nihon'go de hanashimasu ka?

   uchi de mo . . . . Uchi de mo nihon'go de hanashimasu ka?

   anata wa . . . . Anata wa uchi de mo nihon'go de hanashimasu ka?

7. Ryokoo shimashita. . . . . Ryokoo shimashita.

   san'do . . . . San'do ryokoo shimashita.

   Hokkaidoo e . . . . Hokkaidoo e san'do ryokoo shimashita.

   kotoshi . . . . Kotoshi Hokkaidoo e san'do ryokoo shimashita.

176

8. Ken'butsu shimashita ka? . . . . Ken'butsu shimashita ka?

nan'do . . . . Nan'do ken'butsu shimashita ka?

Nikkoo wa . . . . Nikkoo wa nan'do ken'butsu shimashita ka?

12.7.12 Transformation Drill (multiple Relationals)

1. Nihon *de* ben'kyoo shimashita. ⟶ Nihon *de mo* ben'kyoo shimashita.

2. Sono hen ni otearai ga arimasu. ⟶ Sono hen ni mo otearai ga arimasu.

3. Tegami wa Doitsu kara kimashita. ⟶ Tegami wa Doitsu kara mo kimashita.

4. Gin'za de kaimono shimashoo. ⟶ Gin'za de mo kaimono shimashoo.

5. Kuruma de ryokoo shitai desu. ⟶ Kuruma de mo ryokoo shitai desu.

6. Kyooto e ryokoo shimashita. ⟶ Kyooto e mo ryokoo shimashita.

7. Toshokan de hon o karimasu. ⟶ Toshokan de mo hon o karimasu.

8. Asoko ni inu ga imasu yo. ⟶ Asoko ni mo inu ga imasu yo.

12.7.13 Response Drill (multiple Relationals)

1. Kinoo gakkoo *e* ikimashita ka? . . . . Iie, gakkoo e wa ikimasen deshita.

2. Uchi de rekoodo o kikimashita ka? . . . . Iie, uchi de wa kikimasen deshita.

3. Jimusho ni gakusei ga imashita ka? . . . . Iie, jimusho ni wa imasen deshita.

4. Kuni kara tegami ga kimashita ka? . . . . Iie, kuni kara wa kimasen deshita.

5. Den'sha de kimashita ka? . . . . Iie, den'sha de wa kimasen deshita.

6. Hon'ya ni shin'bun ga arimasu ka? . . . . Iie, hon'ya ni wa arimasen.

7. Itsumo hashi de tabemasu ka? . . . . Iie, hashi de wa tabemasen.

8. Furuhon'ya de sagashimashita ka? . . . . Iie, furuhon'ya de wa sagashimasen deshita.

12.7.14 Expansion Drill (*wa . . . wa* contrast)

1. Ikimasu.
   umi e, yama e . . . . Umi e *wa* ikimasu ga, yama e *wa* ikimasen.

2. Koohii o nomimasu.
   asa, ban . . . . Asa wa koohii o nomimasu ga, ban wa nomimasen.

3. Ryokoo shitai desu.
   kuruma de, basu de . . . . Kuruma de wa ryokoo shitai desu ga, basu de wa ryokoo shitaku arimasen.

4. Tanoshikatta desu.
   mae, ima . . . . Mae wa tanoshikatta desu ga, ima wa tanoshiku arimasen.

5. Tegami ga kimashita.
   tomodachi kara, kazoku kara

   .... Tomodachi kara wa tegami ga kimashita ga, kazoku kara wa kimasen deshita.

6. Rusu deshita.
   kesa, kon'ban

   .... Kesa wa rusu deshita ga, kon'ban wa rusu ja arimasen.

7. Ryokoo shimashita.
   kotoshi, kyonen

   .... Kotoshi wa ryokoo shimashita ga, kyonen wa ryokoo shimasen deshita.

12.8 EXERCISES

12.8.1 Insert a Relational in each blank and give an English equivalent for each sentence:

1. Mae (   ) ikitakatta n desu (   ), ima (   ) ikitaku nai n desu.

2. Amerika (   ) (   ) kissaten ga arimasu ka?

3. Sumisu san wa Igirisu kara hikooki (   ) kimashita.

4. Goshujin wa itsu gaikoku (   ) kaerimasu ka?

5. Sen'getsu Hokkaidoo (   ) ryokoo shimashita. Sore kara, Kyooto (   ) (   ) ikimashita.

6. Itsumo hashi (   ) tabemasu ka, fooku (   ) tabemasu ka?

7. Kinoo (   ) yoru dekakemashita ka?

8. Kesa den'wa shitakatta n desu (   ), tsugoo (   ) warukatta n desu.

12.8.2 Ask appropriate questions that fit the following answers:

1. Kesa dekakemashita.

2. Takushii de kaeritai n desu.

3. Iie, yoku nai deshoo.

4. Iie, yomitaku arimasen deshita.

5. Raishuu shitai desu.

6. Pen ka en'pitsu de kakimashoo.

7. Iie, atsuku nakatta desu.

12.8.3 Transform the following into the *deshoo* form:

1. Ishi no niwa wa subarashii desu.

2. Haha wa amari isogashiku arimasen.

3. Biiru o sukoshi nomitai n desu.

4. Hirugohan wa tabetaku arimasen.

5. Kono hon wa muzukashiku arimasen deshita.

12.8.4 Carry on the following dialog in Japanese:

—Were you home yesterday?

—No, I was not home. I came back from Kyōto yesterday evening.

—Oh, is that so? I suppose that the weather was not very good there.

—It was very cold. Besides, it rained.

—That was too bad. But, did you visit Ryōanji Temple, too?

—No, I did not visit Ryōanji Temple. Therefore, I would like to go to Kyōto again.

12.8.5 Answer the following questions in Japanese:

1. Anata wa ryokoo ga suki deshoo?

2. Doko e ryokoo shitai desu ka?

3. Soko e wa nan de ikitai desu ka?

4. Chuugoku e mo ikitai desu ka?

5. Kotoshi ka kyonen doko e ryokoo shimashita ka?

LESSON 13
GIVING

13.1   USEFUL EXPRESSIONS

Ocha o doozo.   "Please have some tea."

Kudamono wa ikaga desu ka/   "How about some fruit?" "Would you like some fruit?"

Doozo okamainaku.₁   "Please do not go to any trouble." "Don't bother."

Chotto matte.₇   "Just a moment." "Hold on." This is the casual and less polite equivalent of *Chotto matte kudasai*.

Ee, itadakimasu.₁   "Yes, thank you." This expression is used to accept an offer of any kind. *Ee* (or *hai*) may be omitted.

Iie, kekkoo desu.₁   "No, thank you." This expression is used to decline an offer of any kind.

13.2   DIALOG

Kazuo's
Mother: Ocha o doozo. Kudamono mo ikaga desu ka/

Ikuo: Doozo okamainaku. Kazuo kun wa mada desu ka/

Mother: Ee, gomen nasai ne. Kazuo wa tomodachi kara₁ eiga no kippu o moraimashita₁.
            Sore de, asa otoototachi to₂ issho ni dekakemashita. Demo, moo sugu kaerimasu.

Ikuo: Soo desu ka. Dewa, moo₃ sukoshi machimasu.

Mother: Ikuo san, gokyoodai wa/

Ikuo: San'nin₄ imasu. Ani to ane to imooto ga hitori₄ zutsu₅ imasu.

Mother: Oniisan ya oneesan wa ikutsu₆ desu ka/

Ikuo: Nijuu yon'sai₄ to hatachi₄ desu.

Mother: Soo desu ka. Chotto matte ne₇ / . . . . Kono arubamu, kirei deshoo. Furan'su no
            tomodachi ga san'satsu₄ kuremashita₈. Kazuo ni₈ issatsu yarimashita₈. Anata ni mo
            agemashoo₈,₉.

Ikuo: Doomo sumimasen.

Mother: Ocha o moo ippai ikaga desu ka/

Ikuo: Hai, itadakimasu. Sumimasen ga, ima nan'ji₄ deshoo ka₁₀.

Mother: Yoji desu kedo. Kazuo, osoi desu nee.

13.3 PATTERN SENTENCES

13.3.1

PM		→	P	
N	R		V	
Tomodachi	KARA[1]		MORAImashita.[1]	

13.3.2

PM		→	P	
N	R		V	
Anata	NI[8]		AGEmashoo.[8]	

13.3.3

PM		→	P	
N	R		V	
Watashi	NI[8]		KUREmashita.[8]	

13.3.4

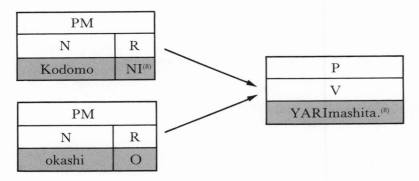

PM	
N	R
Kodomo	NI[8]

PM	
N	R
okashi	O

P
V
YARImashita.[8]

13.3.5

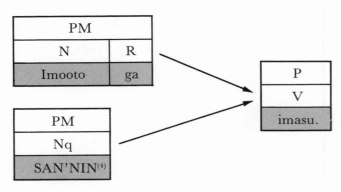

PM	
N	R
Imooto	ga

PM
Nq
SAN'NIN[4]

P
V
imasu.

13.4 NOTES

13.4.1 *Moraimasu,* which means "get or receive (something from someone)" or "is given," functions as a "receiving" Verb. The person who receives is followed by the Relational *wa* or *ga,* the thing given is followed by *o,* and the person who gives by the Relational *kara* "from" or *ni.* However, try to use *kara* at this stage.

Noun (recipient) $\begin{Bmatrix} wa \\ (ga) \end{Bmatrix}$ **+ Noun (giver) +** *kara* **+ Noun (object)** *o* **+** *moraimasu*

Kinoo watashi wa tomodachi kara eiga no kippu o moraimashita.	"I got movie tickets from a friend of mine yesterday."
Dare kara moraimashita ka?	"From whom did [you] get [it]?"
Nani o moraitai n desu ka?	"What do [you] want to be given?"
Jimusho de kami to en'pitsu o moraimashoo.	"Let's get (a sheet of) paper and a pencil at the office."
Boku wa itsumo chichi kara okane o moraimasu.	"I always get money from my father."

Itadakimasu, as indicated in the Useful Expressions section, is used to accept an offer of any kind. The counterparts of the acceptance are *Kekkoo desu, Doozo okamainaku, Iie, ii n desu* "No, thank you." *Okotoba ni amaete itadakimasu* "May I follow your word and accept your offer?" is a more elaborate expression, and *Doozo goen'ryonaku* suggests to the guest to feel at home. *Itadakimasu* may be used in lieu of *moraimasu* to the speaker's superior or even to an equal in order to show politeness. *Moraimasu,* however, is still used when the giver and the receiver are members of the same group, but when the listener and the receiver are members of different groups.

13.4.2 *To* in *otoototachi to* is a Relational meaning "with (younger brothers)." This Relational usually occurs before a Verb and after either a personal name or a Noun that represents an animate object. Occasionally *issho ni* "together" is used with *to.*

Itoo san to hanashimashita.	"[I] talked with Mr. Itō."
Watashi to issho ni ikimashoo.	"Let's go together [with me]."
Ishii san wa donata to imasu ka?	"With whom is Mr. Ishii?"

The Relational *wa* or *mo* may occur after *to,* forming multiple Relationals. See Note 12.4.5.

Anata to wa hanashitaku arimasen.	"[I] don't want to talk with you."
Ishii san to mo ikimashita.	"[I] went [there] with Mr. Ishii, too."

13.4.3 *Moo* used immediately before a number or a numeral usually means "more," as in "one more cup of tea" or "two more (volumes of) books." When *moo* means "already," the accent shifts from *moō* to *m̄oo.* See Note 9.4.11.

Moo issatsu yomimasen ka?	"Won't you read another (one more) volume (book, etc.)?"
Moo sukoshi machimashoo.	"Let's wait a little more."
Moo ichido shirabemashita.	"[I] checked [it] once more."

Tomodachi ga moo gonin kimasu.   "Five more friends [of mine] are coming."

Moo gonin kimashita.   "Five people have already come."

13.4.4 *San'nin* is the combination of the numeral *san* "three" and *-nin*, the counter for people. When you count things or people, there is usually an individual dependent Noun called a counter for each of them. The counter is selected according to the shape, classification, et cetera, of the item you count. The counter is attached to the numeral and formulates the "number," which is a Noun. The counters appearing in this lesson are as follows:

-mai . . . . the counter for thin and flat objects like paper, tickets, sliced things, dishes, et cetera. The numbers with *-mai* are formed regularly.

-nin . . . . the counter for people. Note that the numbers for people are formed irregularly. *Hitori* and *futari* are native numbers. (see Note 13.4.6)

-sai . . . . the counter for age. *Hatachi* is used for "twenty years old."

-satsu . . . . the counter for books, magazines, notebooks, et cetera.

-ji   . . . . the counter indicating "o'clock."

-peeji . . . . the counter meaning "page."

Numeral \ Counter		-mai	-nin	-sai	-satsu	-ji	-peeji
1	ichi		hitori	issai	issatsu		ippeeji
2	ni		futari				
3	san						
4	yon yo-			yo-	yon-	yon-	yo-	yon-
5	go						
6	roku						
7	shichi nana						
8	hachi			hassai hachisai	hassatsu hachisatsu		happeeji hachipeeji
9	kyuu ku			kyuu-	kyuu-	ku-	kyuu-
10	juu			jissai jussai	jissatsu jussatsu		jippeeji juppeeji
(1) how many? or (2) what?	nan-	(1)	(1)	(1)	(1)	(2)	(1) (2)

(Blank columns indicate regular combinations of numerals and counters.)

There are two types of counters: (1) tells "how many," number of objects, and (2) tells a specific point or place from among those in a numerical sequence. Therefore, *nan-* before a counter of the first group means "how many," and *nan-* before a counter of the second group means "what."

(1)	nan'mai	"how many (sheets of paper, etc.)?"
	nan'nin	"how many (people)?"
	nan'sai	"how many years old?"
	nan'satsu	"how many (volumes)?"
(2)	nan'ji	"what time?"
(1) and (2)	nan'peeji	"how many pages?" "what page?"

As you see in the above, the counters with the initials /s/, /h/, /k/, or /t/ become *ss, pp, kk,* or *tt,* respectively after ONE and TEN. /h/ and /k/ become *pp* and *kk,* respectively after SIX and sometimes after EIGHT. /s/, /h/, and /k/ may become *z, b,* and *g,* respectively after THREE and *nan.*

The numbers are quantity Nouns that may be used without any Relational following them. Usually a quantity Noun occurs immediately before the Predicate, between the Predicate Modifier with which the quantity is concerned and the Predicate.

$$\text{Noun} + \begin{Bmatrix} o \\ ga \\ wa \end{Bmatrix} + \text{Predicate} \longrightarrow \text{Noun} + \begin{Bmatrix} o \\ ga \\ wa \end{Bmatrix} + \begin{Bmatrix} \textbf{number} \\ \textbf{quantity Noun} \end{Bmatrix} + \text{Predicate}$$

Kippu o nan'mai kaimashita ka?	"How many tickets did [you] buy?"
San'mai kaimashita.	"[I] bought three (tickets)."
Gakusei wa nan'nin imasu ka?	"How many students are there?"
Gonin imasu.	"There are five (students)."
Hon ga nan'satsu arimasu ka?	"How many books are there?"
Issatsu arimasu.	"There is one (book)."
Ima nan'ji desu ka?	"What time is it now?"
Yoji desu. Mada hayai desu.	"It is four o'clock. It is still early."
Ima nan'sai desu ka?	"How old are [you] now?"
Juuhassai desu.	"[I] am eighteen."

13.4.5 *-Zutsu* is a dependent Noun that is often used after a number or a numeral. It means "each" or "respectively."

Ani to ane ga hitori zutsu imasu.	"[I] have one older brother and one older sister."
Ehon to zasshi o nisatsu zutsu kaimashita.	"[I] bought two picture books and two magazines (respectively)."
Kami o ichimai zutsu agemasu.	"[I] will give one sheet of paper to each of [you]."

13.4.6 *Ikutsu* is an interrogative Noun meaning "how many?" In addition to the numbers introduced before, there are native numbers, as shown below, which are limited to one through ten. Eleven and above follow the ordinary numerals listed in Note 12.4.2.

1	hitotsu	2	futatsu	3	mittsu	4	yottsu	5	itsutsu
6	muttsu	7	nanatsu	8	yattsu	9	kokonotsu	10	too

Ikutsu is the interrogative counterpart of the native numbers. These native numbers occur without any counter following them, and are used to count age (as well as a numeral plus *-sai*), or things like apples, pears, pebbles, coins, balls, candy, et cetera, that have no particular counters.

The usage of the native numbers is the same as that of the numbers.

Otootosan wa ima ikutsu desu ka?	"How old is [your] younger brother?"
Yottsu desu.	"[He] is four years old."
Okashi o hitotsu tabemashita.	"[I] ate a piece of candy."
Pan o futatsu moraimashoo.	"[I] think [I] will have two loaves of bread."

13.4.7 *Chotto matte ne* is an abbreviation of *Chotto matte kudasai ne*. Since Kazuo's mother is an elder and Ikuo is a junior, this omission is acceptable. Never use this expression to any elder or superior.

13.4.8 *Kuremashita* is a Verb meaning "(someone) gave (something) to me or us." The Japanese are rather sensitive in the use of words expressing "giving" or "receiving." Different words should be used according to "who-gives-whom" and "who-gets-from-whom." The differences in these usages come from differences in social status or age, or the degree of respect or politeness that exists between one person who gives and the other who receives.

Agemasu, yarimasu, kuremasu, all mean "give." There are, however, clear distinctions in the usage of these "giving" Verbs. The following are factors in determining which expressions should be used:

1) giver and receiver relationship

2) speaker and listener relationship

3) in-group and out-group relationship

4) hierarchical relationship

5) presence or absence of a person before the speaker.

The symbols below are used in the following charts:

①= speaker Ⓖ = giver ⟶ = given to an equal

②= listener (second person) Ⓡ = receiver ⟋ = given to a superior

③= the third party ⟍ = given to an inferior

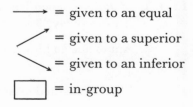 = in-group

------- ⟋ ⟍ = comparative status (equal, lower to higher, higher to lower)

(A)   *a = agemasu*   *y = yarimasu*   *s = sashiagemasu**

(B)   *k = kuremasu*   *ks = kudasaimasu**

*These two Verbs are explained in this Note, but will be drilled in Volume 2, Lesson 1.

(A) *Agemasu, Sashiagemasu,* **and** *Yarimasu*

(a) Given to a third party:

   (1)   None is in-group.

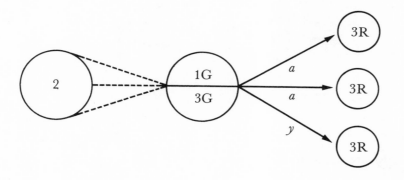

   (2)   ②and ③Ⓡ are in-group.

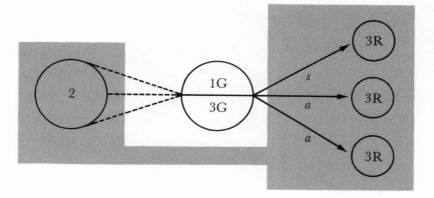

   (3)   ②and Ⓖ are in-group.

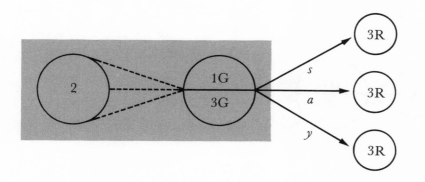

186

(4) (G) and (3R) are in-group.

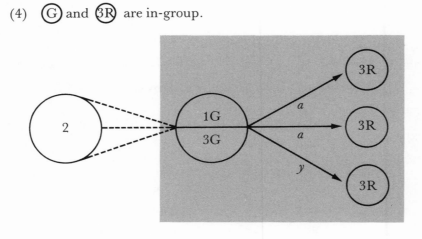

(5) (G), (2) and (3R) are in-group.

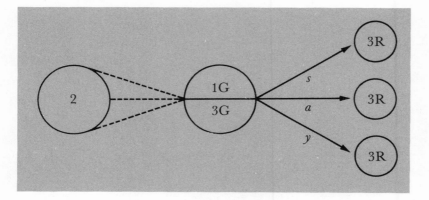

(b) Given to the listener:

   (1) (G) and (2R) are not in-group.

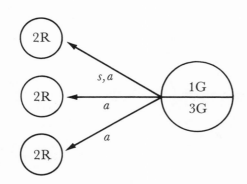

(2) Ⓖ and ②Ⓡ are in-group.

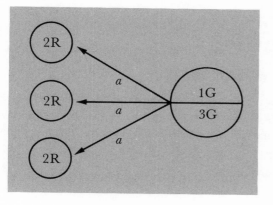

In conclusion, *agemasu* should normally be used with the following exceptions. Assuming that Ⓛ and Ⓖ are equal in status:

1) *Yarimasu* is used when the recipient is the third party, is lower in status than the giver, and is either an out-group of the listener or is an in-group of both giver and listener (a1, a3, a4, and a5).

2) *Sashiagemasu* is used when the recipient is the third party, is higher in status than the giver, and, at the same time, the listener is in an in-group relationship with ①, or ③, or both ① and ③ (a2, a3, a5).

3) Either *sashiagemasu* or *agemasu* is used when the recipient-listener is a superior and is not the giver's in-group (b1).

Agemasu is used when the speaker or someone other than the speaker gives to a third person unless the recipient is a member of the giver's in-group (persons he is closely associated with, such as family, peer group, etc.) or someone who is definitely inferior in age, social status, et cetera.

Watakushi wa tomodachi ni hon o agemashita.   "I gave a book to a friend of mine."

Watakushi wa on'na no hito ni hon o agemashita.   "I gave a book to a lady."

Chichi ga Yamamoto san ni hon o agemashita.   "My father gave a book to Mr. Yamamoto."

Ishii sen'sei wa okusan ni hon o agemashita.   "Mr. Ishii gave a book to his wife."

Even when the recipient is inferior to the giver in age, social status, et cetera, if he (the recipient) is a member of the listener's in-group and the listener is not inferior to the speaker, *agemasu* is used.

Watakushi wa Ishii sen'sei no okosan ni hon o agemasu.   "I will give a book to Mr. Ishii's child."

Ano gakusei wa Watanabe san no otootosan ni hon o agemasu.   "That student is going to give a book to Mr. Watanabe's younger brother."

Yarimasu is used only when the recipient is a younger member of the giver's in-group, or is definitely inferior in age, social status, et cetera to the giver. *Yarimasu* is also used when the recipient is an animal.

Watakushi wa kodomo ni purezen'to o yarimashita.	"I gave a present to my child."
Tanaka san wa inu ni gohan o yarimashita.	"Mr. Tanaka gave food to the dog."
Chichi wa imooto ni okashi o yarimashita.	"My father gave candy to my younger sister."

(B) *Kuremasu* and *Kudasaimasu*

As to *kuremasu* and *kudasaimasu,* the latter is used whenever the giver is a superior, except when the giver and the receiver are the members of the same group but the listener and receiver are not members of the same group. For all other cases, *kuremasu* is used. The following charts illustrate the use of these two "giving" Verbs.

(a)   From out-group:

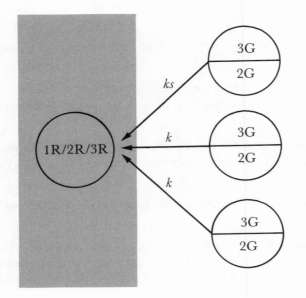

(b)   From in-group:

(1)

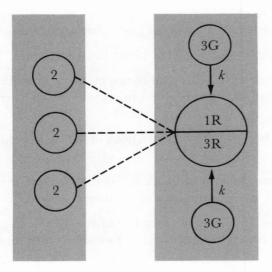

(2)

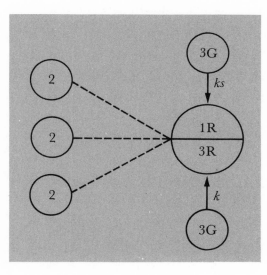

(3)

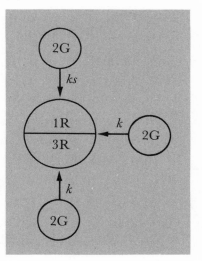

Tomodachi ga watakushi ni hon o kuremashita.	"A friend of mine gave me a book."
Tomodachi ga kanai ni hon o kuremashita.	"A friend of mine gave my wife a book."
Haha wa watashitachi ni hon o kuremashita.	"My mother gave us a book."
Kodomo ga purezen'to o kuremashita.	"My child gave me a present."

The situation of this lesson's dialog exemplifies the relation factors involved in word choice connected with giving and receiving. In the first place the relationship among the three participants may be summarized as follows: Kazuo's mother is obviously superior to her son, Kazuo. Ikuo demonstrates his equality in relation to Kazuo by referring to him as *Kazuo kun;* by implication, then, the mother is also superior to Ikuo. The mother's use of *Ikuo san* when addressing him shows that Ikuo is an outsider and the mother is a female, therefore the mother uses a form indicating distance or out-groupness.

Two groups are involved in these relationships. On the one hand, the family group, on the other, the friend group, and this situation may be illustrated in the following way:

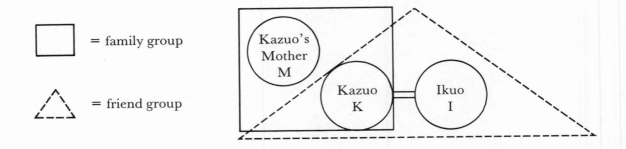

The giving and receiving involved in this dialog presents an even more complex pattern of relationships, as the summary below shows. Kazuo has received movie tickets as a gift from a friend. Kazuo's mother refers to this gift with the word *moraimashita,* which indicates that the giver, who is Kazuo's friend, is more or less Kazuo's peer. Should the giver be Kazuo's superior and be present, then the mother would use a more polite version such as *itadakimashita.*

On the other hand, the mother uses the term *yarimasu* in referring to giving the album to her son, a term which downgrades the receiver, but which is perfectly permissable in the context, since her son is part of her in-group and inferior to her and her friend.

These relationships may be illustrated as follows:

Key

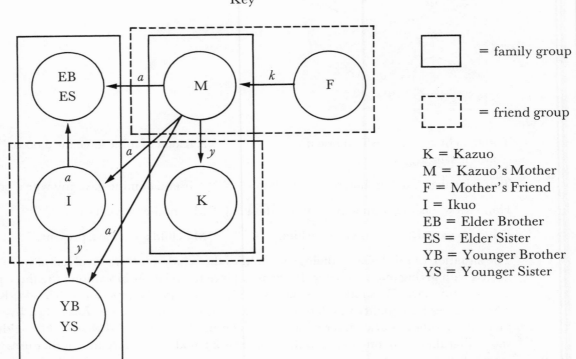

□ = family group

[⌐⌐] = friend group

K = Kazuo
M = Kazuo's Mother
F = Mother's Friend
I = Ikuo
EB = Elder Brother
ES = Elder Sister
YB = Younger Brother
YS = Younger Sister

Ni in *anata ni mo issatsu* is a Relational meaning that the preceding word is the recipient of an action. It is often expressed in English equivalents as the indirect object "to (someone)." In the pattern of "giving," the giver is followed by *ga* or *wa,* the thing given is followed by *o,* and the recipient by *ni.* Note that the giver and the recipient are normally animate in Japanese.

$$\textbf{giver} + \left\{ \begin{array}{l} \textit{ga} \\ \textit{wa} \end{array} \right\} + \textbf{recipient} + \textit{ni} + \textbf{object} + \textit{o} + \left\{ \begin{array}{l} \textit{agemasu} \\ \textit{yarimasu} \\ \textit{kuremasu} \end{array} \right.$$

Anata ni kore o agemasu.   "[I] will give this to you."

Sen'sei ga boku ni kami o ichimai kuremashita.   "The teacher gave me a sheet of paper."

13.4.9   *Agemashoo* here means "I think I shall give." The OO form of a Verb, *-mashoo,* may be used as a suggestion or a proposal of performance which concerns only the speaker, and is in addition to the use introduced in Note 4.4.11 where a suggestion or a proposal of performance involves both the speaker and the hearer. In other words, the subject of a sentence of this connotation is always "I."

Okosan ni kore o agemashoo.   "I think I'll give this to [your] child."

Watashi ga ikimashoo.   "I think I'll go."

Kon'ban den'wa o shimashoo.   "I think I'll make a phone call tonight."

The dialog of this lesson reveals hierarchical groupism, speech level and style, in-group and out-group relationships, and the importance of family grouping.

Hierarchical groupism

In traditional Japanese society, the individual is defined by the whole, by his membership, position, and subsequent role within the whole. Often, the individual's relation to and within the whole is mediated by his membership in a smaller group or groups, further defining his social relations. The group, therefore, and not the individual, is the basic unit of social organization. Furthermore, groups within the social whole, and individuals within those groups, are organized hierarchically, and Japanese society exhibits a vertical rather than a horizontal pattern of institutionalized social relations.

     Group membership, then, influences the entire social situation, and its effect is greatly felt in language. One's social position, as defined by his or her relation to other members of the whole, will determine the very specific types of language he or she uses when addressing other members. Thus, much more than functional communication takes place in the use of Japanese language. The forms used by two individuals in conversation very subtly express the precise social relationship of the two individuals as viewed by the speaker. One addresses a member of the same group in one way, the member of another group in another way. These various forms are required by the social relationship, and the appropriateness of the language used has a direct relationship to the intensity with which one identifies with a specific group. One individual's relation to another is a function of the relative status of the individual within a group and/or the relative status of his or her group within the hierarchy of groups in society, in a strict pattern of superior-inferior relations and degree of closeness.

Speech level and style

Social status and situational roles are important in both Japanese and American culture. Among the differences, especially in relation to Japanese hierarchical groupism considerations are: (1)

that the Japanese language itself reflects a more definite, openly acknowledged emphasis on hierarchy and groupism, and (2) that it provides many and very specific ways of expressing objective and subjective evaluations.

The relative status of the speaker and listener, as well as the subject-person and the object-person, are constant considerations in determining styles and levels of speech. The speaker-listener relationship is revealed in speech style and the subject-object relationship is revealed in level of speech. The speaker's subjective evaluation determines the choice of words, syntax, and affixes, which in turn communicates the message to the listener. The forms and applications of styles and levels will be developed in more detail later.

The Japanese do not have one definite style and level applicable to all second and third persons for all occasions. Styles and levels must be differentiated according to occasions, situations, and conditions. Traditionally, students use a more polite style and level toward teachers, and women use a more polite style and level than men of equivalent social standing.

In-group and out-group

When talking to a second person, the Japanese usually must evaluate the relative relationship existing between him/herself and the second person as well as the relative relationship between a third person referred to and: (1) him/herself; (2) the second person; or (3) other third persons. Generally speaking, the Japanese use one type of speech level and style toward their superiors, and use another toward their inferiors. Sometimes a still different level and style of speech is used toward their peers. Furthermore, they differentiate their usage by classifying those involved in the speech (including third persons referred to) according to group. In a sense, whether an individual is a member of the in-group or whether he stands outside the speaker's group, makes a difference in speech forms used. Therefore, we call this differentiation hierarchical groupism.

The family and familiarism (familialism)

In Japan the family is an extremely important institution. It is the core of the traditional Japanese. Chie Nakane has pointed out that the basic scheme of Japanese social structure consists of an organizational principle modeled on the parent-child vertical relationship rather than the husband-wife horizontal relationship. Evidence of this can be found in various types of institutions in Japan, such as universities and religious communities. The extention of family relationships to other social, economic, political, and cultural groups and its influence on Japanese language usage is quite widespread. We might call this "familialism." Words such as *oyabun* (boss), *kobun* (follower), *oyagokoro* (feeling or love), evidence this tendency.

The traditional structure of the family is based on a central core formed by the mother-child relationship to which is attached the husband-wife or father-child relationship. This is evidenced in the roles of the mother/wife and father/husband respectively. The traditional role of the woman has been to serve as a housewife and mother. She must take care of the children and be able to provide her husband with a place of relaxation from his concerns in the outside world. The husband, on the other hand, has very few social obligations toward his family as the head of the household. He focuses his attention on his duties away from home.

The family is nonetheless a very cohesive and tightly woven unit. Family affairs are considered extremely private, limited to the family circle. This is very much involved with the concept of family honor and the family name, an important value in Japanese morality. If any one member of the family is dishonored, it is a reflection on all the other members. This collective responsibility is in effect to a much greater degree than in America: for example, a girl's marriage possibilities would become practically nullified if her brother were involved in some dishonorable conduct. There are many more examples of the importance of this, although in modern Japan one's family background no longer plays such an absolute role in one's future. There is currently a movement toward the nuclear family rather than the extended family structure.

13.4.10 *Ima nan'ji deshoo ka?* is less abrupt than *Ima nan'ji desu ka?* See Note 11.4.6.

    Soto wa atsui deshoo ka?   "Do you think that it is hot outside?"

13.4.11 When making a social call in Japan, it is customary to bring *omiyage* (a gift) for your hosts, especially if it is a first visit. Similarly, the host or hostess is expected to offer refreshments to the visitor—tea and some fruit, cookies or cakes such as *yookan, sen'bei,* and *mochigashi.* Offering soft drinks shows a more modern influence and, in general, an older host would not offer soft drinks to a guest; neither would a host offer soft drinks to an older guest. In present-day Japan, however, it is common among younger people.

13.5   VOCABULARY

Dialog

kudamono	.......N	fruit
ikaga	......Ni	how? (polite equivalent of *doo*)
Kazuo	.......N	boy's first name
kara	.......R	from (a person) (see 13.4.1)
kippu	.......N	ticket
moraimashita	V	got; received (TA form of *moraimasu←morau*) (see 13.4.1)
to	.......R	with (someone) (see 13.4.2)
moo sugu	....Adv.	any minute now
dewa	.......SI	well
moo	....Adv.	more (see 13.4.3)
machimasu	V	wait (normal form of *matsu*) (Different from the English verb "wait," *machimasu* is a transitive Verb; it follows the direct object Relational *o.*)
Ikuo	.......N	boy's first name
kyoodai	.......N	sister(s) and/or brother(s)
san'nin	.......N	three (people) (see 13.4.4)
hitori	.......N	one (person) (see 13.4.4)
-zutsu	......Nd	each (see 13.4.5)
ikutsu	......Ni	how old?; how many (objects)? (see 13.4.6)
nijuu yon'sai	.......N	twenty-four years old (see 13.4.4)
hatachi	.......N	twenty years old (see 13.4.4)
arubamu	.......N	album
san'satsu	.......N	three volumes (see 13.4.4)
kuremashita	V	(someone) gave (me; us) (TA form of *kuremasu←kureru*) (see 13.4.8)
ni	.......R	to (a person) (see 13.4.8)

issatsu	.......N	one volume (see 13.4.4)
yarimashita	V	gave (TA form of *yarimasu←yaru*) (see 13.4.8)
agemashoo	V	I think I will give (OO form of *agemasu←ageru*) (see 13.4.8 and 13.4.9)
ippai	.......N	a cup (of); a glass (of)
nan'ji	......Ni	what time? (see 13.4.4)
yoji	.......N	four o'clock (see 13.4.4)
osoi	.......A	is late

Notes

kami	.......N	paper
-nin	.....Nd	(counter for people) (see 13.4.4)
-mai	.....Nd	sheet (of) (counter for something thin and flat) (see 13.4.4)
-sai	.....Nd	year(s) (old) (see 13.4.4)
-satsu	.....Nd	volume (counter for books, etc.) (see 13.4.4)
-ji	.....Nd	o'clock (see 13.4.4)
-peeji	.....Nd	page (see 13.4.4)
nan-	......Ni	how many ∼ ?; what ∼ ? (see 13.4.4)
futari	.......N	two (persons)
nan'nin	.....Ni	how many (people)? (see 13.4.4)
hayai	.......A	is early
ehon	.......N	picture book
hitotsu	.......N	one (see 13.4.6)
futatsu	.......N	two
mittsu	.......N	three
yottsu	.......N	four
itsutsu	.......N	five
muttsu	.......N	six
nanatsu	.......N	seven
yattsu	.......N	eight
kokonotsu	.......N	nine
too	.......N	ten
okashi	.......N	candy; sweets; confections
purezen'to	.......N	present; gift
-mashoo	......Dv	OO form of *-masu* (see 13.4.9)

13.6 HIRAGANA PRACTICE

13.6.1 Recognize the difference in each of the following pairs:

お ……おう	[oo]	と ……とう	[too]
こ ……こう	[koo]	ど ……どう	[doo]
ご ……ごう	[goo]	の ……のう	[noo]
そ ……そう	[soo]	ほ ……ほう	[hoo]
ぞ ……ぞう	[zoo]	ぼ ……ぼう	[boo]
も ……もう	[moo]	じょ……じょう	[joo]
よ ……よう	[yoo]	ちょ……ちょう	[choo]
ろ ……ろう	[roo]	ひょ……ひょう	[hyoo]
きょ……きょう	[kyoo]	びょ……びょう	[byoo]
ぎょ……ぎょう	[gyoo]	みょ……みょう	[myoo]
しょ……しょう	[shoo]	りょ……りょう	[ryoo]

13.6.2 Read and write the following:

ひこうき　　とうきょう　　しょくどう　　せんしゅう　　ほっかいどう
べんきょうします　　おとうと　　いもうと　　いきましょうか
しゅうまつ　　どうして　　りょこうしました　　おとうさん
そうでしょう　　もういっぱい　　にっこう　　ちゅうごく

13.7 DRILLS

13.7.1 Pronunciation Drill

ikutsu　hitotsu　futatsu　mittsu　yottsu　itsutsu　muttsu　nanatsu
yattsu　kokonotsu　hitori zutsu　issatsu　nisatsu zutsu

13.7.2 Pattern Drill

1. Kazuo wa tomodachi kara kippu o moraimashita.
2. Tomodachi ga watashi ni arubamu o kuremashita.
3. Anata ni kore o agemashoo.
4. Watashi wa kodomo ni okashi o yarimashita.
5. Kyoodai wa nan'nin desu ka?
6. Imooto to otooto ga hitori zutsu imasu.
7. Oniisan wa ikutsu desu ka?
8. Kazuo wa otoototachi to issho ni dekakemashita.
9. Moo sukoshi machimasu.

13.7.3 Substitution Drill

Watashi wa *tomodachi* ni okashi o agemashita.

1. watashi, haha . . . . Watashi wa haha ni okashi o agemashita.

2. watashi, ani . . . . Watashi wa ani ni okashi o agemashita.

3. otooto, Ikuo san . . . . Otooto wa Ikuo san ni okashi o agemashita.

4. Suzuki san, Yamada san . . . . Suzuki san wa Yamada san ni okashi o agemashita.

5. chichi, Suzuki san . . . . Chichi wa Suzuki san ni okashi o agemashita.

6. watashitachi, sen'sei . . . . Watashitachi wa sen'sei ni okashi o agemashita.

7. ane, haha . . . . Ane wa haha ni okashi o agemashita.

13.7.4 Substitution Drill

Yamada san ga *watashi* ni okashi o kuremashita.

1. Yamada san, imooto . . . . Yamada san ga imooto ni okashi o kuremashita.

2. chichi, watashi . . . . Chichi ga watashi ni okashi o kuremashita.

3. tomodachi, boku . . . . Tomodachi ga boku ni okashi o kuremashita.

4. kanai, watashi . . . . Kanai ga watashi ni okashi o kuremashita.

5. Ikuo san, otoototachi . . . . Ikuo san ga otoototachi ni okashi o kuremashita.

6. Yamada san, watashi no kodomo . . . . Yamada san ga watashi no kodomo ni okashi o
kuremashita.

7. ane, watashi . . . . Ane ga watashi ni okashi o kuremashita.

13.7.5 Substitution Drill

Watashi wa *kodomo* ni okashi o yarimashita.

1. boku, otooto . . . . Boku wa otooto ni okashi o yarimashita.

2. watashi, inu . . . . Watashi wa inu ni okashi o yarimashita.

3. kodomo, inu . . . . Kodomo wa inu ni okashi o yarimashita.

4. ani, imooto . . . . Ani wa imooto ni okashi o yarimashita.

5. shujin, neko . . . . Shujin wa neko ni okashi o yarimashita.

6. haha, kodomotachi . . . . Haha wa kodomotachi ni okashi o yarimashita.

13.7.6 Transformation Drill

1. *Ishii san* wa *Koyama san* ni hon o *agemashita*. ⟶ *Koyama san* wa *Ishii san* kara hon o *moraimashita*.

2. Chichi wa watashi ni kippu o kuremashita. ⟶ Watashi wa chichi kara kippu o moraimashita.

3. Tanaka san wa okusan ni purezen'to o
agemasu. ⟶ Okusan wa Tanaka san kara purezen'to o
moraimasu.

4. Kodomo wa inu ni gohan o yarimashita. → Inu wa kodomo kara gohan o moraimashita.

5. Tomodachi ga watashi ni tegami o kuremashita. → Watashi wa tomodachi kara tegami o moraimashita.

6. Chichi wa imooto ni okane o yarimasu. → Imooto wa chichi kara okane o moraimasu.

7. Ishii san wa tomodachi ni kamera o agemashita. → Tomodachi wa Ishii san kara kamera o moraimashita.

8. Dare ga otooto ni ehon o kuremashita ka? → Otooto wa dare kara ehon o moraimashita ka?

13.7.7 Transformation Drill

1. Kazuo san wa *tomodachi kara* kippu o *moraimashita.* → *Tomodachi wa* Kazuo san ni kippu o *agemashita.*

2. Watashi wa *ani kara* jisho o *moraimashita.* → *Ani wa* watashi ni jisho o *kuremashita.*

3. Chichi wa haha kara koohii o moraimasu. → Haha wa chichi ni koohii o agemasu.

4. Boku wa ane kara kudamono o moraimashita. → Ane wa boku ni kudamono o kuremashita.

5. Tanaka san wa Minoru kun kara tegami o moraimasen. → Minoru kun wa Tanaka san ni tegami o agemasen.

6. Watashi no kodomo wa ano hito kara okashi o moraimashita. → Ano hito wa watashi no kodomo ni okashi o kuremashita.

7. Watakushi wa Suzuki san kara hon o moraimashita. → Suzuki san wa watakushi ni hon o kuremashita.

8. Inu wa kodomo kara gohan o moraimashita. → Kodomo wa inu ni gohan o yarimashita.

13.7.8 E-J Drill (numbers and numerals)

1.	three tickets	. . . . san'mai	11.	page four	. . . . yon'peeji
2.	four people	. . . . yonin	12.	six sheets of paper	. . . . rokumai
3.	five books	. . . . gosatsu	13.	nine o'clock	. . . . kuji
4.	eleven years old	. . . . juuissai	14.	a cup of tea	. . . . ippai
5.	nine pages	. . . . kyuupeeji	15.	how many magazines	. . . . nan'satsu
6.	eight pieces of candy	. . . . yattsu	16.	how old	. . . . ikutsu *or* nan'sai
7.	nine children	. . . . kunin *or* kyuunin	17.	how many people	. . . . nan'nin
8.	one student	. . . . hitori	18.	how many pieces of candy	. . . . ikutsu
9.	four o'clock	. . . . yoji	19.	what page or how many pages	. . . . nan'peeji
10.	five pieces of candy	. . . . itsutsu	20.	how many times	. . . . nan'do

13.7.9 Transformation Drill

1. Anata ni kore o *agemasu*.   ⟶   Anata ni kore o *agemashoo*.

2. Watashi ga hanashimasu.   ⟶   Watashi ga hanashimashoo.

3. Imooto ni yarimasu.   ⟶   Imooto ni yarimashoo.

4. Ashita no asa dekakemasu.   ⟶   Ashita no asa dekakemashoo.

5. Watashi wa koohii o nomimasu.   ⟶   Watashi wa koohii o nomimashoo.

6. Watakushitachi ga koko ni imasu.   ⟶   Watakushitachi ga koko ni imashoo.

7. Nakamura san kara moraimasu.   ⟶   Nakamura san kara moraimashoo.

8. Kippu o san'mai agemasu.   ⟶   Kippu o san'mai agemashoo.

13.7.10 Expansion Drill

1. Agetai desu.   . . . . Agetai desu.

    takusan   . . . . Takusan agetai desu.

    okashi o   . . . . Okashi o takusan agetai desu.

    ano kodomo ni   . . . . Ano kodomo ni okashi o takusan agetai desu.

2. Arimasu.   . . . . Arimasu.

    yon'mai   . . . . Yon'mai arimasu.

    eiga no kippu ga   . . . . Eiga no kippu ga yon'mai arimasu.

    koko ni   . . . . Koko ni eiga no kippu ga yon'mai arimasu.

3. Imasu.   . . . . Imasu.

    hachinin   . . . . Hachinin imasu.

    kodomotachi ga   . . . . Kodomotachi ga hachinin imasu.

    niwa ni   . . . . Niwa ni kodomotachi ga hachinin imasu.

4. Moraitai desu.   . . . . Moraitai desu.

    futatsu ka mittsu   . . . . Futatsu ka mittsu moraitai desu.

    kudamono o   . . . . Kudamono o futatsu ka mittsu moraitai desu.

5. Agemashoo.   . . . . Agemashoo.

    hitotsu zutsu   . . . . Hitotsu zutsu agemashoo.

    okashi o   . . . . Okashi o hitotsu zutsu agemashoo.

    minasan ni   . . . . Minasan ni okashi o hitotsu zutsu agemashoo.

6. Kuremasu.   . . . . Kuremasu.

    nisatsu   . . . . Nisatsu kuremasu.

    ehon o   . . . . Ehon o nisatsu kuremasu.

    ane ga   . . . . Ane ga ehon o nisatsu kuremasu.

7. Yomimashita ka?   . . . .Yomimashita ka?

   nan'peeji   . . . .Nan'peeji yomimashita ka?

   sono hon wa   . . . .Sono hon wa nan'peeji yomimashita ka?

8. Nomitakatta n desu.   . . . .Nomitakatta n desu.

   moo chotto   . . . .Moo chotto nomitakatta n desu.

   biiru o   . . . .Biiru o moo chotto nomitakatta n desu.

9. Moraimashita.   . . . .Moraimashita.

   ichimai zutsu   . . . .Ichimai zutsu moraimashita.

   den'sha to eiga no kippu o   . . . .Den'sha to eiga no kippu o ichimai zutsu moraimashita.

13.7.11 Transformation Drill

1. Okashi o *yottsu* tabemashita.
   ikutsu   ⟶   Okashi o *ikutsu* tabemashita *ka?*

2. Ima yoji desu.
   nan'ji   ⟶   Ima nan'ji desu ka?

3. Kami ga kyuumai arimasu.
   nan'mai   ⟶   Kami ga nan'mai arimasu ka?

4. Zasshi o issatsu moraimashita.
   nan'satsu   ⟶   Zasshi o nan'satsu moraimashita ka?

5. Yamada san wa hatachi desu.
   nan'sai   ⟶   Yamada san wa nan'sai desu ka?

6. Otoko no hito wa kunin imashita.
   nan'nin   ⟶   Otoko no hito wa nan'nin imashita ka?

7. Hon o nijippeeji yomimasu.
   nan'peeji   ⟶   Hon o nan'peeji yomimasu ka?

8. Mainichi nido den'wa shimasu.
   nan'do   ⟶   Mainichi nan'do den'wa shimasu ka?

13.7.12 Substitution Drill

Otooto to *dekakemashita.*

1. tomodachi   . . . .Tomodachi to dekakemashita.

2. haha   . . . .Haha to dekakemashita.

3. hanashi o shimashita   . . . .Haha to hanashi o shimashita.

4. basu o machimashita   . . . .Haha to basu o machimashita.

5. anata   . . . .Anata to basu o machimashita.

6. ryokoo shitai desu   . . . . Anata to ryokoo shitai desu.

7. kazoku   . . . . Kazoku to ryokoo shitai desu.

8. hanashimashoo   . . . . Kazoku to hanashimashoo.

13.8 EXERCISES

13.8.1 Insert appropriate numbers or numerals in the blanks, according to the English words given:

     1. Eiga no kippu o (   ) kaimashita. (four)

     2. Zasshi o (   ) yomimashita. (five)

     3. Ima (   ) desu. (nine o'clock)

     4. Kodomo ga (   ) imasu. (two)

     5. Yamada san wa (   ) desu ka? (how old)

        (   ) deshoo. (twenty-one years old)

     6. Mizu o (   ) moraitai n desu kedo. (a glass of)

13.8.2 Rearrange each group of the following words into a good Japanese sentence:

     1. kono   dare   o   agemasu   ni   kippu   ka

     2. zutsu   o   kodomotachi   okashi   mittsu   ni   yarimashoo

     3. chichi   kamera   boku   kuremashita   o   wa   ni

     4. ka   hon   kinoo   de   nan'satsu   toshokan   karimashita   o

     5. takusan   nee   gakusei   asoko   ga   imasu   ni

13.8.3 Complete each sentence, inserting one of the following words in each blank:

     age(masu)   kure(masu)   yari(masu)   morai(masu)   ni   o   ga   kara

     1. Inu (   ) gohan (   ) (   )mashoo.

     2. Anata wa imootosan (   ) nani (   ) moraimashita ka?

     3. Tomodachi (   ) zasshi (   ) issatsu kuremashita.

     4. Haha wa watashi (   ) kuruma (   ) (   )mashita.

     5. Okosan (   ) ehon (   ) (   )mashoo.

     6. Watashi wa nodo ga kawakimashita. Sore de, haha kara mizu (   ) (   )mashita.

13.8.4 Answer the following questions on the basis of the Dialog:

     1. Ikuo san wa dare no uchi ni imasu ka?

     2. Dare to issho ni imasu ka?

     3. Kazuo san wa ima gakkoo desu ka?

4. Dare ga Kazuo san ni eiga no kippu o agemashita ka?

5. Ikuo san wa imootosan ya otootosan ga imasu ka?

6. Kazuo san no okaasan wa dare kara arubamu o moraimashita ka?

13.8.5 What would you say when:

1. you offer a guest tea?

2. you accept the above offer?

3. you do not accept the above offer?

4. you want to tell someone not to trouble himself for you?

5. you offer a guest another cup of coffee?

6. someone does not show up on time?

LESSON 14
KANA ORTHOGRAPHY AND MINI DIALOGS

(This lesson has been introduced for "passive learning," and the student is not required to study the content for examination. Explanations for note numbers are found in the Cultural Notes section.)

14.1 USEFUL EXPRESSIONS

Itte (i)rasshai.[1]

"Hurry back." This expression is used when seeing someone off. Literally this means "Go and come back." *Itte irasshai* is often contracted to *Itte rasshai*. In polite speech *Itte (i)rasshaimase* may be heard.

Itte mairimasu.[1]

"I'm going." This expression is used by a person who is leaving, in reply to the above expression *Itte (i)rasshai,* and vice versa. Literally this means "I am going and will come back."

Meishi[2] o kudasai.

"Please give me your namecard."

Fooku[3] o kudasai.

"Please give me a fork."

14.2 MINI DIALOGS

14.2.1 Questions and Answers

1) When your Japanese friend sees you walking to the station, he may ask you: *Doko e iku n desu ka?* "Where are you going?" instead of *Doko e ikimasu ka?* and you can answer: *Chotto Shin'juku e ikimasu.*

2) When he sees you wearing a new watch, he may ask you: *Katta n desu ka?* "Did you buy it?" instead of *Kaimashita ka?* and you can answer: *Ee, kinoo kaimashita* or *Iie, chichi ga kuremashita.*

3) When you show up after having kept your Japanese friend waiting, he may say: *Osokatta desu ne. Doo shita n desu ka?* "You came late. What happened?" instead of *Osokatta desu ne. Doo shimashita ka?* and you would answer: *Basu ga kimasen deshita* or *Isogashikatta n desu,* et cetera.

4) When your Japanese friend looks reluctant about going to a movie, you would ask him: *Anata wa eiga ga kirai desu ka?* and you may hear him answer: *Iie, soo ja nai n desu. Okane ga nai n desu* "No, I don't (dislike them). I don't have money." instead of *Iie, soo ja arimasen. Okane ga arimasen.*

5) When your Japanese friend hears that you are going back to your country, he may ask you: *Itsu kaeru n desu ka?* "When are you going back home?" instead of *Itsu kaerimasu ka?* and you would answer: *Raigetsu kaerimasu.*

6) When you ask your Japanese friend about his father, you would say: *Otoosan wa sen'sei desu ka?* and he may answer: *Iie, sarariiman na n desu* "No, he is working for a company." instead of *Iie, sarariiman desu.*

7) When you suggest to your Japanese friend that he have a beer, you would say: *Biiru wa doo desu ka?* and he may answer: *Boku wa nomanai n desu* "I don't drink." instead of *Boku wa nomimasen.*

8) When you want to inquire about the result of your friend's exam, you would ask him: *Shiken wa doo deshita ka?* and he may answer: *Dame datta n desu* "It was no good." instead of *Dame deshita.*

9) When you want to inquire if your Japanese friend had lunch or not, you would ask: *Hirugohan o tabe-mashita ka?* and he may answer *Iie, tabenakatta n desu* "No, I didn't eat it." instead of *Iie, tabemasen deshita.*

10) When you want to inquire if your Japanese friend's English teacher was an American or not, you would ask: *Eigo no sen'sei wa Amerikajin deshita ka?* and he may answer: *Iie, Amerikajin ja nakatta n desu. Igirisujin datta n desu* "No, he wasn't an American. He was an Englishman."

14.2.2 Short Dialogs

1) Jones: おすしを　たべましょうか。
   Satō: わたしは　すしが　すきじゃないんです。
   Jones: ほんとうですか。
   Satō: ええ。さかなが　きらいなんです。

2) Jones: おなかが　すきました。
   Satō: あさごはんを　たべなかったんですか。
   Jones: ええ、たべませんでした。
   Satō: どうして　たべなかったんですか。
   Jones: とても　いそがしかったんです。

3) Jones: パーティーを　しませんか。
   Satō: いいですね。でも、どこで　するんですか。
   Jones: あなたの　うちは　だめですか。
   Satō: うちですか。うちは　とても　ちいさいんですけど。

4) Jones: どうして　まいにち　えいごを　べんきょうしますか。
   Satō: らいねん　アメリカに　いくんです。
   Jones: アメリカの　どこですか。
   Satō: カリフォルニアなんです。

5) Jones: やまもとさんは　えいごが　じょうずですね。
   Satō: ええ、まえ　アメリカに　いたんです。
   Jones: そうですか。あなたは？
   Satō: わたしも　いったんですけど、すぐ　かえりました。

14.2.3 Brief Exchanges

1) Teacher: Onegai ga arimasu kedo, sono e o karitai n desu ga₄ . . .
   "I have a favor to ask. I would like to borrow that picture."

   Student: Sen'sei, doozo.
   "Teacher, please do."

2) Mr. Yamada: Dochira e?
   "Where are you going?"

   Ms. Ishii: Chotto soko made.₅
   "Just [there]."

14.3 KANA ORTHOGRAPHY

The following are the rules of the postwar revised Japanese orthography.

14.3.1 Long Vowels of Hiragana

Long vowels are written by adding one *a gyoo hiragana* to its preceding vowel.

1) Long vowels *a dan kana,* such as あ、か、さ、た、な、は、ま、や、ら、わ、が、 are written by adding あ to the *kana* as follows:

ああ [aa], さあ [saa], はあ [haa], まあ [maa]

2) Long vowels of *i dan kana,* such as い、き、し、ち、に、ひ、み、り、ぎ、 are written by adding い to the *kana* as follows:

いい [ii], おおきい [ookii], おいしい [oishii], ちいさい [chiisai]

3) Long vowels of *u dan kana,* such as う、く、す、つ、ぬ、ふ、む、ゆ、る、ぐ、 are written by adding う to the *kana* as follows:

すう [suu], ふつう [futsuu], ぎゅうにゅう [gyuunyuu]

4) Long vowels of *e dan kana,* such as え、け、せ、て、ね、へ、め、れ、げ、 are written by adding い to the *kana* as follows:

えいが [eiga], えいご [eigo], がくせい [gakusei], とけい [tokei], たいてい [taitei]

But the following words are exceptions:

ええ [ee], ねえ [nee], おねえさん [oneesan]

5) Long vowels of *o dan kana,* such as お、こ、そ、と、の、ほ、も、よ、ろ、ご、 are written by adding う to the *kana* as follows:

おう [oo], そう [soo], どう [doo], もう [moo]

But there are some exceptions:

おおきい [ookii], おおい [ooi], とおい [tooi], とおる [tooru], とおり [toori], こおる [kooru], et cetera

14.3.2 Long Vowels of Katakana

In writing *katakana,* long vowels are shown by writing a bar after the *katakana.* When lines are written horizontally, as is done in this textbook, the bar is horizontal. When the lines are written vertically, the bar is written vertically.

コーヒー [koohii], デパート [depaato], ヨーロッパ [Yooroppa]

14.3.3 Single-Consonant Syllables of Hiragana and Katakana

Single-consonant syllables, such as *t* in *ki-t-to, k* in *ga-k-ko-o, p* in *i-p-pa-i, s* in *i-s-sho,* et cetera, are expressed by つ [tsu] in *hiragana* and ッ [tsu] in *katakana.* Either つ or ッ is usually written slightly smaller.

きっぷ [kippu], ざっし [zasshi], きっと [kitto], クラシック [kurashikku]

14.3.4 Relationals *wa* and *e*

Relationals *wa* and *e* are written as は and へ but are pronounced as *wa* and *e* respectively.

とうきょうへ きます。	[Tookyoo e kimasu.]
どこへ いきましたか。	[Doko e ikimashita ka?]
これは なんですか。	[Kore wa nan desu ka?]
わたくしは おんがくが だいすきです。	[Watakushi wa on'gaku ga daisuki desu.]

14.3.5 Relational *o*

The Relational *o* is written as を.

| おちゃを のみましょう。 | [Ocha o nomimashoo.] |
| なにを しましたか。 | [Nani o shimashita ka?] |

14.3.6 Use of ぢ and づ

In ordinary cases, じ and ず are written for *ji* and *zu* respectively. But in the following cases, ぢ and づ are used instead:

1) When two or more words make a compound, and the initial syllable of the second or the third word is *ji* or *zu* but was originally *chi* or *tsu,* it should be written as ぢ or づ.

It is quite common that a simple *kana* becomes a two-dot *kana* when placed after another word, thus forming a compound.

はな [hana] ＋ ち [chi] ⟶ はなぢ [hanaji]

2) When *ji* follows *chi* or *zu* follows *tsu* in one word, the *ji* and *zu* are written as ぢ and づ.

ちぢむ [chijimu], つづく [tsuzuku]

14.3.7 Foreign words

Conventionally, some foreign words carry sounds close to the original sounds, when they are used in Japanese. In those cases, *katakana* combinations different from those introduced in Lesson 2 may occur. Here are some of them:

e.g.	カリフォルニア	[Kari*fo*runia]	"California"
	ディック	[*Di*kku]	"Dick"
	フォーク	[*fo*oku]	"fork"
	フィラデルフィア	[*Fi*raderu*fi*a]	"Philadelphia"

14.3.8 Marks

1) The small circle [。] indicates the end of a sentence or an utterance, but it does not correspond in function to the comma in English.

これを あげます。 [Kore o agemasu.]

2) The mark [、] indicates a pause.

　さあ、いきましょう。　　　　　　　　　[Saa, ikimashoo.]

3) Quotations are indicated by 「　」.

　「きれいですねえ」と　いいました。　　　["Kirei desu nee" to iimashita.]

14.4　CULTURAL NOTES

14.4.1　Itte (i)rasshai and Itte mairimasu

The two expressions *Itte (i)rasshai* and *Itte mairimasu,* used in parting, illustrate several differences between Japanese and American culture.

First, they are uniform. American usage allows more latitude in choice of words. Moreover, they are merely signals, (that is, the actual content of the expressions is not the point) and as such are mandatory —it would not be permissible to leave or to allow someone to leave without thus acknowledging the fact. Although normally in American culture some utterance would be necessary, this acknowledgment may be either signalized, as in "I'm going now," or substantive as in "I'll be back tomorrow afternoon."

A further point to notice is that both Japanese expressions indicate expectation of return, both the going and the coming back are explicit. While American usage allows for this, it is much more likely to remain implied. "I'll be back soon" obviously implies that the speaker is going, but he or she needn't actually say that. "See you tomorrow" leaves still more unstated.

The expression *Itte (i)rasshai* may be used when the addressee leaves to go to work, school, or to do something not in the normal daily pattern of life—for example, in going shopping, if that is not part of one's usual daily activities. At any rate, both expressions carry a rather light meaning such as the expression "Have a nice time."

14.4.2　Meishi, or Namecards

In a specific conversation, the Japanese needs to immediately determine the specific human relationship involved. Therefore, he will usually use a polite, formal style and level until he can pinpoint the relative social status which pertains to a particular conversation. For this reason the Japanese male—who traditionally has been more exposed to this type of interchange—has developed the custom of exchanging *meishi* or namecards, so that each side will immediately know the other side's position, occupation, status, importance, et cetera. We may call this the accurate identification of the status of the surrounding people, and it is extremely significant if a speaker wishes to conduct proper conversation on the appropriate levels of speech and style. This is also the reason why the Japanese exchange greetings with the utmost caution when first introduced to each other. The exchange of *meishi* allows immediate placement in the appropriate social position, and is still widely practiced today. In fact, if one is offered a card, it would be rude not to reciprocate. It is customary for an inferior to offer his card first.

14.4.3　Gairaigo and Cultural Pluralism (eclecticism)

Words such as *koohii* in Lesson 3, and *depaato, resutoran,* and *kurasu* in Lesson 4 are not native to Japan, but to describe them as non-Japanese would be to overlook an important characteristic of the language and the people. Since the first foreign contacts with China before the Christian era, the Japanese people have enriched their language and culture by assimilating foreign words as well as objects and concepts. The word from the language of the people who introduced the object was simply adopted along with the object. Many words borrowed from the Chinese have been used for so many centuries that they are generally no longer even felt to be foreign.

Again, when Westerners first arrived in Japan, they brought with them many things that the Japanese had never even seen before. Knives and forks, for instance, gave rise to *naifu* and *fooku*. Other words such as *betto* "bed," *kaapetto* "carpet," and *shatsu* "shirt" were similarly adopted for objects the Japanese were unfamiliar with. These adopted words were modified to be acceptable to Japanese pronunciation, yet still maintain a degree of similarity in sound to the original form. Examples of this can be seen in the consonants "l" and "r" which are a source of difficulty for the Japanese attempting to pronounce them. The Japanese would pronounce both "l" and "r" so that they sounded the same. Some other sounds common in English that necessarily are modified in Japanese are "f," "v," and "t"; these becoming "ho" or "fu," "bu," and "chi" or "tsu."

Since the end of World War II the number of English words incorporated in the Japanese language has greatly increased. Many Americans are surprised to discover how many words they can understand once they learn the principles of Japanese pronunciation. These words are called *gairaigo* or loan words. The grammatical structure of the original forms is not necessarily adopted, however. The Japanese do not emphasize differentiation between singular and plural forms of a word that they have adopted.

The Japanese also created "made-in-Japan" loan words by (1) combining two foreign words with different meanings such as *bodii-biru* (body + building), *reen-shuuzu* (rain + shoes); (2) by abbreviating a portion of foreign words such as *an'gura* "underground theater," *eakon* "air conditioner," *apaato* "apartment," *mishin* "sewing machine"; (3) by combining foreign words from different languages such as, *bakan'su seeru* (vacation + sale); (4) by attaching the verb *suru* to a foreign noun such as *haikin'gu suru* or *haiku suru* "to hike," *anaun'su suru* "to announce," *sain suru* "to sign"; (5) by making a foreign word into a native-style Japanese verb such as *saboru* "to be engaged in sabotage" and *ajiru* "to agitate." All of these show the cultural pluralism characteristic of the Japanese. In this sense, Japanese culture evidences its eclectic nature.

14.4.4 Favors or Role Switching

The relationship between a superior (e.g., parents, teachers) and an inferior (e.g., children, students) is affected by the possibility of a favor being done by the inferior for the superior. The altered circumstances may cause a temporary equalizing, or perhaps even a reversal, of the two roles. It is in this sense, that we may understand the relationships between seller and buyer, between a doctor and his patient, between a landlord and his tenant, or between *sen'pai* and *koohai*—the senior and junior members respectively of a profession, a company, or graduates of the same school in different years.

The favor situation, however, is still governed by group consciousness. The greater or lesser degree of intensity with which in-groupness is experienced may in fact intensify the superior-inferior relationship, as in an association of medical doctors. On the other hand, in-groupness may render the role switching superfluous, as in a father who receives a favor from his son. Traditionally the father would not defer to his son even in the favor situation due to the primacy of the father-son, superior-inferior relationship.

14.4.5 Inquisitiveness

Although Mr. Yamada does not seem to be a close friend to Miss Ishii, he asks where she is going. Such inquisitiveness is not as unusual among the Japanese as it would be among Americans, and does not necessarily imply (as it might in a similar situation in America) that Mr. Yamada is interested in dating Miss Ishii. And although Miss Ishii answers his questions, it is not necessary that a Japanese give precise answers to all the questions put to them by an acquaintance. It is perfectly acceptable to answer in less specific terms, as a young American might answer his parents' query, "Where are you going?" with the vague response of "I'm just going out."

14.5 KANA EXERCISES

14.5.1 Make a pair by filling in the blank in *hiragana*:

Example: おとうと　ー（いもうと）

ちち　　　ー（　　　　　）　　ごしゅじんー（　　　　　　）　　おねえさんー（　　　　　　　）

あに　　　ー（　　　　　）　　しゅじん　ー（　　　　　）

おとうさんー（　　　　　）　　せんせい　ー（　　　　　）

14.5.2 Fill in the blank with its antonym in *hiragana*:

Example: むずかしいですー（やさしいです）

おもしろいですー（　　　　　）　　うるさいです　ー（　　　　　　）

きたないです　ー（　　　　　）　　へたです　　　ー（　　　　　　）

おいしいです　ー（　　　　　）　　いそがしいですー（　　　　　　）

あたたかいですー（　　　　　）　　おおきいです　ー（　　　　　　）

いいです　　　ー（　　　　　）　　だいきらいですー（　　　　　　）

すきです　　　ー（　　　　　）　　たかかったですー（　　　　　　）

ちかいです　　ー（　　　　　）　　あつかったですー（　　　　　　）

14.5.3 Read the following *katakana*:

ポスト	プレゼント	プール	テープ
アメリカ	テレビ	カメラ	ペン
レコード	パン	ヨーロッパ	アルバム
スミス	デパート	コーヒー	フォーク
タイプライター	イギリス	ブラウン	ページ
ビール	フランス	レストラン	クラス
ラジオ	ピアノ	メリーランド	
ロシア	ビフテキ	ハワイ	
バス	ドイツ	タクシー	

14.5.4 Write your name in *katakana*:

Example: トーマス・ブラウン　　　　　"Thomas Brown"

14.5.5 Insert appropriate *hiragana* in each blank:

1. こども ＿＿ ＿＿＿＿＿ です。
   (wa) (yattsu)

2. なに ＿ かいますか。
   (o)

3. ＿＿＿＿ですか。
   (soo)

4. ＿＿＿＿＿、 これ ＿ たべま ＿＿＿＿＿。
   (jaa) (o) (shoo)

5. やまもとさん＿＿ にっこうに いました。
   (wa)

6. だれが ＿＿＿＿＿ ＿ ＿＿＿＿＿ しましたか。
   (Kyooto) (e) (ryokoo)

7. ＿＿＿＿＿、 じょうずじゃありません。
   (iie)

8. ＿＿＿＿＿ すみません。
   (doomo)

9. ＿＿＿＿＿ ＿ のみました。
   (ocha) (o)

10. ＿＿＿ ならいました。
    (moo)

11. ＿＿＿＿＿＿＿。
    (sayoonara)

12. きのう どこ ＿ いきましたか。
    (e)

13. ＿＿＿＿＿＿ で えいが ＿ みたかったんです。
    (Tookyoo) (o)

14. とても つめた＿＿＿＿＿です。
    (katta)

15. ＿＿＿＿＿ おかまいなく。
    (doozo)

16. ＿＿＿＿＿＿に ＿ かえりません。
    (issho) (wa)

14.5.6 Read the following sentences:

1. きょうは うちへ かえりません。
2. その みせは あまり きれいじゃありません。
3. あそこで かいましょう。
4. よるは さむかったでしょう。
5. ごはんを たべますか、コーヒーを のみますか。
6. おんがくも よくありません。
7. きのう てんきが よくなかったんです。
8. うちは とうきょうでしょう？

9. わたくしは　にほんごの　べんきょうが　すきです。あなたは？

10. おとうとさんに　えほんを　あげましょう。

11. びょういんは　ちょっと　とおいです。

12. あれも　せんせいの　へやです。

13. りょうあんじへは　いきませんでした。

14. ともだちが　きっぷを　さんまい　くれました。

15. この　ほんは　とても　むずかしかったです。

16. デパートに　いとうさんが　いました。
    departo

17. スミスさんは　がくせいでしょう？

18. まえは　すきじゃありませんでした。

14.5.7 Write the following sentences in *hiragana:*

1. Nani o tabemasu ka?

2. Yamamoto san wa umi ga suki desu.

3. Eki de ano hito o machimashoo.

4. Kuni e kaerimasen.

5. Soko mo jimusho desu yo.

6. Gin'koo ni Kazuo san ga imashita.

7. Amari suki ja arimasen.

8. Soko wa atatakakatta deshoo.

9. Watanabe san wa mae Tookyoo Daigaku no gakusei deshita.

10. Imooto san ni zasshi o agemashoo.

11. Nikkoo e wa ikimasen deshita.

12. Nihon'go wa totemo omoshirokatta desu yo.

13. Ame ga takusan furimashita.

14. Kono jisho mo yoku arimasen.

15. Asoko wa Nikkoo deshoo?

16. Kinoo wa samuku nakatta desu.

17. Ano kissaten wa amari shizuka de wa arimasen.

18. Watakushi no gakkoo wa chotto tooi desu.

19. Mizu o nomimashoo ka?

20. Kippu o gomai moraimashita.

LESSON 15
REVIEW AND APPLICATION

15.1 CONJUGATION
15.1.1 Adjective

	(2)		(1)		(2)		(1)
	atsu*i*						
	samu*i*						
	atataka*i*						
	suzushi*i*						
	mushiatsu*i*						
	tsumeta*i*						
	tanoshi*i*						
	subarashi*i*						
	haya*i*						
	oso*i*						
	chiisa*i*	(n)	*desu* ⟶	~	-*ku nai*	(n)	*desu*
	ooki*i*		*deshoo*				*deshoo*
	too*i*						
	chika*i*						
	yasu*i*						
	taka*i*						
	yo*i* (ii)						
	waru*i*						
	yasashi*i*						
	muzukashi*i*						
	oishi*i*						
	mazu*i*						
	omoshiro*i*						
	tsumarana*i*						
	kitana*i*						
	urusa*i*						
	isogashi*i*						

~ -*katta* ⋮ (n) ⋮ *desu* ⟶ ~ ⋮ -*ku nakatta* ⋮ (n) ⋮ *desu*
deshoo   *deshoo*

15.1.2 Copula—presumptive

	(2)		(1)		(2)		(1)
	hon'too						
	soo						
	rusu		*desu* ⟶	~	*deshoo*		
	yasumi						
	ame						

```
dame            :
shizuka         :
rippa           :
. . . . . . . . . . . . . . . . . . . . . . :   desu   ⟶  ~  :  deshoo
tsumetai        :
tanoshii        :
ii              :
```

15.1.3 Adjectival Derivative

| | (2) | (1) | (2) | (1) |

```
                    (2)                (1)               (2)              (1)
puuru de oyogitai       .
eki de machitai         :
soo iitai               :
den'wa (o) shitai       :
hanashi (o) shitai      :
ryokoo (o) shitai       :
ken'butsu (o) shitai    :   (n)   desu   ⟶  ~  -taku  :  arimasen
arubamu o moraitai      :         deshoo                  nai (n) desu
purezen'to o agetai     :                                 nai (n) deshoo
otooto ni yaritai       :
kuni e kaeritai         :
yuki o mitai            :
         ↓                    ↓                   ↓              ↓
        (2)                  (1)                 (2)            (1)
~    -takatta       :   (n)   desu   ⟶  ~  -taku  :  arimasen deshita
                              deshoo                  nakatta (n) desu
                                                      nakatta (n) deshoo
```

15.2   PATTERNS

15.2.1

Giver / Actor } + { wa / ga / (mo) } recipient + *ni* + object + *o* + { *agemasu* / *yarimasu* / *kuremasu* }

Giver/Actor	wa/ga/(mo)	recipient	ni	object	o	agemasu
a. watakushi boku atashi watashitachi		tomodachi Buraun san anata kimi chichi ane		ocha		
anata kimi anatatachi	wa ga (mo)	tomodachi Buraun san otoosan otootosan	ni	okashi	o	agemasu
shujin kodomo Sumisu san tomodachi		Buraun san ano gakusei		kippu		

b.

watashi		kodomo			
boku		imooto		ehon	
atashi		otooto			
watashitachi					
chichi					
ane					
watashi	wa				
anata	ga	inu	ni	gohan	o yarimasu
ano kata	(mo)	neko		mizu	
sen'sei		tori			
haha					
kodomo					

c.

Yamada san		watakushi			
anata		watashi			
kimi no oniisan		watashitachi			
otoko no hito	ga	boku			
	wa	atashi	ni	purezen'to	o kuremasu
	(mo)	chichi			
		kanai			
		imooto			

15.2.2

$$\text{Recipient} + \begin{Bmatrix} \textit{wa} \\ \textit{ga} \\ \textit{(mo)} \end{Bmatrix} + \text{person} + \textit{kara} + \text{object} + \textit{o} + \textit{moraimasu}$$

watashi		Ikuo kun			
watakushitachi		anata			
boku					
atashi		tomodachi			
anata	wa	Kazuo san	kara	arubamu	o moraimasu
anatatachi					
Minoru kun					
Itoo san					
kodomo					
ane					
shujin					

15.2.3 Quantity Expressions

a.

(go)kazoku		hitori	
(go)kyoodai		futari	
okosan		san'nin	imasu
ani	ga	yonin	(desu)
oniisan	(wa)	gonin	
ane		rokunin	
oneesan		nananin/shichinin	
otooto(san)		hachinin	
		kunin/kyuunin	

214

on'na no hito	:	juunin	ikimasu
	:	juuichinin	kimasu
	ga	issatsu	arimasu
	:	nisatsu	
	:	san'satsu	
	:	yon'satsu	
zasshi	:	gosatsu	agemasu
hon	:	rokusatsu	yarimasu
ehon	o	nanasatsu/shichisatsu	kuremasu
jisho	:	hachisatsu/hassatsu	moraimasu
arubamu	:	kyuusatsu	kaimasu
	:	jissatsu/jussatsu	yomimasu
	:	juuissatsu	karimasu
		ichimai	
	ga	nimai	arimasu
	:	san'mai	
kami	:	yon'mai/yomai	
shin'bun	:	gomai	
rekoodo	o	rokumai	agemasu
kippu	:	shichimai/nanamai	yarimasu
e	:	hachimai	kuremasu
	:	kyuumai/kumai	moraimasu
	:	juumai	kaimasu
	:	juuichimai	
		ippeeji/ichipeeji	
	:	nipeeji	
	:	san'peeji	
	:	yon'peeji	
hon	o	gopeeji	
zasshi	:	rokupeeji	yomimasu
shin'bun	:	nanapeeji/shichipeeji	
	:	happeeji/hachipeeji	
	:	kyuupeeji	
	:	jippeeji/juppeeji	
		hitotsu	
	ga	futatsu	
ishi	:	mittsu	arimasu
	:	yottsu	
	:	itsutsu	
	:	muttsu	
	o	nanatsu	
okashi	:	yattsu	kaimasu
	:	kokonotsu	
	:	too	

		issai	
		nisai	
		san'sai	
chichi		yon'sai	
otoosan		gosai	
haha		rokusai	
okaasan		shichisai/nanasai	
ani		hassai/hachisai	
oniisan		kyuusai	
ane		jissai/jussai	
oneesan		juuissai	
imooto	wa	hatachi	desu
otooto			deshita
kodomo		hitotsu	
okosan		futatsu	
kanai		mittsu	
okusan		yottsu	
shujin		itsutsu	
goshujin		muttsu	
		nanatsu	
Watanabe san		yattsu	
Minoru kun		kokonotsu	
watashi		too	
anata			

		ichiji	
		niji	
		san'ji	
		yoji	
		goji	
		rokuji	
ima	(wa)	shichiji	desu
		hachiji	deshoo
		kuji	
		juuji	
		juuichiji	
		juuniji	

gokazoku	ga		imasu	
kyoodai	wa	nan'nin	(desu)	
			ikimasu	
jisho	ga		arimasu	ka?
		nan'satsu		
zasshi	o		yomimasu	
kippu	ga		arimasu	
		nan'mai		
kami	o		kaimasu	

hon	o	nan'peeji	yomimasu	
okashi	ga		arimasu	
		ikutsu		
ishi	o		kaimasu	
				ka?
goshujin		nan'sai	desu	
	wa		deshita	
okusan		ikutsu	deshoo	
ima	(wa)	nan'ji	desu	
			deshoo	

b.

Buraun san		Ishii san	zasshi		issatsu	agemashoo
chichi		haha	hon			
otooto		imooto	kippu		ichimai	yarimasu
kanai		kodomo	rekoodo			
	to		ni		o	zutsu
kimi						
ani						
min'na		boku	okashi		hitotsu	kuremasu
kodomotachi		ane				
imoototachi						

c.

ehon			nisatsu	agemasu
jisho				yarimasu
				kuremasen ka?
kami	o	moo	nimai	agemashoo
kippu				
okashi			hitotsu	tabemasu

d.

ame	ga		furimasu
yuki			
rekoodo		takusan	kaimasu
		sukoshi	
	o		
hon			
okashi			agemasu
gakkoo			
rekoodo		takusan	arimasu
ehon		sukoshi	
kippu	ga		
hito		oozei	
kodomo		takusan	imasu
		sukoshi	

15.2.4 Relational *to* "with"

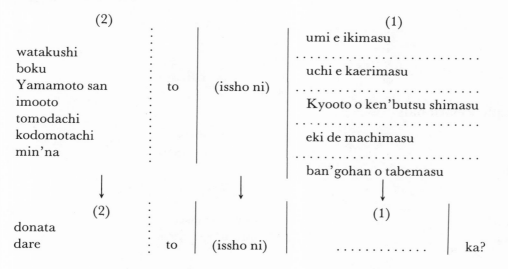

```
        (2)                                    (1)
                          |          |   umi e ikimasu
   watakushi     :        |          | ..........................
   boku          :        |          |   uchi e kaerimasu
   Yamamoto san  :   to   | (issho ni) | ..........................
   imooto        :        |          |   Kyooto o ken'butsu shimasu
   tomodachi     :        |          | ..........................
   kodomotachi   :        |          |   eki de machimasu
   min'na        :        |          | ..........................
                          |          |   ban'gohan o tabemasu

        (2)       :        |    |         (1)
   donata         :        |    |
   dare           :   to   | (issho ni) |   . . . . . . . . . . . |  ka?
```

15.2.5 Relational *kara* "from"

```
      (2)            :                (1)
   Asakusa Eki       :        |   ikimasu
   Yooroppa          :  kara  |   kimasu
   gaikoku           :        |   kaerimasu

      (2)            :                (1)
   doko              :  kara  |   . . . . . . . . . |  ka?
```

15.2.6 Relational *de* "by means of"

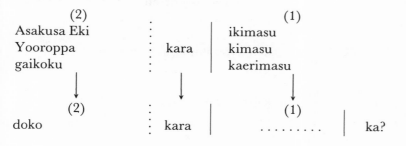

```
      (2)            :                (1)
   den'sha          :        |
   kuruma           :        |   ikimasu
   takushii         :        |   kimasu
   basu             :        |   kaerimasu
   fune             :        |   ryokoo shimasu
   hikooki          :        |
   .................:........|.................
   en'pitsu         :        |
   nihon'go         :        |   kakimasu
   .................:........|.................
   gaikokugo        :        |
   den'wa           :        |   hanashimasu
   .................:   de   |.................
   rajio            :        |
   rekoodo          :        |   kikimasu
   .................:........|.................
   terebi           :        |
   eiga             :        |   mimasu
   .................:........|.................
```

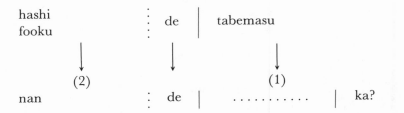

hashi fooku	de	tabemasu

(2) ⟶ de | ⟶ (1)

nan : de | . . . . | ka?

15.2.7 Multiple Relationals

hon'ya	e		kimasu/ ～ -masen
	kara		kaerimasu/ ～ -masen
byooin			

| Kyooto
Yooroppa
niwa
soto | ni | | imasu/ ～ -masen
arimasu/ ～ -masen |

shokudoo			nomimasu/ ～ -masen tabemasu/ ～ -masen
toshokan		wa	ben'kyoo shimasu/ ～ -masen
hon'ya	de	mo	kaimasu/ ～ -masen
pan'ya gaikoku			
kissaten mise byooin			machimasu/ ～ -masen
hikooki	de		ikimasu/ ～ -masen ryokoo shimasu
en'pitsu			kakimasu/ ～ -masen
gaikokugo			hanashimasu/ ～ -masen

15.2.8 Relationals *ka, ya, to*

Buraun san anata		Yamamoto san	ga	imasu den'wa shimasu
ame	ka ya	yuki		furimasu
hashi	to	fooku		sagashimasu
zasshi		shin'bun	o	yomimasu

Kyooto		Nikkoo	o	ken'butsu shimasu
hon		zasshi		karimasu
ehon		arubamu		agemasu
basu		den'sha		machimasu
Nikkoo Asakusa		Shin'juku	e	ryokoo shimasu dekakemasu
kissaten	ka	resutoran	kara	kimasu
toshokan	ya	uchi		ben'kyoo shimasu
shokudoo	to	resutoran	de	kikimasu
gakkoo		toshokan		karimasu ben'kyoo shimasu
Furan'su		Doitsu	ni	imasu arimasu
fune den'sha		hikooki	de	kimasu kaerimasu
hashi		fooku		tabemasu

15.2.9 Time Noun

a. ashita ashita no asa ashita no hiru ashita no ban ashita no yoru asatte rainen raigetsu raishuu	(wa) (mo)	gaikoku kara kaerimasu totemo isogashii desu watakushi wa hima desu
↓		
itsu		. . . . ka?

kyoo kesa kyoo no hiru kon'ban kyoo no yoru kotoshi kon'getsu kon'shuu	(wa) (mo)	den'sha de ikimasu eiga o mimashita ten'ki ga ii desu tsugoo ga warukatta n desu gen'ki desu shizuka deshita

```
↓
itsu            :        |   . . . . . . . . . . . . . . . . .   |   ka?
                :

kinoo           :
kinoo no asa    :
kinoo no hiru   :   (wa)    |   toshokan ni imashita
kinoo no ban    :   (mo)    |   tanoshikatta desu
kinoo no yoru   :           |   hima deshita
ototoi          :
kyonen          :
sen'getsu       :
sen'shuu        :

↓
itsu            :        |   . . . . . . . . . . . . . . . . .   |   ka?

b. mainichi     :        |   dekakemashita
   maiasa       :        |   ben'kyoo shimashita
   maiban       :        . . . . . . . . . . . . . . . . . . . . . .
   maishuu      :        |   isogashii desu
   maigetsu     :        . . . . . . . . . . . . . . . . . . . . . .
   mainen       :        |   hima deshita
```

15.2.10 Adverb

```
                                              chiisai desu
kore         :  wa       |             |      takakatta desu
sore         :  (ga)     |   chotto    . . . . . . . . . . . . . . . . . . . .
kono uchi    :  (mo)     |   totemo    |      kirei desu
                                       |      kirei deshita

             :  o        |             |
sono shin'bun:  (wa)     |   chotto    |      yomimashoo
             :  (mo)     |             |      karimasu


             :           |             |      muzukashiku arimasen
             :           |             |      omoshiroku arimasen deshita
kono eiga    :  wa       |             . . . . . . . . . . . . . . . . . . . .
ano zasshi   :  (mo)     |             |      suki de wa arimasen
             :           |   amari     |      suki ja arimasen deshita
. . . . . . . . . . . . . . :  . . . . |   zen'zen . . . . . . . . . . . . . . . . . . . .
             :  o        |             |
kore         :  (wa)     |             |      tabemasen
             :  (mo)     |             |      nomimasen deshita


anata        :  wa       |             |      chiisakatta desu
. . . . . . . . . . . . :  . . . . . . |             . . . . . . . . . . . . . . . . . .
soko         :  (mo)     |             |      shizuka desu            nee
             :           |   zuibun    |      kirei deshita           ne
. . . . . . . . . . . . :  . . . . . . |             . . . . . . . . . . . . . . . . . .
```

gohan	o (mo)		tabemashita kaimashita
watakushi Buraun san	wa (ga) (mo)	itsumo taitei yoku tokidoki . . . . sugu mata	ikimasu kikimashita
eiga terebi		itsumo taitei tokidoki	omoshiroi desu omoshirokatta desu . . . . ii desu yokatta desu
. . . . nihon'go	wa (ga) (mo)		. . . . heta desu muzukashii desu
heya		tabun	kirei deshoo kitanakatta deshoo
hon			yomimashita
. . . . on'gaku	o (wa) (mo)	moo	. . . . kikimashita
. . . . sono shin'bun		. . . . mada	. . . . yomimasen

15.2.11 Copula *desu* replacing *ni arimasu* and *ni imasu*

(3)		(2)		(1)
chichi				
otoosan				
haha				
okaasan				
oniisan		soto		
ani		niwa		
oneesan		heya		
ane		gakkoo		imasu
kyoodai		uchi		imasen
(go)kyoodai		gaikoku		imashita
kazoku	wa	kuni	ni	imasen deshita
(go)kazoku		koko		
kodomotachi		Tookyoo		
okosan		Amerika		
otooto				
imootosan				
kanai				
okusan				

222

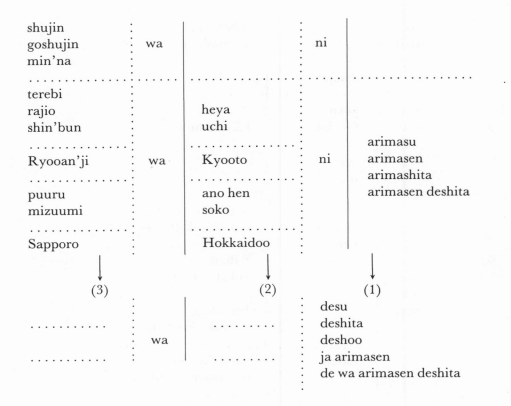

shujin				
goshujin	wa		ni	
min'na				
terebi				
rajio		heya		
shin'bun		uchi		
Ryooan'ji	wa	Kyooto	ni	arimasu
				arimasen
				arimashita
puuru		ano hen		arimasen deshita
mizuumi		soko		
Sapporo		Hokkaidoo		
↓		↓		↓
(3)		(2)		(1)

			desu
			deshita
	wa		deshoo
			ja arimasen
			de wa arimasen deshita

15.2.12 Alternate Question

a.

koohii	ga	oishii desu / suki desu		ocha	ga	oishii desu / suki
		nomimasu				nomimasu
nihon'go	o	naraimashita		chuugokugo	o	naraimashita
toshokan	de	karimasu	ka,	gakkoo	de	karimasu	ka?
uchi	ni	imashita		kissaten	ni	imashita
kotchi	e	ikimashoo		atchi	e	ikimashoo

b.

koohii	wa	oishii desu / suki desu		mazui desu / kirai desu	
		nomimasu		nomimasen	
toshokan	de	karimasu	ka,	hon'ya de kaimasu	ka?
kuni	e	kaerimasu		Chuugoku e ikimasu	
uchi	ni	imashoo		dekakemashoo	

15.3 REVIEW DRILLS

15.3.1 E-J Expansion Drill

1. Ikimashita. . . . . Ikimashita.

   to Nikkō . . . . *Nikkoo e* ikimashita.

   by train . . . . Den'sha de Nikkoo e ikimashita.

   with a friend of mine . . . . Tomodachi to den'sha de Nikkoo e ikimashita.

   last month . . . . Sen'getsu tomodachi to den'sha de Nikkoo e ikimashita.

2. Agemashoo ka? . . . . Agemashoo ka?

   fruit or candies . . . . Kudamono ka okashi o agemashoo ka?

   to Kazuo . . . . Kazuo san ni kudamono ka okashi o agemashoo ka?

   every night . . . . Maiban Kazuo san ni kudamono ka okashi o agemashoo ka?

3. Kaerimashita. . . . . Kaerimashita.

   to my house . . . . Uchi e kaerimashita.

   by taxi . . . . Takushii de uchi e kaerimashita.

   from the station . . . . Eki kara takushii de uchi e kaerimashita.

4. Moraimasen ka? . . . . Moraimasen ka?

   paper and a pencil . . . . Kami to en'pitsu o moraimasen ka?

   from that person over there . . . . Ano hito kara kami to en'pitsu o moraimasen ka?

5. Kuremasu. . . . . Kuremasu.

   movie tickets . . . . Eiga no kippu o kuremasu.

   to us . . . . Watashitachi ni eiga no kippu o kuremasu.

   often . . . . Yoku watashitachi ni eiga no kippu o kuremasu.

   my mother . . . . Haha wa yoku watashitachi ni eiga no kippu o kuremasu.

6. Kakimashita. . . . . Kakimashita.

   a letter . . . . Tegami o kakimashita.

   in Japanese . . . . Nihon'go de tegami o kakimashita.

   together with Mr. Ishii . . . . Ishii san to issho ni nihon'go de tegami o kakimashita.

15.3.2 E-J Substitution Drill

1. *Kinoo* Nikkoo e ikimashita.

1. last month	2. the day before yesterday	3. last week
4. last year	5. this morning	6. before

2. *Mainichi* ame ga furimasu.

1. every week	2. every month	3. every year
4. always	5. sometimes	6. these days

3. *Ashita* kuni e kaerimasu ka?
  1. next week
  2. the day after tomorrow
  3. tonight
  4. next month
  5. next year
  6. soon

4. Hon wa *itsumo* takai n desu.
  1. sometimes
  2. usually
  3. these days

15.3.3 Response Drill (negative response)

1. Kinoo ame ga furimashita ka?

   . . . . *Iie,* kinoo ame ga furimasen deshita.

2. Anata wa oyogi ga suki deshoo?

   . . . . Iie, watashi wa oyogi ga suki ja arimasen.

3. Kyonen no natsu wa atsukatta n desu ka?

   . . . . Iie, kyonen no natsu wa atsuku nakatta n desu.

4. Umi de oyogitai desu ka?

   . . . . Iie, umi de oyogitaku arimasen.

5. Kazoku wa Hokkaidoo desu ka?

   . . . . Iie, kazoku wa Hokkaidoo de wa arimasen.

6. Itoo san to hanashimashita ka?

   . . . . Iie, Itoo san to hanashimasen deshita.

7. Rajio de soo iimashita ka?

   . . . . Iie, rajio de soo iimasen deshita.

8. Kippu o moraitakatta n desu ka?

   . . . . Iie, kippu o moraitaku nakatta n desu.

9. Kyoo suzushii desu ka?

   . . . . Iie, kyoo suzushiku arimasen.

10. Kinoo wa samukatta deshoo?

   . . . . Iie, kinoo wa samuku nakatta n desu.

15.3.4 Transformation Drill (⟶ perfect tense)

1. Doko e ikitai desu ka? ⟶ Doko e ikita*katta* desu ka?

2. Den'wa shitaku nai n desu. ⟶ Den'wa shitaku nakatta n desu.

3. Kazuo kun wa osoi desu nee. ⟶ Kazuo kun wa osokatta desu nee.

4. Sen'sei wa ogen'ki desu ka? ⟶ Sen'sei wa ogen'ki deshita ka?

5. Shiken wa nan'ji desu ka? ⟶ Shiken wa nan'ji deshita ka?

6. Heya wa amari atsuku nai deshoo. ⟶ Heya wa amari atsuku nakatta deshoo.

7. Kyooto e ryokoo shimasu ka? ⟶ Kyooto e ryokoo shimashita ka?

8. Otooto ni okashi o yaritaku arimasen. ⟶ Otooto ni okashi o yaritaku arimasen deshita.

9. Okane ga nai n desu ka? ⟶ Okane ga nakatta n desu ka?

10. Ryokoo wa tanoshiku nai deshoo. ⟶ Ryokoo wa tanoshiku nakatta deshoo.

15.3.5 Substitution and Transformation Drill

1. A: *Koohii* wa ikaga desu ka?

   B: Hai, itadakimasu.

A: *Kudamono* mo hitotsu doozo.

B: Iie, ima wa kekkoo desu.

    1. ocha, okashi   2. koohii, okashi   3. kudamono, okashi

2. C: *Ocha* o doozo.

D: Doozo okamainaku.

C: *Okashi* wa ikaga desu ka?

D: Iie, kekkoo desu.

    1. koohii, okashi   2. kudamono, ocha   3. koohii, gyuunyuu

3. A: Issho ni *eiga e ikimasen* ka?

B: Itsu desu ka?

A: *Ashita* wa doo desu ka?

B: *Ashita* wa chotto tsugoo ga warui n desu.

    1. umi e ikimasu, asatte   2. ryokoo shimasu, kono shuumatsu

    3. kissaten de hanashimasu, ima   4. nomimasu, kon'ban

15.4 REVIEW EXERCISES (Lessons 1–13)

15.4.1 What would you say when:

    1. you greet someone in the afternoon?

    2. you greet someone at night?

    3. you leave someone whom you think will not see you again within the same day?

    4. you want to ask someone if he understands something?

    5. you want to say you understand what someone said?

    6. you want to answer that you do not understand what someone said?

    7. you want someone to listen carefully?

    8. you want someone to wait a minute?

    9. you want to thank someone?

    10. someone thanks you or apologizes to you?

    11. you want to apologize?

    12. you want to express regret or disappointment?

    13. you apologize to someone for what you have done to him?

    14. you visit someone's home and inform him that you are at his door?

    15. you greet someone who has come to visit your home?

226

16. you want to ask someone to speak in Japanese?

17. you accept something to drink or to eat offered by someone?

18. you have finished (are through) drinking or eating something offered by someone?

19. you want to ask someone to read something?

20. you want to ask someone to write something?

21. you have returned home?

22. someone of your family has come home while you are at home?

23. you ask someone to do something for you?

24. you want to congratulate someone?

25. you meet someone whom you have not seen for a long time?

26. you are going to bother someone by visiting him?

27. you want someone to say something once more?

28. you have kept someone waiting?

29. you greet someone in the morning?

30. you are introduced to someone?

31. you are about to leave the place you visited?

32. you want to tell someone to come again?

33. you want to ask someone how he is?

34. you want to tell someone that you are fine (thanks to him)?

35. you want to ask someone politely if he is familiar with it?

36. you want to tell someone to enter?

37. you offer someone tea?

38. you want to tell someone not to trouble himself for you?

39. you offer a guest another cup of tea?

40. you do not accept the above offer?

41. you leave someone at night whom you think you will not see again within the same day?

42. you want to be excused for a moment?

43. you want to ask someone to open (the book on) page five?

44. you want to ask someone to close the book?

45. you leave someone whom you will see again next day?

46. you want someone to take his time?

47. you want to ask someone if something is all right with him?

48. you want to praise someone for his effort?

15.4.2 Transform the code sentence according to the given English sentences:

A. Watanabe san wa sen'sei desu.

    1. Mr. Watanabe was a teacher.

    2. Mr. Watanabe is not a teacher.

    3. Mr. Watanabe must be a teacher.

    4. Mr. Watanabe was not a teacher.

B. Ano eiga wa omoshiroi desu.

    1. That movie is not interesting.

    2. That movie was not interesting.

    3. That movie must be interesting.

    4. That movie must have been interesting.

    5. That movie was interesting.

    6. That movie must not have been interesting.

    7. That movie must not be interesting.

C. Buraun san to hanashimasu.

    1. Let's talk with Mr. Brown.

    2. I didn't talk with Mr. Brown.

    3. I talked with Mr. Brown.

    4. Won't you talk with Mr. Brown?

    5. Shall we talk with Mr. Brown?

D. Kon'ban dekaketai desu.

    1. I do not want to go out tonight.

    2. I did not want to go out tonight.

    3. I wanted to go out tonight.

E. Tsugoo ga ii n desu.

    1. I will not be available.

    2. I was available.

    3. I was not available.

15.4.3 Insert an appropriate Relational in each blank:

    1. Gakkoo (   ) ikimasu.

    2. Minoru (   ) hon desu.

    3. Eiga (   ) mimashoo.

4. Eki (　　　) machimasu.

5. Watakushi (　　　) gakusei desu.

6. Kore (　　　) dare (　　　) kuruma desu ka?

7. Dono shin'bun (　　　) omoshiroi desu ka?

8. Boku (　　　) rekoodo ja arimasen.

9. Anata wa dore (　　　) moraimashita ka?

10. Niwa (　　　) tori (　　　) imasu yo.

11. Okaasan (　　　) uchi (　　　) imashita.

12. Kodomo ga inu (　　　) okashi (　　　) yarimashita.

13. Anata (　　　) zasshi (　　　) yomimasu ka?

　　　"Do you read magazines also (as well as newspaper, etc.)?"

14. Anata (　　　) oyogi (　　　) suki desu ka?

　　　"Do you like swimming also (as well as other people)?"

15. Otootosan (　　　) wa zasshi (　　　) agemashita.

16. Imooto ni (　　　) yarimashita.

　　　"I gave it to my younger sister also (as well as to someone else)."

17. Buraun san (は) Amerika (から) kimashita.

　　　"Mr. Brown came from the States."

18. Supootsu (や) on'gaku ga daisuki desu.

　　　"I like sports, music, et cetera."

19. Kyooto (か) Nikkoo o ken'butsu shitai desu.

　　　"I want to visit Kyōto or Nikkō."

20. Haha wa boku (に) okane (を) kuremashita.

21. Kon'getsu (は) ikimasen (けど), raigetsu (は) ikimasu.

22. Asa (と) yoru (は) suzushii deshoo?

　　　"It will be cool in the morning and at night, won't it?"

23. Eigo (か) furan'sugo (を) naraitakatta n desu.

　　　"I wanted to learn English or French."

24. Den'sha (で) ikimasu ka?

　　　"Are you going by train?"

25. Kazuko san (と) den'wa (で) hanashimashita.

　　　"I talked with Kazuko on the phone."

26. Kore (は) takakatta desu (が), are (は) yasukatta n desu yo.

27. Shujin (も) yomimasen deshita.

    "My husband didn't read it either."

28. Otooto (と) issho ni kissaten (で) ocha (を) nomimashita.

29. Watakushi (は) yama (が) suki desu.

30. Anata wa donata (に) tegami (を) moraitai n desu ka?

15.4.4 Write down an appropriate answer to each of the following questions:

A. 1. Anata no gokazoku wa nan'nin desu ka?

   2. Ima anata to issho ni imasu ka?

   3. Kyoodai wa nan'nin desu ka?

   4. Oniisan (oneesan, imootosan, *or* otootosan) wa ikutsu desu ka?

B. 1. Anata no kuni wa doko desu ka?

   2. Kuni no oten'ki wa doo desu ka?

   3. Natsu wa atsui deshoo?

   4. Ame ga takusan furimasu ka?

   5. Anata no kuni de wa yuki ga furimasu ka?

C. 1. Anata wa ryokoo ga suki desu ka?

   2. Doko e ikitai desu ka?

   3. Dare to issho ni ikitai desu ka?

   4. Nan de ikimasu ka?

D. 1. Anata wa nihon'go o hanashimasu ne?

   2. Donata kara naraimashita ka?

   3. Nihon'go no ben'kyoo wa muzukashii desu ka, yasashii desu ka?

   4. Anata wa doitsugo ya furan'sugo mo hanashimasu ka?

   5. Chuugokugo mo naraitai desu ka?

15.4.5 Make appropriate questions that will lead to the following answers:

1. Sen'getsu ryokoo shimashita.

2. Kuji desu.

3. Imooto wa ima yattsu desu.

4. Ano kata wa Yamamoto sen'sei desu yo.

5. Iie, moraimasen deshita.

6. Pan'ya wa soko ni arimasu.

7. Eiga wa omoshiroku nakatta desu.

8. Kore wa Itoo san no heya desu.

9. Nisatsu zutsu agemashita.

10. Den'sha de uchi e kaerimashita.

11. Kodomo wa futari imasu.

12. Hai, totemo oishikatta desu.

13. Kore ga yokatta n desu.

14. Inu to tori ga imashita.

15. Iie, kirei deshita yo.

16. San'mai arimashita.

17. Iie, hima ja arimasen deshita.

18. Maigetsu Kan'da de hon o kaimasu.

19. Iie, hashi de wa tabemasen. Fooku de tabemasu.

15.4.6 Complete each sentence by inserting, in each blank, one of the Sentence Interjectives listed below. (Use each word only once.)

demo, sore ni, soshite, sore kara, ee, iie, hai, sore de

1. Boku wa gakusei desu. (   ), ani wa gakusei ja arimasen.

2. Watakushi wa kyonen Doitsu e ikimashita. (   ), Furan'su e ikimashita.

3. Sumisu san wa inu ga suki desu. (   ), neko mo suki desu yo.

4. "Oniisan wa itsumo gyuunyuu o nomimasu ka?" "(   ), nomimasu."

5. "Kotoshi no fuyu wa yuki ga furimashita ka?" "(   ), furimasen deshita."

6. Kinoo wa totemo isogashikatta n desu. (   ), ben'kyoo shimasen deshita.

7. Kinoo Nikkoo o ken'butsu shimashita. (   ), yoru uchi e kaerimashita.

8. "Ano kissaten wa kirei desu ka?" "(   ), totemo."

15.4.7 Choose one of the following words for each of the blanks:

agemashita   kuremashita   yarimashita

1. Yamamoto san wa chichi ni kippu o_____.

2. Chichi wa haha ni biiru o_____.

3. Haha wa otooto ni ehon o_____.

4. Watashi wa imooto ni okashi o_____.

5. Otooto wa chichi ni ocha o_____.

6. Watashi wa chichi ni hon o_____.

7. Yamamoto san wa watashi ni tegami o_____.

8. Watashi wa Yamamoto san ni rekoodo o_____.

9. Yamamoto san wa tomodachi ni kippu o_____.

10. Yamamoto san wa ani ni jisho o_____.

11. Watashi wa anata ni koohii o_____.

12. Anata wa watashi ni kono hon o_____.

13. Anata wa imootosan ni nani o_____ka?

14. Anata wa Yamamoto san ni nani o_____ka?

15. Imooto wa anata ni nani o_____ka?

15.4.8 Ask one of your classmates:

1. how many are in his (her) family?

2. where they are?

3. if he (she) wants to visit Kyōto next month?

4. what time it is?

5. how many books he (she) reads every month?

6. how many times he (she) went (came) to Japan?

7. if he (she) wants to go home (to your home town)?

8. how (by what means) he (she) comes to class?

15.4.9 Carry on the following dialog:

—It's been hot these days, hasn't it? Wouldn't you like to swim today?

—Yes, I'd like to. But I am not available today.

—Why?

—Tomorrow is my mother's birthday. So I am going to buy a present today. (birthday *tan'joobi*)

—Are you? How old is your mother?

—She is fifty-two.

—What are you going to give her?

—I would like to give her a watch. (watch *tokei*)

—How nice!

15.5 AURAL COMPREHENSION

15.5.1 みのる　「あついですね。」
こやま　「ジュース* か　コカコーラ† を　あげましょうか。」

*juusu ''juice''　　†kokakoora ''Coca-Cola''

みのる　　「すみません。じゃあ、コカコーラを　もらいたいんですけど。」
こやま　　「どうぞ。」
みのる　　「ああ、おいしい。」
こやま　　「つめたいでしょう。もういっぱい　どうですか。」
みのる　　「いいえ、けっこうです。ごちそうさま。」

15.5.2　すずき　　「ブラウンさんは　りょこうが　すきでしょう？」
　　　　　ブラウン　「ええ、だいすきです。よく　いきますよ。」
　　　　　すずき　　「がいこくへも？」
　　　　　ブラウン　「ええ、がいこくへも　ときどき　いきます。フランスや　ドイツや　イギリスへも
　　　　　　　　　　　いきました。」
　　　　　すずき　　「いいですね。あなたは　フランスごや　ドイツごを　はなしますか。」
　　　　　ブラウン　「あまり　じょうずじゃありませんけど、すこし　はなします。」
　　　　　すずき　　「こんどは　どこへ　いきたいですか。」
　　　　　ブラウン　「ちゅうごくへ　いきたいんですけど、おかねが　ないんです。だから、たぶん
　　　　　　　　　　　この　へんで　りょこうします。」

　　　　　すずき　　「やまもとさんは　あした　やすみでしょう？」
15.5.3　やまもと　「ええ、クラスが　ないんです。」
　　　　　すずき　　「なにを　しますか。」
　　　　　やまもと　「あさは　うちに　いますけど、よるは　ともだちの　うちの　パーティー* へ
　　　　　　　　　　　いきます。」
　　　　　すずき　　「なんの　パーティーですか。」
　　　　　やまもと　「たんじょうび† の　パーティーです。」
　　　　　すずき　　「おおぜい　いきますか。」
　　　　　やまもと　「たぶん　くにんか　じゅうにんでしょう。」
　　　　　すずき　　「たのしいでしょうね。」

　　　　　*paatii ''party''　　　†tan'joobi ''birthday''

15.5.4　わたなべ　「あさっては　なかむらさんの　たんじょうびですね。プレゼントを　あげませんか。」
　　　　　いとう　　「そうですね。なにが　いいでしょう？」
　　　　　わたなべ　「はなは　どうですか。なかむらさんは　はなが　すきですよ。」
　　　　　いとう　　「いいですね。どこで　かいますか。」
　　　　　わたなべ　「えきの　はなやは？」
　　　　　いとう　　「ああ、あそこ。いつ　かいましょうか。」
　　　　　わたなべ　「なかむらさんは　あさって　がっこうへ　きます。あさっての　あさ　かいましょう。」

15.5.5　いとう　　「ブラウンさん、おそいですね。」
　　　　　いしい　　「ええ、おそいですね。あの　ひとは　いつも　はやいんですけど。」
　　　　　いとう　　「そうですね。もうすこし　まちましょうか。」
　　　　　いしい　　「ええ、まちましょう。」

15.5.6 きょう ともだちと いっしょに かまくらの うみへ いきたかったんですが、ともだちの つごうが わるかったんです。それで、ざんねんでしたけど、かまくらへは いきませんでした。でも、おとうとと いっしょに プールへ いきました。おとうとは まだ ここのつですが、およぎが とても じょうずです。いちにちじゅう いっしょに およぎました。つかれました* が、たのしかったです。

*tsukaremashita ''got tired''

15.5.7 きょうは やすみでした。きのうは てんきが よかったんですが、きょうは いちにちじゅう あめが ふりました。それで、あさは としょかんへ いきました。ほんと ざっしを いっさつ ずつ よみました。ひる うちへ かえりました。かないと いっしょに ひるごはんを たべました。それから、レコードで おんがくを ききました。

15.5.8 ぼくの かぞくは ごにんです。ちちと ははと いもうとと おとうとと ぼくです。みんな とうきょうに います。ぼくたちは まえ きょうとに いました。きょうとは ふゆ さむかったですが、ゆきは あまり ふりませんでした。
　ちちは サラリーマン です。まいにち かいしゃ* へ いきます。ははは うちに います。ピアノ† が じょうずです。おとうとは じゅうにさい、いもうとは やっつです。おとうとは スポーツが すきですが、いもうとは ほんが だいすきです。だから、ぼくは ときどき いもうとに ほんを やります。せんげつは がいこくの えほんを やりました。えが とても きれいでした。

*kaisha ''company''　　†piano ''piano''

APPENDIX I
ABBREVIATIONS

A	. . . .	Adjective	*takai, isogashii, yoi*
Adv.	. . . .	Adverb	*totemo, tokidoki, tabun*
B	. . . .	Base	
C	. . . .	Copula	*desu, deshita, deshoo*
D	. . . .	Derivative	
Da	. . . .	adjectival Derivative	*-tai, -takatta, -taku (nai)*
Dv	. . . .	verbal Derivative	*-masu, -masen, -mashita, -mashoo*
E	. . . .	Predicate Extender	*(ja) arimasen, (-ku) arimasen, (-ku) nai, (-ku) nakatta*
I	. . . .	Inflection	
N	. . . .	Noun	
Na	. . . .	adjectival Noun	*kirei, shizuka, gen'ki*
Nd	. . . .	dependent Noun	*-kata, -hen, -mai, -san*
Ni	. . . .	interrogative Noun	*doko, ikutsu, itsu, nani*
N	. . . .	ordinary Noun	*gakkoo, kami, ashita, gomai*
NM	. . . .	Noun Modifier	*watakushi no (hon), sono (hito)*
P	. . . .	Predicate	
PC	. . . .	Pre-Copula	*n (desu)*
PM	. . . .	Predicate Modifier	(Adverb, time Noun, N+R, number)
PN	. . . .	Pre-Noun	*kono, sono, ano, dono*
R	. . . .	Relational	
Rc	. . . .	clause Relational	*(-masu) ga, ... (desu) kedo, ...*
Rp	. . . .	phrase Relational	*no, to, ya, wa, mo, ga, o, e, ni, de*
S	. . . .	Sentence	
SI	. . . .	Sentence Interjective	*hai, ee, iie, jaa, soshite, dakara, demo, a*
SP	. . . .	Sentence Particle	*ka, yo, ne, nee*
V	. . . .	Verb	*ikimasu, yomimasu, furimasu, arimasu*

APPENDIX II
SENTENCE STRUCTURE

$$S = SI + PM \left\{ \begin{array}{l} (NM)^{*1} \left\{ \begin{array}{l} PN \\ N + (R)^{*2} \\ Adv.^{*3} \\ P^{*4} \end{array} \right\}^{*5} + N + (R) \\ \\ (Adv.) + Adv. + (R) \\ P^{*6} + (R) \end{array} \right\} // P \left\{ \begin{array}{l} \left\{ \begin{array}{l} V\,[B + I + D] \\ A\,[B + I + D] \\ (NM) + N + (R) + C \end{array} \right\} + (R) + (E)^{*7} + (PC)^{*8} + (C)^{*9} \end{array} \right\} + SP$$

*1 (NM) = NM optional

*2 (R) = R optional

*3 Adv. is only followed by Na such as *kirei,* adverbially used N such as *san'nin, kyoo,* or place N such as *ushiro, ue.*

*4 limited to final-clause Predicate such as *iku, itta.*

*5 $\left\{ \; \right\}$ = specification or limitation

*6 limited to TE, KU, TARI, Stem forms. R is obligatory for TARI, Stem forms, but optional for TE, KU forms.

*7 (E) = E optional

*8 (PC) = PC optional

*9 (C) = C optional

APPENDIX III
RELATIONALS

Relational		Lesson	Functions	Example Sentences
de	Rp	4	place of action [in; at; on, etc.]	*Gakkoo de naraimashita.*
de	Rp	12	means [by means of; with]	*Den'sha de kaerimashoo.*
e	Rp	3	direction [to]	*Umi e ikimasen ka?*
ga	Rp	5	subject	*Den'wa ga arimasu.*
ga	Rc	9	reversal reasoning [but; although]	*Ten'ki ga warukatta desu ga, dekakemashita.*
			[and]	*Sono eiga o mimashita ga, omoshirokatta desu.*
ka	Rp	11	[or]	*Koohii ka ocha o nomimashoo.*
kara	Rp	12	place of departure [from]	*Doko kara kimashita ka?*
		13	source [from]	*Tomodachi kara moraimashita.*
kedo	Rc	12	reversal reasoning [but; although]	*Ikitai n desu kedo, tsugoo ga warui n desu.*
mo	Rp	4, 7 / 12	inclusion [also; too]	*Koohii mo nomimasu.* / *On'gaku mo suki desu.* / *Kyooto e mo ryokoo shimashita.*
		8	[(not) either]	*Shin'bun mo yomimasen.* / *Rekoodo mo yoku arimasen.* / *Uchi ni mo imasen.*
ni	Rp	5	location [in; at; on, etc.]	*Soko ni arimasu.*
		13	indirect object [to (a person)]	*Anata ni agemashoo.*
no	Rp	7	qualification or modification of Noun [of; in, etc.]	*Kore wa watakushi no heya desu.* / *Nihon'go no hon o kaimasu.* / *Gin'za no mise de kaimashita.*
o	Rp	3	direct object	*Terebi o mimasu ka?*

Relational		Lesson	Functions	Example Sentences
to	Rp	5	exhaustive listing [and]	*Kami to en'pitsu o kaimashita.*
		13	involvement [with]	*Okusan to issho ni kimasen ka?*
wa	Rp	7, 12	topic	*Kore wa hon desu.* *Kinoo wa Nikkoo ni imashita.*
		9, 12	in negation	*On'gaku wa kikimasen.* *Osake wa suki ja arimasen.* *Nikkoo e wa ikimasen deshita.*
		9, 12	contrast	*Hon wa yomimasu ga, zasshi wa yomimasen.* *Ima wa suki desu ga, mae wa kirai deshita.*
ya	Rp	9	sample listing [and (the like)]	*Kyooto ya Nara e ikimashoo.*

APPENDIX IV
CONJUGATION TABLES
NORMAL FORM

1. Verb

Lesson	Form	Imperfect Affirmative	Imperfect Negative	Perfect Affirmative	Perfect Negative	OO form
a	13	agemasu (ageru)	agemasen	agemashita	agemasen deshita	agemashoo
	4	arimasu	arimasen	arimashita	arimasen deshita	(arimashoo)
b	4	ben'kyoo (o) shimasu (suru)	ben'kyoo (o) shimasen	ben'kyoo (o) shimashita	ben'kyoo (o) shimasen deshita	ben'kyoo (o) shimashoo
d	4	dekakemasu (dekakeru)	dekakemasen	dekakemashita	dekakemasen deshita	dekakemashoo
	12	den'wa (o) shimasu (suru)	den'wa (o) shimasen	den'wa (o) shimashita	den'wa (o) shimasen deshita	den'wa (o) shimashoo
f	11	furimasu (furu)	furimasen	furimashita	furimasen deshita	(furimashoo)
h	8	hairimasu (hairu)	hairimasen	hairimashita	hairimasen deshita	hairimashoo
	7	hanashimasu (hanasu)	hanashimasen	hanashimashita	hanashimasen deshita	hanashimashoo
i	11	iimasu (iu)	iimasen	iimashita	iimasen deshita	iimashoo
	3	ikimasu (iku)	ikimasen	ikimashita	ikimasen deshita	ikimashoo
	5	imasu (iru)	imasen	imashita	imasen deshita	imashoo
k	3	kaerimasu (kaeru)	kaerimasen	kaerimashita	kaerimasen deshita	kaerimashoo
	3	kaimasu (kau)	kaimasen	kaimashita	kaimasen deshita	kaimashoo
	4	kaimono (o) shimasu (suru)	kaimono (o) shimasen	kaimono (o) shimashita	kaimono (o) shimasen deshita	kaimono (o) shimashoo
	4	kakimasu (kaku)	kakimasen	kakimashita	kakimasen deshita	kakimashoo

Lesson / Form		Imperfect		Perfect		OO form
		Affirmative	Negative	Affirmative	Negative	
k	9	karimasu (kariru)	karimasen	karimashita	karimasen deshita	karimashoo
	12	ken'butsu (o) shimasu (suru)	ken'butsu (o) shimasen	ken'butsu (o) shimashita	ken'butsu (o) shimasen deshita	ken'butsu (o) shimashoo
	4	kikimasu (kiku)	kikimasen	kikimashita	kikimasen deshita	kikimashoo
	3	kimasu (kuru)	kimasen	kimashita	kimasen deshita	kimashoo
	13	kuremasu (kureru)	kuremasen	kuremashita	kuremasen deshita	(kuremashoo)
m	13	machimasu (matsu)	machimasen	machimashita	machimasen deshita	machimashoo
	4	mimasu (miru)	mimasen	mimashita	mimasen deshita	mimashoo
	13	moraimasu (morau)	moraimasen	moraimashita	moraimasen deshita	moraimashoo
n	7	naraimasu (narau)	naraimasen	naraimashita	naraimasen deshita	naraimashoo
	3	nomimasu (nomu)	nomimasen	nomimashita	nomimasen deshita	nomimashoo
o	11	oyogimasu (oyogu)	oyogimasen	oyogimashita	oyogimasen deshita	oyogimashoo
r	12	ryokoo (o) shimasu (suru)	ryokoo (o) shimasen	ryokoo (o) shimashita	ryokoo (o) shimasen deshita	ryokoo (o) shimashoo
s	9	sagashimasu (sagasu)	sagashimasen	sagashimashita	sagashimasen deshita	sagashimashoo
	3	shimasu (suru)	shimasen	shimashita	shimasen deshita	shimashoo
	4	shokuji (o) shimasu (suru)	shokuji (o) shimasen	shokuji (o) shimashita	shokuji (o) shimasen deshita	shokuji (o) shimashoo
	7	shookai (o) shimasu (suru)	shookai (o) shimasen	shookai (o) shimashita	shookai (o) shimasen deshita	shookai (o) shimashoo
t	3	tabemasu (taberu)	tabemasen	tabemashita	tabemasen deshita	tabemashoo

Form Lesson		Imperfect		Perfect		OO form
		Affirmative	Negative	Affirmative	Negative	
y	13	yarimasu (yaru)	yarimasen	yarimashita	yarimasen deshita	yarimashoo
	5	yobimasu (yobu)	yobimasen	yobimashita	yobimasen deshita	yobimashoo
	9	yomimasu (yomu)	yomimasen	yomimashita	yomimasen deshita	yomimashoo

Forms in parentheses are not to be used at this stage.

2. Verbal Derivative

Dictionary Form	Stem Form	TA Form	OO Form
-masu	-mase(n)*	-mashita	-mashoo

*(n) will be explained in later volumes.

Tense

Imperfect		Perfect		
Affirmative	Negative	Affirmative	Negative	OO Form
-masu	-masen	-mashita	-masen deshita	-mashoo

3. Adjective

Adjectives introduced in LEARN JAPANESE Volume I are as follows:

atatakai	11	chikai	8	mazui	8	isogashii	8
suzushii	11	tooi	8	muzukashii	9	kitanai	8
atsui	11	hayai	13	yasashii	9	subarashii	12
samui	11	osoi	13	omoshiroi	9	tanoshii	12
mushiatsui	11	ii; yoi	8	tsumaranai	9	tsumetai	11
chiisai	8	warui	8	takai	9	urusai	8
ookii	8	oishii	8	yasui	9	(nai	9)

242

Any Adjective in Japanese inflects as shown in the charts below:

Dictionary Form	TA Form	KU Form
taka*i*	taka*katta*	taka*ku*

Tense

Imperfect		Perfect	
Affirmative	Negative	Affirmative	Negative
-i (n) desu	-ku arimasen -ku nai (n) desu	-katta (n) desu	-ku arimasen deshita -ku nakatta (n) desu

4. Copula

Dictionary Form	TA Form	OO Form
desu	deshita	deshoo

Tense

Imperfect		Perfect		OO Form
Affirmative	Negative	Affirmative	Negative	
desu	ja arimasen de wa arimasen	deshita	ja arimasen deshita de wa arimasen deshita	deshoo

Adjectival Nouns as well as Nouns occur before the Copula.
Adjectival Nouns introduced in LEARN JAPANESE Volume I are as follows:

hima	5	suki	8
joozu	7	kirai	8
heta	7	daisuki	8
shizuka	7	daikirai	8
nigiyaka	7	gen'ki	8
kirei	7	dame	8
		rippa	9

5. Adjectival Derivative

Dictionary Form	TA Form	KU Form
-ta*i*	-ta*katta*	-ta*ku*

Tense

Imperfect		Perfect	
Affirmative	Negative	Affirmative	Negative
-tai	-taku arimasen -taku nai (n) desu	-takatta (n) desu	-taku arimasen deshita -taku nakatta (n) desu

APPENDIX V
DIALOG—ENGLISH AND HIRAGANA EQUIVALENTS

DIALOG—English Equivalent

3.2   After class

Mr. Yamada:	Miss Ishii, aren't you going (back) home with me?
Miss Ishii:	I am going to the Kanda now.
Mr. Yamada:	To the Kanda?
Miss Ishii:	Yes, I am going to buy books. What are you going to do, Mr. Yamada? Are you going (back) home right away?
Mr. Yamada:	No, I am going to drink coffee at a coffee shop.
Miss Ishii:	You often go to a coffee shop, Mr. Yamada!
Mr. Yamada:	Yes, I go (there) every day. Miss Ishii, are you coming to school tomorrow?
Miss Ishii:	Yes, I am.
Mr. Yamada:	Well, see you again tomorrow.
Miss Ishii:	Yes, good-bye.

4.2   Monday at school

Mr. Itō:	Ms. Koyama, did you go out yesterday?
Ms. Koyama:	No, I did not go out. I am going to have an exam tomorrow. So, I studied at home all day long.
Mr. Itō:	Good! I did not study at all.
Ms. Koyama:	Really? What did you do?
Mr. Itō:	I saw a movie at Shinjuku. After that, I also did some shopping at the department store.
Ms. Koyama:	Did you?
Mr. Itō:	Do you have classes the day after tomorrow, Ms. Koyama?
Ms. Koyama:	No, I don't.
Mr. Itō:	Then, won't you go to Kamakura with me? And, let's dine at a restaurant at night.
Ms. Koyama:	How nice! Let's go.

5.2   On the street

Mr. Tanaka:	Mr. Suzuki, is there a telephone in this vicinity?
Mr. Suzuki:	There is one over there, you see.

Mr. Tanaka:	Well, excuse me for a moment. I'll come (back) soon.

. . . .

Mr. Tanaka:	Sorry to have kept you waiting.
Mr. Suzuki:	Don't mention it. Shall we go (now)?
Mr. Tanaka:	Yes. Oh, there is Mr. Yamada! Shall we call (out his name)? . . . Mr. Yamada!
Mr. Yamada:	Oh, hello.
Mr. Suzuki:	Hi. You were at the Shinjuku Station yesterday, weren't you?
Mr. Yamada:	Yes, I went to a movie. How about you, Mr. Suzuki?
Mr. Suzuki:	I went to a bookstore and a bank. Do you have some free time today, Mr. Yamada?
Mr. Yamada:	Yes, I do.
Mr. Suzuki:	Mr. Tanaka is coming to my house now. Aren't you coming with us?
Mr. Yamada:	Yes, thank you. I will come (and bother you).

7.2   A tour of the campus

Mr. Smith:	What is that over there?
Ms. Koyama:	That is a library.
Mr. Smith:	Pretty! How about that one?
Ms. Koyama:	That one? It is a cafeteria. Shall we have tea?
Mr. Smith:	Yes, we are thirsty, aren't we?

. . . .

Prof. Nakamura:	Ms. Koyama.
Ms. Koyama:	Oh, Professor Nakamura. I will introduce my friend to you. This is Mr. Smith. This is Professor Nakamura.
Prof. Nakamura:	How do you do?
Mr. Smith:	Glad to meet you.
Prof. Nakamura:	Are you a student of this university, too?
Mr. Smith:	No, I am not. I am a graduate student at the University of Maryland.
Prof. Nakamura:	Mr. Smith, where did you study the Japanese language?
Mr. Smith:	I studied it at the University of Hawaii. But, I am not good at it yet.
Ms. Koyama:	Professor, we'd better be leaving now.
Prof. Nakamura:	Really? Come again to spend a leisurely time.
Mr. Smith:	Yes, thank you. I will.

8.2 Going to a coffee shop

Yamamoto: Aren't you Mr. Watanabe?

Watanabe: Oh, Mr. Yamamoto. I didn't see you for a long time. How are you?

Yamamoto: Fine, thank you. And you?

Watanabe: Fine, thank you.

Yamamoto: By the way, are you busy now?

Watanabe: No, I am not very busy.

Yamamoto: Won't you stop for a while and have some tea in that area?

Watanabe: All right. . . . There is a coffee shop there, you see. Are we going into (that coffee shop)?

Yamamoto: That (coffee) shop is not good. The coffee there is awful. Besides, the shop is not clean, either. Let's go to the Denen.

Watanabe: Is that place far?

Yamamoto: No, it is near from here. Come this way.

Watanabe: Do you often go to that coffee shop?

Yamamoto: Yes, I go there frequently. The coffee there is very good. The music is good, too.

Watanabe: You are fond of music, Mr. Yamamoto!

Yamamoto: Yes, I love it. Now, this is the (coffee) shop. Let's go in.

9.2 Talking about books and things

Ishii: Do you often read magazines, newspapers, and the like?

Itō: No, I do not read magazines, newspapers, and the like so often. But, as for books I read them often, you know.

Ishii: Books are expensive these days, aren't they?

Itō: They certainly are! So, I always borrow them at the library.

Ishii: I usually borrow books at the library, too, but I sometimes buy them.

Itō: Is that book yours or the library's?

Ishii: It is mine. I bought this at a secondhand bookstore the day before yesterday. I tried to find it at the library, but it wasn't there.

Itō: It's a very fine book. Was it expensive?

Ishii: No, it wasn't.

Itō: Did you already read it?

Ishii: Yes, I did.

Itō: How was it?

Ishii: It was very interesting. Won't you read it, too?

Itō: Is it all right?

Ishii: Yes, please take your time.

11.2   Suzuki visits Minoru

Suzuki: Are you home, Minoru?

Minoru: Oh, Mr. Suzuki. Please come on in.

Suzuki: Yes, thank you.

Minoru: It's been raining continuously. It must have been hot and humid outside.

Suzuki: No, it wasn't so hot and humid. Is it going to be rainy tomorrow, too?

Minoru: The weather will be fine tomorrow. They said so on the radio.

Suzuki: That's good. I suppose you like swimming, Minoru. Won't you swim with me in the sea or in the swimming pool?

Minoru: When is it?

Suzuki: How about tomorrow?

Minoru: Tomorrow? I won't be available on this weekend. The fact is I am going home tomorrow.

Suzuki: To your home? Your home is in Tōkyō, isn't it?

Minoru: No, it's in Hokkaidō.

Suzuki: Oh, is it? Then, are your family all in Hokkaidō?

Minoru: My father and mother are in Sapporo, but my older brother and older sister are in Tōkyō.

Suzuki: Isn't the summer in Sapporo cool?

Minoru: It isn't very cool. It will probably be hot already about this time.

12.2   Sightseeing

Takada: Miss Brown, you weren't home yesterday, were you?

Brown: No, I went to Nikkō. But, how do you happen to know?

Takada: I phoned you twice yesterday.

Brown: Oh, I'm sorry about that. Anything you want to talk to me about?

Takada: No, nothing particular. I just wanted to have a talk with you. Did you go to Nikkō by train?

Brown: Yes. I didn't want to go by train, but I went by the Tōbu Line from the Asakusa Station.

Takada:	You must have liked Nikkō.
Brown:	Yes, it was very beautiful. But, there were a lot of people.
Takada:	Did you go to the lake, also?
Brown:	Yes, I did, but the weather was not good, you know.
Takada:	That was too bad. I visited Kyōto last month.
Brown:	Did you see the stone garden of the Ryōanji Temple? That is wonderful, isn't it?
Takada:	I didn't go to the Ryōanji Temple. But, I would like to visit there next time.
Brown:	Although I also want to go sightseeing to Kyōto, I don't have time.

13.2   Giving

Kazuo's Mother:	Please have tea. How about some fruit, too?
Ikuo:	Please don't go to any trouble. Hasn't Kazuo come back yet?
Mother:	No, I'm sorry. Kazuo was given movie tickets by (from) one of his friends. Therefore, he went out together with his younger brothers in the morning. But, I am sure he is coming back soon.
Ikuo:	Is he? Then, I will wait some more time.
Mother:	Ikuo, do you have brothers or sisters?
Ikuo:	I have three. They are an older brother, an older sister, and a younger sister, respectively.
Mother:	How old are your older brother and older sister?
Ikuo:	They are twenty-four years old and twenty years old.
Mother:	Are they? Just a moment, please. . . . Aren't these albums pretty? A friend of mine in France gave me three. I gave one to Kazuo. I think I will give one to you, also.
Ikuo:	Thank you very much.
Mother:	How about another cup of tea?
Ikuo:	Yes, I will. Excuse me, but what time is it now?
Mother:	It's four o'clock. Kazuo is late (in coming home)!

DIALOG—Hiragana Equivalent

3.2   After class

やまだ	「いしいさん、いっしょに かえりませんか。」
いしい	「これから、ちょっと かんだへ いきます。」
やまだ	「かんだへ？」
いしい	「ええ、ほんを かいます。やまださんは なにを しますか。すぐ うちへ かえりますか。」
やまだ	「いいえ、きっさてんで コーヒーを のみます。」
いしい	「やまださんは よく きっさてんへ いきますね。」

やまだ　　「ええ、まいにち　いきます。いしいさん、あした　がっこうへ　きますか。」
いしい　　「ええ、きます。」
やまだ　　「じゃあ、また　あした。」
いしい　　「ええ、さようなら。」

4.2　　Monday at school

いとう　　「こやまさん、きのう　でかけましたか。」
こやま　　「いいえ、でかけませんでした。あした　しけんが　あります。それで、うちで
　　　　　　いちにちじゅう　べんきょうを　しました。」
いとう　　「えらいですね。わたしは　ぜんぜん　べんきょうしませんでした。」
こやま　　「そうですか。なにを　しましたか。」
いとう　　「しんじゅくで　えいがを　みました。それから、デパートで　かいものも
　　　　　　しました。」
こやま　　「そうですか。」
いとう　　「こやまさん、あさって　クラスが　ありますか。」
こやま　　「いいえ、ありませんけど。」
いとう　　「じゃあ、いっしょに　かまくらへ　いきませんか。そして、よる　レストランで
　　　　　　しょくじを　しましょう。」
こやま　　「いいですね。いきましょう。」

5.2　　On the street

たなか　　「すずきさん、この　へんに　でんわが　ありますか。」
すずき　　「あそこに　ありますよ。」
たなか　　「じゃあ、ちょっと　しつれい。すぐ　きます。」

....

たなか　　「おまちどおさま。」
すずき　　「どう　いたしまして。いきましょうか。」
たなか　　「ええ。あ、そこに　やまださんが　いますよ。よびましょうか。……やまださん。」
やまだ　　「あ、こんにちは。」
すずき　　「こんにちは。やまださん、きのう　しんじゅくえきに　いましたね。」
やまだ　　「ええ、えいがへ　いきました。すずきさんは？」
すずき　　「ちょっと　ほんやと　ぎんこうへ　いきました。やまださん、きょう　おひまが
　　　　　　ありますか。」
やまだ　　「ええ、ありますけど。」
すずき　　「いま　たなかさんが　うちへ　きます。いっしょに　きませんか。」
やまだ　　「ええ、ありがとう。おじゃまします。」

7.2　　A tour of the campus

スミス　　「あれは　なんですか。」
こやま　　「としょかんです。」

250

スミス　　　「きれいですねえ。それは？」
こやま　　　「それですか。しょくどうです。おちゃを　のみましょうか。」
スミス　　　「ええ、のどが　かわきましたね。」

....

なかむら　　「こやまさん。」
こやま　　　「あ、なかむらせんせい。ともだちを　しょうかいします。スミスさんです。こちらは
　　　　　　　なかむらせんせいです。」
なかむら　　「はじめまして。」
スミス　　　「どうぞ　よろしく。」
なかむら　　「あなたも　ここの　がくせいですか。」
スミス　　　「いいえ、そうじゃありません。メリーランドだいがくの　だいがくいんの
　　　　　　　がくせいです。」
なかむら　　「スミスさんは　どこで　にほんごを　ならいましたか。」
スミス　　　「ハワイだいがくで　ならいました。でも、まだ　じょうずじゃありません。」
こやま　　　「せんせい、わたしたちは　そろそろ　しつれいします。」
なかむら　　「そうですか。また　ゆっくり　いらっしゃい。」
スミス　　　「はい、ありがとうございます。」

8.2　　Going to a coffee shop

やまもと　　「わたなべさんじゃありませんか。」
わたなべ　　「あ、やまもとさん。しばらく。おげんきですか。」
やまもと　　「ええ。わたなべさんも？」
わたなべ　　「ええ、おかげさまで。」
やまもと　　「ところで、いま　いそがしいですか。」
わたなべ　　「いいえ、あまり　いそがしくありませんけど。」
やまもと　　「ちょっと　その　へんで　おちゃを　のみませんか。」
わたなべ　　「いいですね。……そこに　きっさてんが　ありますよ。はいりますか。」
やまもと　　「その　みせは　よくありません。コーヒーが　まずいんです。それに、みせも
　　　　　　　きれいじゃありません。でんえんへ　いきましょう。」
わたなべ　　「そこは　とおいですか。」
やまもと　　「いいえ、ちかいですよ。こっちです。」
わたなべ　　「やまもとさんは　その　きっさてんへ　よく　いきますか。」
やまもと　　「ええ、よく　いきます。そこの　コーヒーは　とても　おいしいんです。おんがくも
　　　　　　　いいです。」
わたなべ　　「やまもとさんは　おんがくが　すきですねえ。」
やまもと　　「ええ、だいすきです。さあ、この　みせです。はいりましょう。」

9.2　　Talking about books and things

いしい　　　「いとうさんは　よく　ざっしや　しんぶんを　よみますか。」
いとう　　　「いいえ、ざっしや　しんぶんは　あまり　よみません。でも、ほんは　よく
　　　　　　　よみますよ。」
いしい　　　「このごろ　ほんが　たかいですね。」
いとう　　　「ほんとうですね。だから、ぼくは　いつも　としょかんで　かります。」
いしい　　　「わたしも　たいてい　としょかんで　かりますが、ときどき　かいます。」
いとう　　　「その　ほんは　いしいさんのですか、としょかんのですか。」

いしい　「わたしのです。おととい　ふるほんやで　かいました。としょかんで　さがしましたが、
　　　　なかったんです。」
いとう　「ずいぶん　りっぱですね。たかかったですか。」
いしい　「いいえ、たかくありませんでした。」
いとう　「もう　よみましたか。」
いしい　「ええ、よみました。」
いとう　「どうでしたか。」
いしい　「とても　おもしろかったです。いとうさんも　よみませんか。」
いとう　「いいんですか。」
いしい　「ええ、どうぞ　ごゆっくり。」

11.2　Suzuki visits Minoru

すずき　「みのるくん、いますか。」
みのる　「あ、すずきさん。どうぞ　おはいりください。」
すずき　「おじゃまします。」
みのる　「よく　ふりますねえ。そとは　むしあつかったでしょう？」
すずき　「いいえ、あまり　むしあつくなかったですよ。あしたも　あめですか。」
みのる　「あしたは　てんきが　いいでしょう。ラジオで　そう　いいましたよ。」
すずき　「それは　よかった。みのるくんは　およぎが　すきでしょう？　うみか　プールで
　　　　いっしょに　およぎませんか。」
みのる　「いつですか。」
すずき　「あしたは　どうですか。」
みのる　「あしたですか。この　しゅうまつは　つごうが　わるいんです。じつは、あした
　　　　くにへ　かえります。」
すずき　「くにへ？　みのるくんの　うちは　とうきょうでしょう？」
みのる　「いいえ。ほっかいどうです。」
すずき　「おや、そうですか。じゃあ、ごかぞくは　みなさん　ほっかいどうですか。」
みのる　「ちちと　ははは　さっぽろに　いますが、あにと　あねは　とうきょうです。」
すずき　「さっぽろの　なつは　すずしいんでしょう？」
みのる　「あまり　すずしくないんです。いまごろは　もう　たぶん　あついでしょう。」

12.2　Sightseeing

たかだ　「ブラウンさん、きのうは　るすでしたね。」
ブラウン　「ええ、にっこうへ　いきました。でも、どうして　ごぞんじですか。」
たかだ　「きのう　にど　でんわしました。」
ブラウン　「そう、それは　すみませんでした。なにか　ごようですか。」
たかだ　「いいえ、べつに。ちょっと　はなしを　したかったんです。にっこうへは
　　　　でんしゃで？」
ブラウン　「ええ。でんしゃで　いきたくなかったんですけど、あさくさえきから　とうぶで
　　　　いきました。」
たかだ　「にっこうは　よかったでしょう。」
ブラウン　「ええ、とても　きれいでした。でも、ひとが　おおぜい　いました。」
たかだ　「みずうみへも　いきましたか。」
ブラウン　「ええ、いきましたけど、てんきが　よくなかったんです。」

たかだ　「それは　ざんねんでしたね。わたしは　せんげつ　きょうとけんぶつを　しました。」
ブラウン　「りょうあんじの　いしの　にわを　みましたか。あれは　すばらしいですね。」
たかだ　「りょうあんじへは　いきませんでした。でも、こんど　いきたいです。」
ブラウン　「わたしも　また　きょうとけんぶつを　したいんですけど、ひまが　ないんです。」

13.2　Giving

かずおの
　はは　「おちゃを　どうぞ。くだものも　いかがですか。」
いくお　「どうぞ　おかまいなく。かずおくんは　まだですか。」
はは　「ええ、ごめんなさいね。かずおは　ともだちから　えいがの　きっぷを
　　　もらいました。それで、あさ　おとうとたちと　いっしょに　でかけました。でも、
　　　もうすぐ　かえります。」
いくお　「そうですか。では、もうすこし　まちます。」
はは　「いくおさん、ごきょうだいは？」
いくお　「さんにん　います。あにと　あねと　いもうとが　ひとりずつ　います。」
はは　「おにいさんや　おねえさんは　いくつですか。」
いくお　「にじゅうよんさいと　はたちです。」
はは　「そうですか。ちょっと　まってね。……この　アルバム、きれいでしょう？
　　　フランスの　ともだちが　さんさつ　くれました。かずおに　いっさつ　やりました。
　　　あなたにも　あげましょう。」
いくお　「どうも　すみません。」
はは　「おちゃを　もういっぱい　いかがですか。」
いくお　「はい、いただきます。すみませんが、いま　なんじでしょうか。」
はは　「よじですけど。かずお、おそいですねえ。」

APPENDIX VI
GLOSSARY

Numbers refer to lessons in which the words first occur. Numerals and numeral-counter combinations are not listed in this section. See Notes 12.4.2 and 13.4.4.

(A)

a	SI	5	oh; ah
aa	N	9	in that way
agemasu	V	13	give (normal form of *ageru*) (see 13.4.8)
aki	N	11	autumn; fall
amari	Adv.	8	(not) very much; (not) very often (see 8.4.4)
ame	N	11	rain
Amerika	N	3	the United States of America; America
amerikajin	N	7	an American
anata	N	7	you
ane	N	11	(my) older sister
ani	N	11	(my) older brother
ano	PN	8	that over there (see 8.4.6)
are	N	7	that one over there (see 7.4.1)
arimasen	E	7	(see 7.4.12 and 8.4.5)
arimasen deshita	E+C	9	perfect tense form of *arimasen* (see 9.4.10 and 9.4.12)
arimasu	V	4	have (see 4.4.4); is situated (normal form of *aru*) (see 5.4.6)
arubamu	N	13	album
asa	N	11	morning
asagohan	N	4	breakfast; morning meal
Asahi	N	9	Asahi (Newspaper)
Asakusa	N	12	an amusement center in downtown Tōkyō
asatte	N	4	the day after tomorrow
ashita	N	3	tomorrow (see 3.4.13 and 11.4.5)
asoko	N	5	that place over there; over there (see 5.4.4)
atashi	N	9	I (used by women) (see 9.4.3)
atatakai	A	11	is warm (sometimes *attakai*)
atchi	N	8	that way; that one

atsui	A	11	is hot

(B)

ban	N	11	evening; night
ban'gohan	N	4	supper; evening meal
basu	N	12	bus
ben'kyoo	N	4	study
ben'kyoo (o) shimasu	V	4	study (normal form of *ben'kyoo (o) suru*)
betsu ni	Adv.	12	nothing particular (see 12.4.3)
bifuteki	N	3	beefsteak
biiru	N	3	beer
boku	N	9	I (used by men) (see 9.4.3)
Buraun	N	12	Brown
byooin	N	9	hospital

(C)

chichi	N	11	(my) father (see 11.4.14)
chiisai	A	8	is small; is little (in size)
chikai	A	8	is near
chotto	Adv.	3	for a while (see 3.4.4); a little (see 8.4.4)
Chuugoku	N	7	China
chuugokugo	N	7	Chinese language
chuugokujin	N	7	a Chinese

(D)

daigaku	N	7	university; college
daigakuin	N	7	graduate school
daikirai	Na	8	dislike very much
daisuki	Na	8	like very much
dakara	SI	8	so; therefore
dame	Na	8	no good
dare	Ni	5	who? (see 5.4.3)
de	R	3	at; in (see 3.4.11 and 4.4.6)
de	R	11	by means of (see 12.4.6)
dekakemasu	V	4	go out; set out (normal form of *dekakeru*)

demo	SI	7	but; however
Den'en	N	8	name of a coffee shop
den'sha	N	12	electric train; streetcar
den'wa	N	5	telephone
den'wa (o) shimasu	V	12	make a phone call (normal form of *den'wa (o) suru*)
depaato	N	4	department store
deshita	C	9	TA form of *desu* (see 9.4.12)
deshoo	C	11	OO form of *desu* (see 11.4.6, 11.4.8, and 13.4.10)
desu	C	7	(see 7.4.3); equivalent of *ni arimasu* or *ni imasu* (see 11.4.11)
dewa	SI	13	well
de wa arimasen	C+R+E	7	formal equivalent of *ja arimasen* (see 7.4.12)
de wa arimasen deshita	C+R+E+C	9	negative perfect tense form of *desu* (see 9.4.12)
-do	Nd	12	time(s) (see 12.4.2)
Doitsu	N	7	Germany
doitsugo	N	7	German language
doitsujin	N	7	a German
doko	Ni	3	what place?; where? (see 3.4.10)
donata	Ni	5	who? (polite equivalent of *dare*) (see 5.4.3)
dono	PN	8	which? (see 8.4.6)
doo	N	9	how? (see 9.4.12)
dooshite	Adv.	12	how?; why? (see 12.4.1)
doozo	SI	9	please
dore	Ni	7	which one? (see 7.4.1)
dotchi	Ni	8	which way?; which one?

(E)

e	R	3	to (a place) (see 3.4.5)
e	N	8	painting(s); picture
ee	SI	3	yes (see 3.4.7)
ehon	N	13	picture book
eiga	N	4	movie
eigo	N	7	English language

eki	N	5	station
en'pitsu	N	12	pencil

(F)

fooku	N	12	fork
fune	N	12	boat; ship
Furan'su	N	7	France
furan'sugo	N	7	French language
furan'sujin	N	7	a Frenchman
furimasu	V	11	(rain or snow) fall (normal form of *furu*) (see 11.4.2)
furuhon'ya	N	9	secondhand bookstore
futari	N	13	two (persons)
futatsu	N	13	two (see 13.4.6)
fuyu	N	11	winter

(G)

ga	R	4	(see 4.4.3, 5.4.3, 5.4.6, and 8.4.10)
ga	Rc	9	but; although (see 9.4.5)
gaikoku	N	7	foreign country; abroad
gaikokugo	N	7	foreign language
gaikokujin	N	7	foreigner
gakkoo	N	3	school
gakusei	N	7	student
gen'ki	Na	8	healthy; in good spirits
-getsu	Nd	12	month
gin'koo	N	5	bank
Gin'za	N	3	Ginza Street or a shopping center of Tōkyō
-go	Nd	7	language (see 7.4.14)
go-	(prefix)	11	(see 11.4.12)
gohan	N	3	meal; boiled rice
goshujin	N	11	someone else's husband
gyuunyuu	N	3	cow's milk

(H)

haha	N	11	(my) mother
hai	SI	3	yes (formal equivalent of *ee*) (see 3.4.7)
hairimasu	V	8	go in (normal form of *hairu*)
hanashi	N	12	a talk; tale
hanashimasu	V	7	speak; talk (normal form of *hanasu*)
haru	N	11	spring
hashi	N	12	chopsticks
hatachi	N	13	twenty years old (see 13.4.4)
Hawai	N	3	Hawaii
hayai	A	13	is early
-hen	Nd	5	area; vicinity (see 5.4.1 and 8.4.6)
heta	Na	7	unskillful; poor (at)
heya	N	4	room
hikooki	N	12	airplane
hima	Na	5	free time
hiru	N	11	noon (it sometimes means ''lunch'')
hirugohan	N	4	lunch; noon meal
hito	N	8	person
hitori	N	13	one (person) (see 13.4.4)
hitotsu	N	13	one (see 13.4.6)
Hokkaidoo	N	11	Hokkaidō Prefecture (northern island of Japan)
hon	N	3	book
-hon	Nd	13	counter for thin and long objects (see 13.4.4)
hon'too	N	9	true; real
hon'ya	N	5	bookstore (see 5.4.8)

(I)

ichinichijuu	N	4	all day long; throughout the day
Igirisu	N	7	England
igirisujin	N	7	an Englishman
ii	A	8	is good (see 8.4.3)
iie	SI	3	no (see 3.4.7)
iimasu	V	11	say (normal form of *iu*)

ikaga	Ni	13	how? (polite equivalent of *doo*)
ikimasu	V	3	go (normal form of *iku*) (see 3.4.14)
Ikuo	N	13	boy's first name
ikutsu	Ni	13	how old?; how many (objects)? (see 13.4.6)
ima	N	5	now
ima goro	N	11	about this time; at this time
imasu	V	5	exist (normal form of *iru*) (see 5.4.2 and 5.4.6)
imooto	N	11	(my) younger sister
inu	N	5	dog
ippai	N	13	a cup (of); a glass (of)
ishi	N	12	stone
Ishii	N	3	family name
isogashii	A	8	is busy
issho ni	Adv.	3	together; with [me, us, etc.]
Itoo	N	4	family name
itsu	Ni	11	when? (see 11.4.5)
itsumo	Adv.	9	always; usually
itsutsu	N	13	five

(J)

jaa	SI	4	well
ja arimasen	C+R+E	7	negative of *desu* (see 7.4.12)
ja arimasen deshita	C+R+E+C	9	perfect tense form of *ja arimasen* (see 9.4.12)
-ji	Nd	13	o'clock (see 13.4.4)
jimusho	N	5	office
-jin	Nd	7	(see 7.4.14)
jisho	N	3	dictionary
jitsu wa	SI	11	the fact is; in fact
joozu	Na	7	skillful; proficient; good (at)

(K)

ka	SP	3	(see 3.4.3 and 9.4.7)
ka	R	11	or (see 11.4.9)

kaerimasu	V	3	go back; come back (normal form of *kaeru*) (see 3.4.14)
-kai	Nd	13	counter for floor (see 13.4.4)
kaimasu	V	3	buy (normal form of *kau*)
kaimono	N	4	shopping
kaimono (o) shimasu	V	4	do shopping (normal form of *kaimono (o) suru*)
kakimasu	V	4	write (normal form of *kaku*)
Kamakura	N	4	a historical city near Tōkyō
kamera	N	3	camera
kami	N	13	paper
kanai	N	11	my wife
Kan'da	N	3	Kanda Street or a book center of Tōkyō
(o)kane	N	5	money
kara	R	12	from (a place) (see 12.4.8); from (a person) (see 13.4.1)
karimasu	V	9	borrow (normal form of *kariru*)
-kata	Nd	8	person (see 8.4.6)
kazoku	N	11	family (see 11.4.12 and 11.4.14)
Kazuo	N	13	boy's first name
kedo	Rc	4	although; but (see 4.4.10 and 12.4.7)
ken'butsu	N	12	sightseeing
ken'butsu (o) shimasu	V	12	see the sights of; visit (normal form of *ken'butsu (o) suru*)
kesa	N	11	this morning
kikimasu	V	4	listen to; hear (normal form of *kiku*) *(Kikimasu* is a transitive Verb: the Relational *o* occurs with this Verb to show a direct object. *Teepu o kikimasu.)*
kimasu	V	3	come (normal form of *kuru*) (see 3.4.14)
kimi	N	9	you (used by men)
kinoo	N	4	yesterday (see 11.4.5)
kippu	N	13	ticket
kirai	Na	8	dislike
kirei	Na	7	pretty; clean *(Kirei* is not an Adjective but an adjectival Noun. Adjectives never end in *-ei.)* (see 7.4.4)
kissaten	N	3	coffee shop
kitanai	A	8	is dirty; is unclean; is messy

kochira	N	7	this person (direction; one) (see 7.4.9)
kodomo	N	11	child (see 11.4.14)
koko	N	5	this place; here (see 5.4.4)
kokonotsu	N	13	nine
kon'ban	N	11	tonight
kon'do	N	12	this time (in the future or in the past) (see 12.4.12)
kon'getsu	N	12	this month
kono	PN	8	this (see 8.4.6)
kono goro	N	9	these days
kon'shuu	N	12	this week
koo	N	9	in this way
koohii	N	3	coffee
kore	N	7	this one (see 7.4.1)
kore kara	Adv.	3	from now
kotchi	N	8	this way; this one (see 8.4.9)
kotoshi	N	12	this year
Koyama	N	4	family name
kudamono	N	13	fruit
-kun	Nd	11	equivalent of -san (used by men) (see 11.4.1)
kuni	N	7	country; home (town; country)
kurasu	N	4	class
kuremasu	V	13	give [me] (normal form of kureru) (see 13.4.8)
kuruma	N	12	car
kyonen	N	12	last year
kyoo	N	3	today
kyoodai	N	13	sister(s) and/or brother(s)
Kyooto	N	12	old capital of Japan; Kyōto Prefecture

(M)

machimasu	V	13	wait (normal form of matsu) (Different from the English verb "wait," machimasu is a transitive Verb; it follows the direct object Relational o.)
mada	Adv.	7	(not) yet; still (see 7.4.15)
mae	N	9	before
mai-	(prefix)	12	every ~ (see 12.4.10)

-mai	Nd	13	sheet (of) (counter for something thin and flat) (see 13.4.4)
maiasa	N	12	every morning
maiban	N	12	every night
maigetsu	N	12	every month
mainen	N	12	every year
mainichi	N	3	every day
Mainichi	N	9	Mainichi (Newspaper)
maishuu	N	12	every week
-masen	Dv	3	(see 3.4.2 and 3.4.3)
-masen deshita	Dv+C	4	(see 4.4.2)
-mashita	Dv	4	TA form of -masu (see 4.4.1)
-mashoo	Dv	4	OO form of -masu (see 4.4.11 and 13.4.9)
-masu	Dv	3	(see 3.4.2)
mata	Adv.	12	again
mazui	A	8	is tasteless; does not taste good
Meriiran'do	N	7	Maryland
mimasu	V	4	see (normal form of miru) (or "watch" as in "watch TV")
minasan	N	11	everyone (see 11.4.13)
min'na	N	11	all; everyone (see 11.4.13)
Minoru	N	11	boy's first name
mise	N	8	shop; store
mittsu	N	13	three
mizu	N	3	water
mizuumi	N	12	lake
mo	R	4	also; too (see 4.4.9, 7.4.10, 11.4.5, and 12.4.5)
mo	R	8	(not) either (see 8.4.8, 11.4.5, and 12.4.5)
moo	Adv.	9	already (see 9.4.11)
moo	Adv.	13	more (see 13.4.3)
moo sugu	Adv.	13	any minute now
moraimasu	V	13	receive; get (normal form of morau) (see 13.4.1)
mushiatsui	A	11	is hot and humid
muttsu	N	13	six

muzukashii	A	9	is difficult

(N)

n (desu)	PC	8	(see 8.4.3)
nai	A	9	there is not; is nonexistent (see 9.4.8)
nai	E	11	negation (see 11.4.4)
Nakamura	N	7	family name
namae	N	7	name
nan	Ni	7	what? (see 7.4.2)
nan-	Ni	13	how many ~ ?; what ~ ? (see 13.4.4)
nanatsu	N	13	seven
nani	Ni	3	what? (see 3.4.10)
nanigo	Ni	7	what language? (see 7.4.14)
nan'ji	Ni	13	what time? (see 13.4.4)
nan'nin	Ni	13	how many (people)? (see 13.4.4)
naraimasu	V	7	study; take lessons; is taught; learn (normal form of *narau*) (Note that *naraimasu* is not always equivalent to "learn.")
natsu	N	11	summer
ne	SP	3	(see 3.4.12)
nee	SP	7	(see 7.4.5)
neko	N	5	cat
-nen	Nd	12	year (see 12.4.10)
ni	R	5	in; at (see 5.4.2)
ni	R	13	to (a person) (see 13.4.8)
nigiyaka	Na	7	lively; cheerful; noisy; bustling
Nihon	N	3	Japan
nihon'go	N	4	Japanese language
nihon'jin	N	7	a Japanese
Nikkoo	N	12	city in Tochigi Prefecture (famous for the Tōshōgū Shrine)
-nin	Nd	13	(counter for people) (see 13.4.4)
niwa	N	12	garden
no	R	7	(see 7.4.11 and 9.4.6)
nodo	N	7	throat (see 7.4.7)
nomimasu	V	3	drink (normal form of *nomu*)

(O)

o	R	3	(see 3.4.8)
o-	(prefix)	5	(see 5.4.10)
ocha	N	3	tea; green tea
oishii	A	8	is tasty; is good; is delicious
okaasan	N	11	(someone else's) mother
okane	N	5	money
okashi	N	13	candy; sweets; confections
okosan	N	11	(someone else's) child
okusan	N	11	(someone else's) wife
omoshiroi	A	9	is interesting
onaka	N	7	stomach (see 7.4.7)
oneesan	N	11	(someone else's) older sister
on'gaku	N	8	music
oniisan	N	11	(someone else's) older brother
on'na no hito	N	5	woman
ookii	A	8	is big; is large
oozei	Adv.	12	a lot of people (see 12.4.9)
osoi	A	13	is late
otearai	N	5	toilet; rest room
otoko no hito	N	5	man
otoosan	N	11	(someone else's) father
otooto	N	11	(my) younger brother
ototoi	N	4	the day before yesterday
oya	SI	11	oh!; oh?; my!
oyogi	N	11	swimming
oyogimasu	V	11	swim (normal form of *oyogu*)

(P)

pan	N	3	bread
pan'ya	N	5	bakery
-peeji	Nd	13	page (see 13.4.4)
pen	N	12	pen
posuto	N	5	mailbox; postbox

purezen'to	N	13	present; gift
puuru	N	11	swimming pool

(R)

raigetsu	N	12	next month
rainen	N	12	next year
raishuu	N	12	next week
rajio	N	11	radio
rekoodo	N	4	record
rekoodoya	N	5	musical record shop
resutoran	N	4	restaurant
rippa	Na	9	fine; magnificent
rusu	N	12	is out; is not at home
ryokoo	N	12	trip; travel
ryokoo (o) shimasu	V	12	travel; take a trip (normal form of *ryokoo (o) suru*)
Ryooan'ji	N	12	Ryōanji Temple in Kyōto (famous for its stone garden)

(S)

saa	SI	8	now!
sagashimasu	V	9	look for (normal form of *sagasu*) (*Sagashimasu* is a transitive Verb; it follows the direct object Relational *o.*)
-sai	Nd	13	year(s) (old) (see 13.4.4)
samui	A	11	is cold (weather)
-san	Nd	3	Mr.; Mrs.; Miss (see 3.4.1)
Sapporo	N	11	capital city of Hokkaidō
-satsu	Nd	13	volume (counter for books, etc.) (see 13.4.4)
sen'getsu	N	12	last month (see 12.4.10)
sen'sei	N	7	teacher (see 7.4.8)
sen'shuu	N	12	last week
shiken	N	4	examination; test
shimasu	V	3	do (normal form of *suru*)
shin'bun	N	9	newspaper
Shin'juku	N	4	a shopping center of Tōkyō
shizuka	Na	7	quiet
shokudoo	N	5	dining room (hall); cafeteria; eating place

shokuji	N	4	meal; eating a meal
shokuji (o) shimasu	V	4	dine; eat a meal (normal form of *shokuji (o) suru*)
shookai (o) shimasu	V	7	introduce (normal form of *shookai (o) suru*)
shujin	N	11	(my) husband
-shuu	Nd	12	week (see 12.4.10)
shuumatsu	N	11	weekend
soko	N	5	that place; there
sono	PN	8	that (see 8.4.6)
soo	N	7	in that way; so
sore	N	7	that one (see 7.4.1)
sore de	SI	4	so; accordingly (see 4.4.5)
sore kara	SI	4	afterwards; and (then)
sore ni	SI	8	besides; moreover (see 8.4.7)
sorosoro	Adv.	7	it's about time (see 7.4.17)
soshite	SI	4	and
sotchi	N	8	that way; that one
soto	N	11	outside
subarashii	A	12	is wonderful
sugu	Adv.	3	soon
suki	Na	8	like; fond of
sukoshi	Adv.	12	a little (see 12.4.9)
Sumisu	N	7	Smith
supootsu	N	8	sport
Suzuki	N	5	family name
suzushii	A	11	is cool

(T)

tabemasu	V	3	eat (normal form of *taberu*)
tabun	Adv.	11	probably; perhaps
-tachi	Nd	7	(turns the preceding animate Noun into plural) (see 7.4.16)
-tai	Da	12	want to (do) (see 12.4.4)
taipuraitaa	N	3	typewriter

taitei	Adv.	9	generally; in most cases
takai	A	9	is expensive
takusan	Adv.	12	a lot (see 12.4.9)
takushii	N	12	taxi
Tanaka	N	5	family name
tanoshii	A	12	is pleasant
tatemono	N	9	building
teepu	N	4	tape
tegami	N	4	letter (correspondence)
ten'ki	N	11	weather
ten'pura	N	3	tempura; Japanese fry; fritter
terebi	N	4	television; TV set
to	R	5	and (see 5.4.9)
to	R	13	with (someone) (see 13.4.2)
tokidoki	Adv.	9	sometimes; once in a while
tokoro de	SI	8	by the way; incidentally (see 8.4.2)
tomodachi	N	7	friend
too	N	13	ten
Toobu	N	12	the Tōbu line
tooi	A	8	is far
Tookyoo	N	3	capital of Japan
tori	N	5	bird; chicken (meat)
toshokan	N	7	(school or public) library
totemo	Adv.	8	very (see 8.4.4)
tsugoo	N	11	convenience (see 11.4.10)
tsumaranai	A	9	is uninteresting; is dull; is unimportant
tsumetai	A	11	is cold (thing)

(U)

uchi	N	3	home; house
umi	N	11	sea; seaside
urusai	A	8	is noisy; is annoying

(W)

wa	R	3	(see 3.4.9, 7.4.2, 8.4.10, 9.4.2, and 12.4.5)
warui	A	8	is bad

watakushi	N	4	I (the contracted form *watashi* may also be used) (see 4.4.8)
watakushitachi	N	7	we (see 7.4.16)
Watanabe	N	8	family name
watashi	N	4	I (the contracted form of *watakushi*) (see 4.4.8)

(Y)

ya	R	9	and (selective) (see 9.4.1)
-ya	Nd	5	-store; -dealer (see 5.4.8)
yama	N	11	mountain
Yamada	N	3	family name
Yamamoto	N	8	family name
yarimasu	V	13	give (normal form of *yaru*) (see 13.4.8)
yasashii	A	9	is easy
yasui	A	9	is inexpensive
yasumi	N	11	vacation; holiday; closed; absent
yattsu	N	13	eight
yo	SP	5	(see 5.4.5)
yobimasu	V	5	call (normal form of *yobu*)
yoi	A	8	is good (see 8.4.3 and 9.4.9)
yoku	Adv.	3	often; a good deal
yomimasu	V	9	read (normal form of *yomu*)
Yomiuri	N	9	Yomiuri (Newspaper)
Yooroppa	N	12	Europe
yoru	N	4	night
yottsu	N	13	four
yuki	N	11	snow
yuubin'kyoku	N	5	post office

(Z)

zasshi	N	9	magazine
zen'zen	Adv.	4	not at all (see 7.4.15)
zuibun	Adv.	9	extremely; quite
-zutsu	Nd	13	each (see 13.4.5)

APPENDIX VII
INDEX TO NOTES